Lecture Notes in Artificial Intell

Edited by J. G. Carbonell and J. Siekmann

Subseries of Lecture Notes in Computer Science

Karl Tuyls   Pieter Jan 't Hoen
Katja Verbeeck   Sandip Sen (Eds.)

Learning and Adaption in Multi-Agent Systems

First International Workshop, LAMAS 2005
Utrecht, The Netherlands, July 25, 2005
Revised Selected Papers

 Springer

Series Editors

Jaime G. Carbonell, Carnegie Mellon University, Pittsburgh, PA, USA
Jörg Siekmann, University of Saarland, Saarbrücken, Germany

Volume Editors

Karl Tuyls
Universiteit Maastricht
Tongersestraat 6, Maastricht, The Netherlands
E-mail: k.tuyls@cs.unimaas.nl

Pieter Jan 't Hoen
Center for Mathematics and Computer Science (CWI)
Kruislaan 413, P.O. Box 94079, 1090 GB Amsterdam, The Netherlands
E-mail: hoen@cwi.nl

Katja Verbeeck
Vrije Universiteit Brussel
Faculty of Sciences (WE), Department of Computer Science
Pleinlaan 2, 1050 Brussels, Belgium
E-mail: kaverbee@vub.ac.be

Sandip Sen
University of Tulsa
Department of Mathematical and Computer Sciences
600 S. College, Tulsa, OK 74104, USA
E-mail: sandip-sen@utulsa.edu

Library of Congress Control Number: 2006923098

CR Subject Classification (1998): I.2.11, I.2, C.2.4

LNCS Sublibrary: SL 7 – Artificial Intelligence

ISSN   0302-9743
ISBN-10   3-540-33053-4 Springer Berlin Heidelberg New York
ISBN-13   978-3-540-33053-0 Springer Berlin Heidelberg New York

Springer is a part of Springer Science+Business Media

springer.com

© Springer-Verlag Berlin Heidelberg 2006
Printed in Germany

Typesetting: Camera-ready by author, data conversion by Scientific Publishing Services, Chennai, India
Printed on acid-free paper   SPIN: 11691839   06/3142   5 4 3 2 1 0

Preface

This book contains selected and revised papers of the International Workshop on Learning and Adaptation in Multi-Agent Systems (LAMAS 2005), held at the AAMAS 2005 Conference in Utrecht, The Netherlands, July 26.

An important aspect in multi-agent systems (MASs) is that the environment evolves over time, not only due to external environmental changes but also due to agent interactions. For this reason it is important that an agent can learn, based on experience, and adapt its knowledge to make rational decisions and act in this changing environment autonomously.

Machine learning techniques for single-agent frameworks are well established. Agents operate in uncertain environments and must be able to learn and act autonomously. This task is, however, more complex when the agent interacts with other agents that have potentially different capabilities and goals. The single-agent case is structurally different from the multi-agent case due to the added dimension of dynamic interactions between the adaptive agents.

Multi-agent learning, i.e., the ability of the agents to learn how to cooperate and compete, becomes crucial in many domains. Autonomous agents and multi-agent systems (AAMAS) is an emerging multi-disciplinary area encompassing computer science, software engineering, biology, as well as cognitive and social sciences. A theoretical framework, in which rationality of learning and interacting agents can be understood, is still under development in MASs, although there have been promising first results.

The goal of this workshop was to increase awareness and interest in adaptive agent research, encourage collaboration between machine learning (ML) experts and agent system experts, and give a representative overview of current research in the area of adaptive agents. The symposium served as an inclusive forum for the discussion of ongoing or completed work concerning both theoretical and practical issues. An important part of the workshop was to model MASs for different applications and to develop robust ML techniques.

Contributions in this book cover topics on how an agent can learn, using ML techniques, to act individually or to coordinate with one another towards individual or common goals, which is still an open issue in real-time, noisy, collaborative and adversarial environments. The book start with an extensive overview article on cooperative and competitive multi-agent learning, which also contains a description of the contributions of this book and places them in context with the state of the art. It is a good starting point for newcomers in the field, wishing to read a self-contained overview of the state of the art in multi-agent learning, and also a good introduction for experts wishing to explore the contributions of this book.

We hope that our readers will enjoy reading the efforts of the researchers. A special word of gratitude also goes to our invited speakers, Peter Stone and Ann Nowé.

The first invited talk, "Multi-Robot Learning for Continuous Area Sweeping", by Peter Stone, University of Texas at Austin, USA, has been shaped into the paper: "Multi-Robot Learning for Continuous Area Sweeping", by Mazda Ahmadi and Peter Stone.

In their paper they study the problem of multi-agent continuous area sweeping. In this problem agents are situated in a particular environment in which they have to repeatedly visit every part of it such that they can detect events of interest for their global task and coordinate to minimize the total cost. Events are not uniformly distributed, such that agents need to visit locations non-uniformly. The authors formalize this problem and present an initial algorithm to solve it. Moreover they nicely illustrate their approach with a set of experiments in a routine surveillance task.

The second invited talk of the workshop was by Ann Nowé, professor of computer sciences at the university of Brussels, Belgium, resulting in the paper: "Learning Automata as a Basis for Multiagent Reinforcement Learning", by Ann Nowé, Katja Verbeeck and Maarten Peeters. In their work they start with an overview on important theoretical results from the theory of learning automata in terms of game theoretic concepts and consider them as a policy iterator in the domain of reinforcement learning problems. Doing so they gradually move from the variable structure automaton, mapping to the single-stage single-agent case, over learning automata games, mapping to the single-stage multi-agent case, to interconnected learning automata, considering multistage multi-agent problems. The authors also show the most interesting connection with the field of ant colony optimization.

Acknowledgements

When organizing a scientific event like LAMAS, a word of gratitude is always in place. This book would not have been produced without the help of many persons. First of all, the organizers would like to thank the members of the PC, who guaranteed a scientifically strong and interesting LNCS volume. Secondly, we would like to express our appreciation to the invited speakers, Ann Nowé and Peter Stone, for their distinguished contribution to the workshop program. Finally, we also would like to thank the authors of all contributions for submitting their scientific work to the LAMAS workshop!

December 2005

Karl Tuyls
Pieter Jan 't Hoen
Katja Verbeeck
Sandip Sen
Tulsa

Organization

Organizing Committee

Co-chairs: Karl Tuyls
                                      Pieter Jan 't Hoen
                                      Katja Verbeeck
                                      Sandip Sen

Program Committee

Stephane Airiau	Han La Poutré	Jan Ramon
Bikramjit Banerjee	Michael Littman	Sandip Sen
Ana Lucia Bazzan	Peter McBurney	Peter Stone
Sander Bohté	Ann Nowé	Kagan Tumer
Michael Goodrich	Simon Parsons	Danny Weyns
Daniel Kudenko	Steve Phelps	David Wolpert

Additional Referees

Jacob Crandall
Alexander Helleboogh
Koen Mertens

Table of Contents

An Overview of Cooperative and Competitive Multiagent Learning

Pieter Jan 't Hoen[1], Karl Tuyls[2], Liviu Panait[3],
Sean Luke[3], and J.A. La Poutré[1,4]

[1] Center for Mathematics and Computer Science (CWI),
P.O. Box 94079, Amsterdam 1090 GB, The Netherlands
[2] Computer Science Department (IKAT), Tongersestraat 6,
University of Maastricht, The Netherlands
[3] George Mason University, Fairfax, VA 22030
[4] TU Eindhoven, De Lismortel 2, Eindhoven 5600 MB, The Netherlands
hoen@cwi.nl, k.tuyls@cs.unimaas.nl,
{lpanait, sean}@cs.gmu.edu, hlp@cwi.nl

Abstract. *Multi-agent systems* (MASs) is an area of distributed artificial intelligence that emphasizes the joint behaviors of agents with some degree of autonomy and the complexities arising from their interactions. The research on MASs is intensifying, as supported by a growing number of conferences, workshops, and journal papers. In this survey we give an overview of multi-agent learning research in a spectrum of areas, including reinforcement learning, evolutionary computation, game theory, complex systems, agent modeling, and robotics.

MASs range in their description from cooperative to being competitive in nature. To muddle the waters, competitive systems can show apparent cooperative behavior, and vice versa. In practice, agents can show a wide range of behaviors in a system, that may either fit the label of cooperative or competitive, depending on the circumstances. In this survey, we discuss current work on cooperative and competitive MASs and aim to make the distinctions and overlap between the two approaches more explicit.

Lastly, this paper summarizes the papers of the first International workshop on Learning and Adaptation in MAS (LAMAS) hosted at the fourth International Joint Conference on Autonomous Agents and Multi Agent Systems (AAMAS'05) and places the work in the above survey.

1 Introduction

Multi-agent systems (MASs) is an area of distributed artificial intelligence that emphasizes the joint behaviors of agents with some degree of autonomy and the complexities arising from their interactions. The research on MASs is intensifying, as supported by a growing number of conferences, workshops, and journal papers. This book of the first International workshop on Learning and Adaptation in MAS (LAMAS), hosted at the fourth International Joint Conference on Autonomous Agents and Multi Agent Systems (AAMAS'05), is a continuation of this trend.

K. Tuyls et al. (Eds.): LAMAS 2005, LNAI 3898, pp. 1–46, 2006.

The goal of the LAMAS workshop was to increase awareness and interest in adaptive agent research, encourage collaboration between Machine Learning (ML) experts and agent system experts, and give a representative overview of current research in the area of adaptive agents. The workshop served as an inclusive forum for the discussion of ongoing or completed work concerning both theoretical and practical issues. More precisely, researchers from the multi-agent learning community presented recent work and discussed their newest ideas for a first time with their peers. An important part of the workshop was dedicated to model MASs for different applications and to develop robust ML techniques. Contributions cover on how an agent can learn using ML techniques to act individually or to coordinate with one another towards individual or common goals. This is an open issue in real-time, noisy, collaborative and possibly adversarial environments.

This introductory article has a twofold goal. The first is to give a broad overview of current MASs research. We present our overview of MASs research from the two main perspectives to be found in the literature; the cooperative and competitive perspective. Secondly, we briefly present an overview of the included papers and invited contributions and place them in the global context of ongoing research.

In cooperative systems, as suggested by the label, the agents pursue a common goal. Such systems are characterized by the fact that the designers of the MAS are free in their design of the agents. The agents can be built and learn with extensive knowledge of the system and the agents can expect benevolent intentions from other agents. Note that we do not claim that it is easy to design a cooperative MAS to have good emergent behavior, on the contrary!

In contrast to cooperative MASs, agents in a competitive MAS setting have non-aligned goals, and individual agents seek only to maximize their own gains. Recent work in competitive MASs has aimed at moving Reinforcement Learning (RL) techniques from the domain of single-agent to multi-agent settings. There is a growing body of work, algorithms and evaluation criteria, which we cover in the second part of our survey. Furthermore, this section also covers a growing body of work on non-cooperative agents [189] for economical and societal settings that have received increasing interest only in recent years. Such agents have their own, possibly conflicting goals and aim for local optimization. Their owners can e.g. be competing companies or autonomous departments within a bigger organization, where the multi-agent systems should facilitate trading, allocation, or planning between these owners, e.g. by means of negotiation or auctioning.

The rest of this document is structured as follows. Section 2 first informally introduces agents playing simple matrix games. We use this section to initially introduce the concepts of play, and whether the agents can be labeled as cooperative, competitive, or as something in between. Section 3 presents our overview of cooperative MASs. Section 4 continues with our overview of competitive MASs. Sections 3 and 4 are intended to be largely self contained, although there are cross-links between the sections. Section 5 presents the papers of this LAMAS proceedings and places this work in the context of the survey of MASs work, Sections 3 and 4. Lastly, Section 6 concludes with an agenda of future research opportunities for MASs. Appendix A includes some basic Game Theory (GT) concepts universal to the domain of cooperative and competitive MASs as a general background for readers not familiar with the subject.

The next section continues with a discussion on the labels of cooperative and competitive as applied to MASs.

2 Agents Classified as Cooperative or Competitive

Multi-Agent Systems range in their description from cooperative to being competitive in nature. To muddle the waters, competitive systems can show apparent cooperative behavior, and vice versa. In practice, agents in a system, depending on the circumstances, can show a wide range of behaviors that may either fit the label of cooperative or competitive.

The fundamental distinction between systems labeled as cooperative or competitive is that for the former the agents are designed with as goal the maximization of a group utility. Competitive agents are solely focused on maximizing their own utility. We, in this section, label the agents as either utilitarian or selfish to stress more their intention, i.e. their design goal, than their actual behavior. For example, a competitive/selfish agent may cooperate with other agents in a temporary coalition. The selfish intentions of the agent are met due to a larger expected reward from cooperation. On the other hand, a cooperative/utilitarian agent may seem competitive if it accidentally hogs a resource to the detriment of other agents in its group. In complex cooperative systems, agents can easily hinder the other agents as the complexity of the interactions increase. The label utilitarian or selfish stresses more the intentional stance of the agent (and of its designer), as opposed to its apparent behavior.

The utilitarian stance for cooperative systems, as already mentioned in the introduction, is also reflected in the design of the agents. Commonly, a cooperative system is designed by one party (be that one designer or a team) to achieve a set of agreed upon goals. The behavior, or the algorithm that learns the behavior of the agents, is largely under the control of the designers of the system. This allows for possible intricate coordination to be a priori implemented in the system and many interactions in the system can be anticipated. An agent can essentially expect good intentions from other agents in the system. This is not the case for the competitive setting. Each agent is created by separate designers that all aim to achieve their own goals. This makes cooperation between selfish agents, even if this is rational, a more difficult and risky task. The designer of a competitive agent must also expend effort in considering the types of exploitive behavior that will be encountered. This distinction in design of agents for a cooperative or competitive setting must be kept in mind when choosing the range of strategies the agents can choose from.

2.1 Setting

In the following, we give a sample of the type of interactions that can be observed between agents. We discuss how these are a consequence of the utilitarian or selfish intentional stance.

We restrict our discussion to the well known two-agent, two-action matrix games. For a complete taxonomy we refer the reader to [132]. Of importance is that the listed games give an exhaustive overview of the types of settings that the agents can encounter. This gives a sound basis to inspect how agents can handle these types of games, both from the utilitarian and the selfish stance. We can then classify the agent behavior as either (apparent) cooperative, (apparent) competitive, or indistinguishable.

[132] classifies games from the perspective of selfish agents; the agents focus on maximizing their own gain, i.e. their private utility. Game theoretical notions prevail in the discussion of the choice of strategies of the agents. We take a slightly broader view and also focus on utilitarian agents and how they would play in the selected games. Utilitarian agents focus on achieving the highest possible group utility, i.e. the sum of their individual rewards.

Note that we only consider play between two selfish agents or between two utilitarian agents. We consider either a system of agents where all agents are intended to achieve a common goal, or a system of agents where all agents expect the worst. We do not cover the intricacies of a cooperative system that has to deal with selfish agents. For a more complete discussion of this topic, we refer the reader to [106] and Section A for a discussion on Evolutionary Stable Strategies.

The agents in the games know the complete payoff matrices. They know their own reward and that of their opponents for all joint actions[1]. They simultaneously must choose an action and receive their part of the reward based on the picked joint action. What they may not know is how the other agent, be that a malicious opponent or a benevolent agent, will play.

Note that we here as yet restrict ourselves to the single play of the presented matrix games. Agents may also have to learn these payoffs during repeated play of the game. We will give examples of this, along with a more formal treatment, in Section 4. After this initial exposition, we discuss how the choice of strategies can change due to repeated play.

2.2   Types of Games

From the viewpoint of selfish agents, [132] broadly classifies the matrix games as either trivial, games of no conflict, games of complete opposition, or as games of partial conflict. The latter is also called a mixed motive game. We discuss each of the categories below. For each category, we sketch the game, give an example, and discuss how selfish and utilitarian agents would cope with the game.

Trivial games: In trivial games (TG), the expected reward of an agent does not depend on the choice of action of the other agent. In Table 1, we show such a trivial game. The Row player can choose either action $A1$ or $B1$ while the Column player can choose from actions $A2$ or $B2$. The items in the table show the rewards for the Row player and Column player respectively for choice of action Ai or Bi respectively. For this game, the rewards of one player are not

---

[1] Agents in most Game Theory literature know the payoff matrix before play.

Table 1. A trivial game

TG	A2	B2
A1	2,2	2,2
B1	2,2	2,2

influenced by the choice of actions of the opponent. Such a game is therefore not of great interest in terms of formulating a best strategy. This strategy is based on what they think they should play given the logical action chosen by the opponent, a non-issue in this case.

Due to the simple nature of this game, there is no intrinsic difference in play between utilitarian and selfish agents.

No conflict games: In no-conflict games (NCG), both players benefit from choosing one, unambiguous joint action. Neither player benefits, in terms of individual rewards, by deviating from this logical choice. Consider the game in Table 2:

Table 2. A no-conflict game

NCG	A2	B2
A1	4,4	2,3
B1	3,2	2,2

Both the Row and Column player prefer the joint action $A1A2$ (we give first the Row, and the Column player action) as this gives the most individual reward. Neither player has an incentive to choose another action when the sole goal is maximizing the private utility for selfish agents. $A1A2$ is also the logical choice of action for the utilitarian players. We stress that in both cases, the Row and Column player individually choose $A1$ and $A2$ respectively without prior negotiations; the players base their individual choice solely on their own strategic reasoning.

Note that the Row player may prefer to play $B1A2$ when the Row player aims to maximize the relative utility of play; the Row player wants to have more utility than the Column player. This aspect is not an issue for utilitarian players.

As for trivial games, there is little difference in play between utilitarian and selfish agents. One distinction that can be made is that a utilitarian row player will not pick action $B1$ as such a player is not interested in achieving a higher reward than the other player. More importantly, this choice of action will lower the utility of the group and should be avoided.

Games of Complete opposition (also known as zerosum games): In games of complete opposition (CO), the gain of one agent is a loss for the other agent. The Table 3 shows a typical zerosum game (rewards for one joint action sum to 0). These games are characterized by fierce competition. On average, an agent can expect to have zero reward.

For selfish players, games of complete opposition are a difficult scenario. The best strategy for an unknown opponent, from a game theoretical viewpoint, is

Table 3. A game of complete opposition

CO	A2	B2
A1	0,0	2,-2
B1	1,-1	-3,3

to play a random strategy; all actions are equally probable. More technically, this is a mixed strategy. See Section A for a more formal definition. For two utilitarian agents, the game is also problematical as coordination of joint actions, by definition of a zerosum game, will not lead to a higher aggregated reward.

Games of Partial Conflict Mixed Motive Games: Games of partial conflict (PC) allow for both agents to choose profitable actions, but the agents prefer different joint actions. The latter point is the distinction between the no-conflict games and the mixed-motive games. We give an example in Table 4.

Table 4. A partial conflict game

PC1	A2	B2
A1	2,7	-1,-10
B1	1,-5	10,1

The Row agent prefers joint action $B1B2$. The Column agent prefers joint action $A1A2$. Blindly choosing $B1$ by the Row player and $A2$ by the Column player results in joint action $B1A2$ that is preferred by neither player.

Games of partial conflict are difficult for selfish agents. Optimal play is achieved through a mixed strategy that maximizes expected utility. This aspect is handled in more detail in Appendix A.

Utilitarian agents that have as goal to maximize the group utility have a more clearcut strategy; choose the joint action that maximizes the total utility. For Table 4, joint action $B1B2$ is the clear choice. For Table 5, the utilitarian agents are however faced with the choice of playing joint action $A1A2$ or $B1B2$. The agents must however make their choices individually, with no a priori information of the action that will be played by the other agent.

Table 5. A second no-conflict game

PC2	A2	B2
A1	3,3	1,1
B1	1,1	3,3

2.3 Repeated Play

The above section has presented play for agents for single shot play of a selection of typical matrix games. We now focus on how the game can change if two agents repeatedly play the same game. Repeated play opens opportunities, especially to selfish agents, not available in single shot play of the game.

Force-vulnerable or Threat-vulnerable: [132] lists two opportunities in repeated play for selfish agents. Games can be threat-vulnerable or force-vulnerable. A player is called a disgruntled if he fails to achieve his most preferred outcome in initial play of the game. For example, the outcome for the disgruntled Row player is $A1A2$. Two cases can be distinguished: (i) Row's largest payoff is in $A1B2$, and (ii) Row's largest payoff is in $B1B2$.

Consider the first case. Row can only achieve this desired outcome if the Column player shifts away from the original outcome while Row sticks to $A1$. Now by threatening to shift unilaterally to $B1$, Row can effect an outcome where Column gets a smaller payoff than if Column where to shift unilaterally. This game is hence threat-vulnerable. The Row player can induce the Column player to switch by threatening to play an action that is even less preferred by the Column player.

For the second case, suppose now that Row's payoff in $B1B2$ is larger than in $A1A2$. The Column player can be induced to switch to this joint action if first the Row player actually switches to play $B1$. The Column player may then switch to $B2$ if the payoff for the Column player in $B1B2$ is higher than the payoff in $B1A2$. Such a game is called force-vulnerable.

Exploitation: In repeated play a player may learn about the strategy of the opponent. For example, in the games of complete opposition, the Row player may learn that the Column player is not purely random and has a slight bias for playing $B2$. This gives the Row player the opportunity to play action $A1$ more often for payoff Table 3. For the single shot game, Game Theoretical considerations lead the Row player to play a perfect random strategy for the game of complete opposition. This behavior can change in repeated play as one player learns more of the opposing player and exploitation opportunities are observed.

Threat or Retributive strategies: We have discussed how games may be threat vulnerable. More generally, solutions to games that are not reachable in single play can be achieved in iterated play due to the possibility of retributive actions. A famous example is the Tit-for-Tat strategy [7] in iterated play of the Prisoner's Dilemma, of which an example is shown in Table 6:

Table 6. A Prisoner's Dilemma game

PD	A2/C	B2/D
A1/C	3,3	0,5
B1/D	5,0	1,1

Players receive a reward for jointly cooperating ($A1A2$), but receive a higher reward by unilaterally defecting ($A1B2$ or $B1A2$). The players however achieve a lower reward for a joint defection ($B1B2$). The dominant strategy in the single shot version of the game is to defect, due to the reasoning that the opponent will defect.

In repeated play of the game, a higher reward can be achieved by both players, be they selfish or utilitarian, by repeatedly jointly cooperating. Defections may be less common as a player has the possibility to threaten to punish a defection with defections of its own. This is encoded in the Tit-for-Tat strategy that initially starts the game by cooperating. A defection by the opponent is punished by a defection in the next round of play. The Tit-for-Tat player then reverts to playing cooperation until the next defection by the opponent. Players can achieve a high individual reward over multiple trials of the game, while the threat of retribution guards the player against exploitation by a malicious opponent.

In general, in repeated play, joint solutions of the game by selfish players are possible that are not apparent in single shot play of the game. Future interactions between agents allow for strategies that incorporate threats against exploitation, and at the same time allow for risky joint play.

Give and take: For the games of partial opposition, i.e. the mixed motive games, two agents are each able to gain in each round of play. The agents however have opposed preferences for the choice of joint actions in terms of received individual reward. Repeated play of the same game allows for give and take by both players to achieve a higher aggregated reward than if both players aggressively continuously strive for their own preferred action.

In Table 7, two utilitarian players are indifferent between play of $A1A2$, $A1B2$, or $B1A2$. As long as $B1B2$ is not played, the two agents together reap the highest possible reward. The situation is more complex for two selfish agents.

Table 7. A game of *Give* and *Take*

GT	A2	B2
A1	3,3	2,4
B1	4,2	2,2

Two selfish agents are indifferent between $A1A2 - A1A2$, $A1B2 - B1A2$, and $B1A2 - A1B2$ played over two iterations of the game. Both would prefer to receive a reward of 8 over two iterations; the row player would prefer $B1A2 - B1A2$ to be played. There is however the risk of playing $B1B2$ if the column player reasons in a similar manner. The utilitarian players can unilaterally choose to play the safe action $A1$ and $A2$ respectively for the role of Row and Column player as they are only concerned about the group utility.

The selfish players have basically also the above choice; repeatedly play $A1A2$ as a safe, guaranteed joint action. They can also settle for the option of the more complex interleaving of $B1A2$ with $A1B2$. The selfish agents are indifferent between the two strategies in terms of expected reward, although the latter interleaving is more difficult to achieve. For the strategy of repeated play of $A1A2$, both selfish agents have an incentive to deviate. The row player can unilaterally switch to $B1$ and the Column player can decide to unilaterally switch to $B2$ to try to reap the higher reward. This can lead the players to wind up playing $B1B2$, where neither player has a strong incentive to unilaterally switch back.

Observe once again Table 4. Two selfish agents should play $A1A2$ $\frac{9}{14}$ of the time and $B1B2$ $\frac{5}{14}$ of the time for both agents to reap the same average reward.

This is a difficult coordination pattern to achieve. This pattern however achieves a higher reward than any mixed strategies the agents can choose due to the risk of penalties for actions $A1B2$ and $B1A2$. Unilaterally striving for their own preferred action by the Row or Column player will lead to lower reward than for the fine grained coordination. The game in Table 5 is hence a challenge for selfish algorithms.

In this section, we have sketched the differences between cooperative and competitive agents using simple matrix games. We have discussed the intricacies that arise when classifying the behavior of an agent from the perspective of single play of a game, and the possible changes in behavior for repeated play of the same game. Sections 3 and 4 then delve into the existing literature covering the state-of-the-art research on cooperative and competitive MASs.

3 Cooperative MASs

In this section, we will focus on the application of *machine learning* to problems in the MAS area. Machine learning explores ways to get a machine agent to discover on its own, often through repeated trials, how to solve a given task. Machine learning has proven a popular approach to solving multi-agent systems problems because the inherent complexity of many such problems can make solutions by hand prohibitively difficult. Automation is attractive. We will specifically focus on problem domains in which the multiple agents are *cooperating* to solve a joint task or to maximize utility; as opposed to *competing* with one another. This is covered in Section 4. We call this specific sub-domain of interest *cooperative multi-agent learning*. Despite the relative youth of the field, the number of cooperative multi-agent learning papers is large, and we hope that this survey will prove helpful in navigating the current body of work.

We argue there are two major categories of cooperative multi-agent learning approaches. The first one, *team learning*, applies a single learner to search for behaviors for the entire team of agents. Such approaches are more along the lines of traditional machine learning techniques, but they may have scalability problems as the team size increases. To keep the search space manageable, team learning techniques might assign identical behaviors to multiple team members.

A second category of techniques, *concurrent learning*, uses multiple concurrent learning processes. Rather than learning behaviors for the entire team, concurrent learning approaches typically employ a learner for each team member, in the hope that this reduces the joint space by projecting it into N separate spaces. However, the presence of multiple concurrent learners makes the environment non-stationary, which is a violation of the assumptions behind most traditional machine learning techniques. For this reason, concurrent learning requires new (or significantly modified versions of) machine learning methods.

The last section covers inter-agent communication.

3.1 Team Learning

In team learning, there is a single learner involved: but this learner is discovering a set of behaviors for a team of agents, rather than a single agent. Team learning is an easy approach to multi-agent learning because it can use standard single-agent machine learning techniques: there is a single entity that performs the learning process. Unfortunately, team learning may have problems when scaling to complex domains involving large numbers of agents: given an environment with S states, a team with N agents might be in as many S^N states (assuming multiple agents might be in the same state). This explosion in the state space size can be overwhelming for learning methods that explore the space of state utilities (such as reinforcement learning), but it may not as drastically affect techniques that explore the space of behaviors (such as evolutionary computation) [80, 140, 145]. For such reasons, evolutionary computation seems easier to scale up, and it is by far the most widely used team learning technique.

Team learning may be divided into two broad categories: *homogeneous* and *purely-heterogeneous* team learning. Homogeneous learners develop a single agent behavior which is used by every agent on the team. Purely-heterogeneous team learners develop a unique behavior for each agent - such approaches hold the promise of better solutions through agent specialization, but they must cope with larger search spaces. There exist approaches in the middle-ground between these two categories: for example, divide the team into groups, where group mates share the same behavior. We refer to these as *hybrid* team learning methods.

Choosing among these approaches depends on whether specialists are needed in the team or not. Balch[2] [9] suggests that domains where single agents can perform well (for example, foraging) are particularly suited for homogeneous learning, while domains that require task specialization (such as robotic soccer) are more suitable for heterogeneous approaches. Potter et al [127] suggest that the number of different skills required to solve the domain, and not domain difficulty, is a determinant factor requiring a heterogeneous approach.

Homogeneous Team Learning: The assumption that all agents have the same behavior drastically reduces the learning search space. Research in this area includes analyses of the performance of the homogeneous team discovered by the learning process [68], comparisons of different learning paradigms [140], or the increased power added by indirect [131] and direct [83] communication abilities. Learning rules for cellular automata is an oft-overlooked paradigm for homogeneous team learning (a survey of this area is presented in [109]).

Purely-Heterogeneous Team Learning: In heterogeneous team learning, the team is composed of agents with different behaviors, with a single learner trying to improve the team as a whole. This approach allows for more diversity in the team at the cost of increasing the search space. The bulk of research in heterogeneous team learning has concerned itself with the requirement for or the emergence

---

[2] Although both the work of Balch and that of Potter et al employ concurrent learning processes, their findings are particularly apropos to our discussion here.

of specialists. For example, Luke and Spector [98] compares different strategies for evolving heterogeneous team behaviors. Their results show that restricted breeding (preventing cross-breeding of behaviors for different specialists) works better than unrestricted breeding, which suggests that the specialization allowed by the heterogeneous team representation conflicts with the inter-agent genotype mixture allowed by the free interbreeding. However, the question is not fully answered, as the contradictory result in [69] shows.

Hybrid Team Learning: In hybrid team learning, the set of agents is split into several groups, with each agent belonging to exactly one group. All agents in a group have the same behavior. One extreme (a single group), is equivalent to homogenous team learning, while the other extreme (one agent per group) is equivalent to heterogeneous team learning. Hybrid team learning thus permits the experimenter to achieve some of the advantages of each method. Luke et al compare the fully homogeneous results with a hybrid combination that divides the team into six groups of one or two agents each, and then evolves six behaviors, one per group [97]. Although homogeneous teams performed better, the authors suggest that hybrid teams might have outperformed the homogeneous ones given more time. Hara and Nagao [67] introduce a method that automatically discovers the optimum number of groups and their compositions.

3.2 Concurrent Learning

The most common alternative to team learning in cooperative multi-agent systems is concurrent learning, where multiple learning processes attempt to concurrently improve parts of the team. Most often, each agent has it own unique learning process to modify its behavior.

Concurrent learning and team learning each have their champions and detractors. While concurrent learning outperforms both homogeneous and heterogeneous team learning in [30, 79], team learning might be preferable in other situations [108]. When then would each method be preferred over the other? Jansen and Wiegand [81] argue that concurrent learning may be preferable in domains for which some decomposition is possible and helpful, and when it is useful to focus on each subproblem to some degree independently of the others.

The central challenge for concurrent learning is that each learner is adapting its behaviors in the context of other co-adapting learners over which it has no control. In single-agent scenarios (where traditional machine learning techniques are applicable), a learner explores its environment, and while doing so, improves its behavior. Things change with multiple learners: the agents' adaptation to the environment can change the environment itself in a way that makes that very adaptation invalid. This is a significant violation of the basic assumptions behind most traditional machine learning techniques.

There are three directions in concurrent learning research. First, research on the *credit assignment* problem deals with how to apportion the team reward to the individual learners. Second, there are challenges in the *dynamics of learning*. Such research aims to understand the impact of co-adaptation on the learning processes. Third, some work has been done on *modeling other agents* in order to improve the interactions (and collaboration) with them.

3.3 Credit Assignment

When dealing with multiple learners, one is faced with the task of divvying up among them the reward received through their joint actions. The simplest solution is to split the team reward equally among each of the learners, or in a larger sense, divide the reward such that whenever a learner's reward increases (or decreases), *all* learners' rewards increase (decrease). This credit assignment approach is usually termed *global reward*.

There are many situations where it might be desirable to assign credit in a different fashion, however. Clearly if certain learners' agents did the lion's share of the task, it might be helpful to specially reward those learners for their actions, or to punish others for laziness. Similarly, Wolpert and Tumer [197] argue that global reward does not scale well to increasingly difficult problems because the learners do not have sufficient feedback tailored to their own specific actions. In other situations credit assignment *must* be done differently because global reward cannot be efficiently computed, particularly in distributed computation environments. For example, in a robotics foraging domain, it may not be easy to globally gather the information about all items discovered and foraged.

If team reward is not equally divided among the agents, what options are there, and how do they impact on learning? One extreme is to assess each agent's performance based solely on its individual behavior. This approach discourages laziness because it rewards agents only for those tasks they have actually accomplished. However, agents do not have any rational incentive to help other agents, and greedy behaviors may develop. We call this approach *local reward*.

Balch [8, 10] argues that local reward leads to faster learning rates, but not necessarily to better results than global reward. Using local reward leads to better performance in a foraging domain and to worse performance in a simulated soccer domain, as compared to global reward. A few other credit assignment schemes have been proposed as well. Chang et al [33] take a different approach to perform credit assignment: each agent employs a Kalman filter to compute its true contribution to the global reward. Rather than apportion rewards to an agent based on its contribution to the team, one might instead apportion reward based on how the team would have fared differently were the agent not present. Wolpert and Tumer [197] call this the *Wonderful Life Utility*, and argue that it is better than both local and global reward, particularly when scaling to large numbers of agents.

The wide variety of credit assignment methods have a significant impact on our coverage of research in the dynamics of learning, which follows in the next section. Our initial focus will be on the study of concurrent learning processes in fully cooperative scenarios, global reward is used. But other credit assignment schemes may run counter the researchers' intention for the agents to cooperate, resulting in dynamics resembling general-sum or even competitive games, which we also discuss in the next section.

3.4   The Dynamics of Learning

When applying single-agent learning to stationary environments, the agent experiments with different behaviors until hopefully discovering a globally optimal behavior. In dynamic environments, the agent may at best try to keep up with the changes in the environment and constantly track the shifting optimal behavior. Things are even more complicated in multi-agent systems, where the agents may adaptively change each others' learning environments. We believe two tools have the potential to help model and analyze the dynamics of concurrent learners across multiple learning techniques. The first one, Evolutionary Game Theory, EGT was successfully used to study the properties of cooperative coevolution [48, 195], to visualize basins of attraction to Nash equilibria for cooperative coevolution [121], and to study trajectories of concurrent Q-learning processes [176, 166]. The other tool combines information on the rate of behavior change per agent, learning and retention rates, and the rate at which other agents are learning as well, to model and predict the behavior of existing concurrent learners.

Many studies in concurrent learning have investigated the problem from a game-theoretic perspective. A important concept for such investigations is that of a Nash equilibrium, which is a joint strategy (one strategy for each agent) such that no single agent has any rational incentive (in terms of better reward) to change its strategy away from the equilibrium. As the learners do not usually have control over each others' behaviors, creating alliances to escape this equilibrium is not trivial. For this reason, many concurrent learning methods will converge to Nash equilibria, even if such equilibria correspond to suboptimal team behaviors.

Fully Cooperative Scenarios: Research in simple stateless environments shows that multiple cooperating concurrent learners can greatly benefit from being optimistic about their teammates: the goal is not to match well your current teammates, but to expect them to improve as well due to their learning [85, 122]. Scaling up to environments with states is computationally demanding. Wang and Sandholm [185] present the *Optimal Adaptive Learning* algorithm, which is guaranteed to converge to optimal Nash equilibria if there are a finite number of actions and states; unfortunately, the time required for the algorithm to achieve such optimality guarantees may be exponential in the number of agents. Environments where the state can only be partially observed (usually due to the agents' limited sensor capabilities) represent even more difficult (also more realistic) settings. The task of finding the optimal policies in partially observable Markov decision process (POMDP) is PSPACE-complete [124], and it becomes NEXP-complete for decentralized POMDPs [17]. Preliminary research for such domains is presented in [125, 114].

General Sum Games: Unequal-share credit assignment techniques can inadvertently place learning in rather non-cooperative scenarios. For such reasons, general sum games are applicable to the cooperative learning paradigm, even though in some situations such games may not be in any way cooperative. Following the early work of Littman [92], there has been significant recent research in concurrent (and not necessarily cooperative) learning for general-sum games [26]. Concurrent learning algorithms for such settings[3] range from Nash-Q [76], Friend-or-Foe Q-learning [93], EXORL ([161]), Correlated-Q [62], to WoIF [27].

3.5 Teammate Modeling

A final area of research in concurrent learning is teammate modeling: learning about other agents in the environment so as to make good guesses of their expected behavior, and to act accordingly (to cooperate with them more effectively, for example). For example, agents may use Bayesian learning to create models of other agents, and use such models to anticipate their behavior [32]. Suryadi and Gmytrasiewicz [162] present a similar agent modeling approach consisting of learning the beliefs, capabilities and preferences of teammates. As the correct model cannot usually be computed, the system stores a set of such models together with their probability of being correct, given the observed behaviors of the other agents. On the other hand, modeling teammates is not a must for better coordination [146]. Finally, Wellman and Hu suggest that the resulting behaviors are highly sensitive to the agents' initial beliefs, and they recommend minimizing the assumptions about the other agents' policies [192].

3.6 Learning and Communication

For some problems communication is a necessity; for others, communication may nonetheless increase agent performance. We define *communication* very broadly: altering the state of the environment such that other agents can perceive the modification and decode information from it. Among other reasons, agents communicate in order to coordinate more effectively, to distribute more accurate models of the environment, and to learn subtask solutions from one another.

But are communicating agents really *multi-agent*? Stone and Veloso argue that unrestricted communication reduces a multi-agent system to something isomorphic to a single-agent system [160]. They do this by noting that without any restriction, the agents can send complete external state information to a "central agent", and to execute its commands in lock-step, in essence acting as effectors for the central agent.

Explicit communication can also significantly increase the learning method's search space, both by increasing the size of the external state available to the agent (it now knows state information communicated from other agents), and by increasing the agent's available choices (perhaps by adding a "communicate with agent i" action). As noted in [40], this increase in search space can hamper learning an optimal behavior by more than communication itself may help.

Direct Communication: Many agent communication methods employ, or assume, an external communication method by which agents may share information

---

[3] The algorithms are usually tested on general-sum and competitive domains, and only very rarely in cooperative problems.

with one another. The method may be constrained in terms of throughput, latency, locality, agent class, etc. Examples of direct communication include shared blackboards, signaling, and message-passing. The literature has examined both hard-coded communication methods and learned communication methods, and their effects on cooperative learning overall. Tan [169] and Berenji and Vengerov [15] suggest that cooperating learners can use communication to share different knowledge about the environment in order to improve team performance. Other research provides the agents with a communication channel but does not hard-code its purpose; the task is for the agents to discover a language for communication [183].

Indirect Communication: Indirect communication methods are those which involve the *implicit* transfer of information from agent to agent through modification of the world environment. Examples of indirect communication include: leaving footsteps in snow, leaving a trail of bread crumbs in order to find one's way back home, and providing hints through the placement of objects in the environment (perhaps including the agent's body itself). Much of the indirect communication literature has drawn inspiration from social insects' use of pheromones to mark trails or to recruit other agents for tasks [75]. Pheromones are chemical compounds whose presence and concentration can be sensed by fellow insects [22], and like many other media for indirect communication, pheromones can last a long time in the environment, though they may diffuse or evaporate. Several pheromone-based learning algorithms have been proposed for foraging problem domains (such as [110]).

This section has presented cooperative MASs. The next section continues with MASs from a competitive perspective.

4 Competitive MASs

4.1 Preamble

The previous section has presented an overview of the literature concerning cooperative MASs. These systems are characterized by the fact that the agents implicitly or explicitly have as common goal to work together. The agents are benevolent and choose actions to promote the overall utility of the system. This is not an easy task, as discussed in Section 3, but the programmers of the agents in principle are free to design the agents that cooperate and truthfully exchange information to promote the desired cooperation. This is however not the case for more competitive settings where the individual agents have non-aligned goals.

Competition in inherent in human interaction. The field of economics is founded on this principle. Game Theory is an analytical offshoot where the goal is to mathematically analyze the strategies required for detailed scenarios, smaller in domain than usually encountered in economics. Electronic Agents in competitive settings have been introduced and studied for broadly two types of settings that we cover here:

- E-commerce;Market-Based Games; bargaining/negotiations, markets and market mechanisms, and auctions.
- Multi-Agent RL (MARL) usually for more restricted settings; matrix games.

The above two distinctions are not exhaustive for the field of competitive agents as a whole. They are however two dominant streams of research. We treat each in a separate section below, although there are overlaps.

4.2   Design of Adaptive Software Agents for Market-Based Multi-agent Games

General. Non-cooperative agents [189] for economical and societal settings, or competitive agents for short, received increasing interest only in recent years. Such agents have their own, possibly conflicting goals and aim for local optimization. Their owners can e.g. be competing companies or autonomous departments within a bigger organization, where the multi-agent systems should facilitate trading, allocation, or planning between these owners, e.g. by means of negotiation or auctioning.

Due to the advances in the use of Internet technology, providing technology for autonomous or competitive parties has become crucial, both for computer science and for its applications [123, 82]. For competitive agents in a multi-agent system, the question is how such a system can work properly. Here, inspired by economics, competitive games appear to be important. Several important problems have very recently been addressed.

A game is given by a set of rules regarding some players that interact with each other, and it determines who gets which payoff at the end [18, 54, 111, 118, 119]. Examples are negotiation, auctioning, formation of interaction networks between parties, production decisions in an oligopoly economy, or planning and scheduling with self-interested parties [89, 138, 4]. In this section, we focus on prominent competitive games as above (i.e., games between competitive players [4].), viz. market games, and in particular, we mainly consider various types of negotiation and auctioning.

Various forms of negotiations and auctions exist. Examples of negotiation [18, 111, 19] are one-issue negotiations and multi-issue negotiation (dealing with just one or with multiple issues, respectively); bilateral negotiations between two parties; one party that negotiates simultaneously with multiple other parties about one or more goods; etcetera. Similarly, many types of auctions exist [89], such as classical auctions like the English ascending bid auction, the Dutch clock auction, the single sealed bid second price auction (Vickrey auction); multi-issue auctions; double auctions (buyers and sellers bid simultaneously, as in many financial markets); reverse auctions (procurement auctions); combinatorial auctions (for the allocation of a collection of multiple goods) [142]; etcetera.

In these market games, participating agents have to determine several aspects. Of course, the direct values of the bid or the bidding strategy is important

---

[4] We thus do not only address with "competitive games" the special constant-sum game, but the more general class of games played by competitive agents.

to be determined. Similarly, other aspects can be important to get to good bidding behavior, like models of the (changing) preferences of the opponents in the market games, the (changing) actual strategies used by the opponents, or the actual value of the good at hand (e.g. being private, common, with externalities or with complementarities).

Some of the auctions have the properties that strategic behavior by the agents is filtered out and therefore not relevant: the "truth-revealing" auctions (e.g., Vickrey auctions, and VCG auctions: Vickrey-Clark-Grooves). Most market games, however, allow strategic behavior by agents to influence the outcomes of these games. Also, the bidding process in "truth-revealing auctions" becomes strategy-dependent as well at the moment that these auctions appear in a repeated or concurrent fashion (e.g. [16, 43]). An example is formed by simultaneous auctions on the Internet, all dealing with similar goods, where an agent just needs to acquire one good. Therefore, strategy determination is important for agents playing in these multiple market games.

Thus, strategies, information and knowledge related to the market games are needed for individual agents. These are studied in fields like game theory and micro economics [18, 54, 111, 102]. Although recent game theory gives valuable insights, its settings and results are often highly stylized, and not applicable in or powerful enough for multi-agent systems [82, 44].[5]

Relations to other disciplines: Related scientific disciplines are (evolutionary) game theory and economics. For competitive game settings with the above described characteristics, strategies and relevant knowledge for competitive software agents are not readily available from these disciplines, as already indicated above. In general, these disciplines address such settings at a higher abstraction level, while not taking into account the actual computational tractability of and learnability of strategies and related parameters. Issues address especially how and which equilibria can be reached or obtained [144, 53], for more idealized and abstract settings of learning in repeated games [53, 187] (with e.g. the usage of mathematical Bayesian rules [6] or coordinated learning in stylized games). This does not concern computational efficiency (or tractability) considerations, but rather whether strategies are computable (i.e., on Turing machines) [53, 112, 49]. Some of the insights, however, can be used for multi-agent systems, thus especially at a higher abstraction level or for more stylized settings, including the use of impossibility results.

Adaptive Solutions: Participation of an agent in one competitive game cannot be seen in its isolation, is interdependent of e.g. the future and the past, and of e.g. slowly unraveling information about e.g. allocations, interdependencies, and (private) valuations. The strategy of an agent should thus be adaptive. This is also due to the limited capabilities of agents, as is also acknowledged by modern game theory and economics, stating that agents are not fully rational:

---

[5] We will briefly further discuss the relevance of the areas (evolutionary) game theory and (micro-) economics later.

[6] e.g. with infinite positive priors distributions.

– the players in the market games are heterogeneous agents which are boundedly rational [139, 150, 6]: diverse agents that e.g. have only partial (incomplete) information (and knowledge) and limited computing power. [7]

Thus solutions to compute adaptive strategies are needed [82, 178]: adaptive
solutions, which build on experience, and which determine, adapt and learn strategies and related models and knowledge. Adaptive solutions determine the strategies via appropriate models, that contain the strategy variables as well as other
appropriate parameters, representations, and relationships, and for which parameter settings have to be determined by intelligent computational techniques.

Since market games are more context dependent than e.g. matrix games, the
issues that must be learnt can be broader than for matrix games. Actually,
market games are often embedded in some sort of (application) setting, which
determines some of the opponent types and preferences, or e.g. some of the
repeated game settings. Depending on the closeness of the market game to an
application setting, the game settings can be considered to be more fundamental,
applicable or even applied.

Learning Agents: Feasible adaptive techniques for agents playing in market
games are e.g. fuzzy techniques, evolutionary algorithms, various (learning)
heuristics, neural networks, simulated annealing, and graphical models. Combining competitive agent systems and learning techniques for market-based
games is currently appearing as one of the important ways to go in the research
on multi-agent systems.

Until now, several papers on adaptive strategies on single or multiple competitive games in multiagent systems have appeared. Papers mainly presenting various kinds of heuristics, with possibly fuzzy or probabilistic models, are e.g. [1, 5,
21, 23, 44, 45, 56, 57, 72, 77, 100, 116, 134, 152, 154, 180]. Results with fully learning approaches as well as a focus on multiple competitive games have been rather
limited until now. We will give some representative references in the sequel.

Typically, learning should be done in some kind of "multiple" settings. I.e.,
learning can be done in the "classical" way of repeated one-shot games, or one
game with one opponent during the stepwise progress of the game. However, due
to the tight connections with the economic and social application fields, learning
can and should also be done in e.g. repeated interrelated games or concurrent
games, learning while playing against e.g. multiple opponents, or about multiple
goods. We will encounter instances in the sequel.

Opponent Modeling. In several settings, opponent modeling can be of importance in order to derive good game outcomes [45, 88, 91, 136, 137, 154, 155].
In such models, (approximations of) preferences of opponents are represented,
which can form the base for the actual agent strategy. This is especially important, when trade-offs between game outcomes between the different players
can be made and some kind of Pareto-efficiency is involved, e.g. like in multi-
issue negotiation. Opponent models can be determined for one opponent or for a

---

[7] This does of course not only affect an agent because of its own abilities, but also via
the abilities of its opponent agents.

class (type) of opponents. In the latter case, a distinction can be made between starting with a pre-existing opponent model (offline modeling) vs. starting from scratch and learning opponent models while repeatedly playing games (online modeling). Learning techniques that have been applied are e.g. simulated annealing [88], probabilistic approaches [154, 155], graphical models [136, 137], neural networks and evolutionary algorithms [21, 91]. Alternatively, opponent modeling papers exist for e.g. combinatorial auctions, in order to reduce the search space for the auctioneer (e.g. [78]).

In a related but different way, preference elicitation is an important issue. In this case, the modeling of some human (or agent) is done in a cooperative way, in order to get the preferences into an appropriate model: a user preference model for market games. This model can then be used in an agent when playing in market games, on behalf of that person. So, in this case, the agent is instructed which goals to reach, by means of the preference model. The learning process differs in that it is supposed to be carried out with a cooperating, willing "opponent": the human being. Several papers with different objectives and learning techniques exist in this area. Learning techniques include neural networks, evolutionary algorithms, and heuristics to obtain fuzzy constraints [20, 66, 99]. This area of research is close to the more general area of preference elicitation and knowledge acquisition from humans [74], but has a different objectives in that it concerns decision making during negotiations.

Market and Strategy Modeling. In other settings, models of opponent preferences are less relevant, and parameters concerning the goods about which the market game is played, or the aggregate (anonymous) market behavior (determined by a substantial amount of fairly anonymous agents) is of more importance. In case of the underlying good, one may think of a good of which its valuation can be determined from participation in multiple games. E.g., the actual value for a seller of a customer click on a web advertisement can usually not be determined beforehand. This can be learning by approaches with e.g. neural networks or evolutionary algorithms [21]. Also, the valuation of a good can depend on the allocation of other goods to (other) agents [21, 165], leading to allocative interdependencies. The level of adaptivity of the involved agents can also influence the respective individual payoffs [165]. Similarly, aggregate market behavior is of importance. This means so much as e.g: what is the typical winning price for certain types of goods in certain types of markets [21, 193], which can be done by various learning techniques. We also refer to the trading agent competition (TAC) below. Some typical settings and results exist e.g. for multiple games with an aggregated stochastic approach [1, 23], for multiple goods in repeated auctions with bounded budgets [180], one-to-many negotiations [57, 116], concurrent games with price prediction [120] or valuation estimation [130], or using evolutionary or fuzzy neural techniques for one or multiple goods in overlapping auctions [5, 71]. Also, more specific and tailored models can be designed for market (price) prediction, e.g. for financial markets. This, however, quickly reaches an other discipline, viz., regression and prediction methods, especially if these markets are complex; this is outside the scope of this paper. Finally, market behavior determined by bidding agents can also be studied by simulations, in the form of evolutionary algorithms standing for populations of agents strategies, from which also proper bidding strategies can be obtained [58, 5, 31, 55].

In case of market games on complex goods, strategies could be decomposed in some substrategies, that deal with different aspects of or paradigms in the game. E.g., a negotiation strategy can be decomposed into the concession strategy (how much to concede in the overall value of a bid) and the Pareto-search strategy (search for Pareto-optimal deals) [45, 152, 153]. The concession strategy could be seen as market and strategy modeling, the Pareto-search strategy could be seen as opponent modeling.

Models of Application Settings. Application settings and models that go further than the conventional game theoretic stylizations are important for this field. Market games are often studied related to more specific application models. We briefly mention some settings and models, e.g.

- The trading agent competitions: TAC [167, 191, 194] and TAC SCM (supply chain management) [167]. Both competitions deal with a modeled application settings, viz., a) travel agencies that have to buy and sell holiday trips consisting of complementary or substitutable constituents, and b) a 2-phase supply chain for computer manufacturing and sales, respectively. Both deal with several types of market mechanism for the distribution of goods and services with complementarities and substitutables, and the agents have to design strategies for both bidding in multiple games and determination of what to buy. Approaches that have been presented until now, are e.g. price prediction, equilibrium analysis, decision theory, and some forms of machine learning (like Reinforcement Learning) (e.g. [35, 61, 70, 159] or [193] for a survey).
- Market-based scheduling, resource allocation, and logistics [36, 190, 101, 134, 164].
- Information goods with negotiation and (dynamic) pricing [28, 57, 63, 86, 87, 149, 156, 152, 153].

Co-learning and Evaluation: State and Open Issues. In addition to the development of adaptive systems for agents in market games, other aspects become important as well.

When applying adaptive techniques for competitive agents in multiagent systems, the quality of an adaptive strategy for an agent depends on the (adaptive) strategies of other agents. In the case that all agents use truly adaptive strategies as well, various forms of colearning occurs. Up to now, such environments of multiple agents are still rather restricted and mainly address learning in cooperative systems and e.g. stochastic (general-sum) games [147, 188]. Approaches and requirements address e.g. various settings with stationary opponent agents and best response, evolutionary simulations [3, 5, 31, 55, 46, 58, 64, 171], self-play (many results [37], also for co-evolution, e.g. [177]), or, for market settings, leveled learning and opponent modeling [77, 181], adaptivity and individual profits [165], and some mixed approaches (e.g. [184]). Thus, learning in a dynamic environment containing colearning competitive agents has still received limited attention, and still substantial questions exist about what feasible and relevant environments are [25, 37, 47, 143, 148, 158, 184, 188]. Environments of more or less arbitrary opponent agents are not possible in general (i.e., several impossibility results exist [112, 113]). Therefore, appropriate classes of competitive opponent agents have to be given for which best learning strategies must be determined [148] (the "AI agenda"), while other robust evaluation criteria for resulting strategies must be determined and satisfied (e.g. [25, 37]). Still, appropriate further insight needs to be acquired for the effects of co-learning and for the way in which adaptive strategies can be evaluated.

4.3 MARL

In this section we give an overview of the state of art in multi-agent RL (MARL). This section is strongly inspired by the recent work of[128],[129], and [148], . These papers discuss current state of the art MARL algorithms and introduce new evaluation criteria (i.e. the AI agenda) for judging MARL algorithms. We also refer the interested reader to [13], [84], and [95] for alternative overview papers. We discuss a number of notable MARL algorithms along with novel evaluation criteria for competitive multi-agent RL learning. We have a bit of a chicken and the egg scenario as novel criteria are under development and are supported by novel learning algorithms that, of course, perform extremely well for the newly introduced norms. We first discuss the novel criteria, and then separately discuss the remaining algorithms. The next section begins with the basic concepts of Multi-Agent RL and the often chosen problem domain of matrix games.

Competitive Agents and Reinforcement Learning for Matrix games.
In this section we introduce some concepts from Reinforcement Learning. We repeat concepts from Game Theory in Section 3 and cast these to the the MARL perspective for the sake of reference.

In general, let S denote the set of states in the game and let A_i denote the set of actions that agent/player i may select in each state $s \in S$. Let $a = (a_1, a_2, \ldots, a_n)$, where $a_i \in A_i$ be a join action for n agents, and let $A = A_1 \times \cdots \times A_n$ be the set of possible joint actions. **Zero-sum games** are games where the rewards of the agents for each joint action sum to zero. **General sum games** allow for any sum of values for the reward of a joint action.

A **strategy (or policy)** for agent i is a probability distribution $\pi(\cdot)$ over its actions set A_i. Let $\pi(S)$ denote a strategy over all states $s \in S$ and let $\pi(s)$ (or π_i) denote a strategy in a single state s. A strategy may be a **pure strategy** (an agent selects an action deterministically) or according to a **mixed strategy** (a strategy that plays a random action, according a probability distribution). A **joint strategy** played by n agents is denoted by $\pi = (\pi_i, \ldots, \pi_n)$. Also, let a_{-i} and π_{-i} refer to the joint action and strategy of all agents except agent i.

We focus on the more restricted **matrix game**, defined by a set of matrices $R = \{R_1, \ldots, R_n\}$. Matrix games are the chosen domain for most recent MARL applications. We further restrict our presentation to two-player, two-action games as these are well classified [132] and often used. The algorithms presented in the rest of the paper are of course applicable to more general settings.

Let $R(\pi) = (R_1(\pi), \ldots, R(\pi_n))$ be a vector of expected payoffs when the joint strategy π is played. Also, let $R_i(\pi_i, \pi_{-i})$ be the expected payoff to agent i when it plays strategy π_i and the other agents play π_{-i}. A strategy then is **dominant** if, regardless of what any other players do, the strategy earns a player a larger payoff than any other strategy. Let $R_i(\begin{bmatrix} a_i \\ a_{-i} \end{bmatrix})$ be the payoff for agent i playing action a_i while the other agents play action a_{-i}. A strategy π_i is dominant, if and only if

$$\forall \pi_i' \forall \pi_{-i} \sum_{a_i, a_{-i}} \pi_i(a_i) \pi_{-i}(a_{-i}) R_i(\begin{bmatrix} a_i \\ a_{-i} \end{bmatrix}) >= \sum_{a_i, a_{-i}} \pi_i'(a_i) \pi_{-i}(a_{-i}) R_i(\begin{bmatrix} a_i \\ a_{-i} \end{bmatrix}) \quad (1)$$

Each individual matrix game has certain classic game theoretic values. The **minimax** value for player i is $m_i = \max_{\pi_i} \min_{a_{-i}} R_i(\pi_i, a_i)$, i.e. the least reward that can be achieved if the game is known and the game is only played once. A **Best-Response** (BR) to the opponents strategy π_{-i} is defined by

$$BR = \pi^* = max_\pi R_i(\pi, \pi_{-i}). \quad (2)$$

This is the most expected reward that can be gained playing assuming the game is known, the game is only played once, and the opponent strategy is known.

A **Nash Equilibrium** (Nash-Equilibrium) is then a joint strategy such that no agent may unilaterally change its strategy without lowering its expected payoff in the one shot play of the game. Nash [115] showed that every n player matrix game has at least one such Nash-Equilibrium. A **Pareto optimal** solution of the game is a joint strategy such that no agent may unilaterally increase its expected payoff without making another agent worse off. A joint strategy π_1 is said to **Pareto dominate** a strategy π_2 if the expected payoff for π_1 is at least as high as for π_2 and higher for at least one of the agents. A joint strategy is **Pareto deficient** if it is not Pareto optimal.

We assume that an agent can observe its own payoffs as well as the actions taken by all agents in each stage game, but only after the fact. All agents concurrently choose their actions. A possible adaption of the policy of the agents, i.e. learning as a result of observed opponent behavior, only takes effect in the next stage game. Each agent aims to maximize its reward for iterated play of the same matrix game, playing the same opponent.

Evaluation Criteria. *General Background:* Classic Reinforcement Learning [163, 186] aims to converge to stationary policy π for an individual agent that maximizes the expected discounted future payoffs. This amounts to

$$\max_\pi E(\sum_{\tau=t}^{T} \gamma^{\tau-t} R^\tau(\pi)) \quad (3)$$

where T may be finite or infinite and $0 < \gamma < 1$ is the discount factor. An alternative measure is the average reward over the last t epochs. Both approaches however implicitly assume the agent is optimizing relative to a stationary environment, an assumption that in general does not hold for MARL. All current MARL algorithms therefore incorporate some modeling of the opponent in some form or other to include the opponent as part of the (changing) environment against which an agent is optimizing.

It should be noted that [113] prove that in general it is impossible to perfectly learn to play optimally against an adaptive opponent and at the same time perfectly estimate the policy of this opponent. Whether this theoretical result is relevant for specific games must be kept in mind. To complicate matters, [179] analyzes from an information theoretical perspective how much an agent can hinder an opponent in modeling by displaying limited random behavior, purely to hide its real preferences. Such strategic behavior is an example of how complex interactions between agents can be and how difficult it can be to learn a good policy when using an opponent model.

[34] introduces a first general classification of competence of MARL algorithms. The ranking of algorithms is based on the crossproduct of their possible strategies and their possible beliefs about the opponent's strategy. An agent's possible strategy can be classified based upon the amount of history it has in its memory. An agents beliefs mirrors the strategy classification. The different categories are supposed to be leagues of players. A fair opponent is any opponent from the same league or less. The idea is that a new learning algorithm should ideally be able to beat any fair opponent. [11] add to this classification scheme with new criterion of reactivity (see later in this section).

The focus to date in MARL algorithms has been mainly on game theoretical equilibriums from single shot games, i.e Nash-Equilibrium, Pareto-Optimal, minimax, etc .... Best-Response and Nash-Equilibrium are intertwined through the circular argument that if both players play BR players will arrive at a mirrored minimax outcome, a Nash-Equilibrium. This is the heart of **Fictitious play**; see [29], and [53].

A recent critique against the focus on such equilibriums has been launched by [128]. This work lists some well-known problems. Nash-Equilibrium are for example known not to be appropriate in repeated games, see also the Folk Theorem. The work of [96] shows how to construct equilibriums for players that are interested in average payoffs for repeated games in polynomial time. It is however unknown how the players should learn these during play as they discover the structure of the game, and the play of their opponents. Also problematical is the existence of multiple Nash-Equilibrium; how do the players choose to which they should converge if the criteria is convergence to a, not the, Nash-Equilibrium. Lastly, one-sided converge to a Nash-Equilibrium by one of the players may make it miss out on exploitation opportunities if the opponents do not follow suit. Algorithms aiming at a Nash-Equilibrium typically achieve this by updating their policy towards the BR with respect to the current policies of their opponents. Players will then, if all follow similar strategies, arrive at individual minimax values of the game, which is a Nash-Equilibrium. Such properties have been proved for converge to Nash-Equilibrium in self-play in zero sum games [92], but have proved less tractable for general sum games. [128] provide suggestions for different criteria for evaluating MARL algorithms. Their main focus is on the **AI Agenda**.

The AI Agenda poses as evaluation criteria as to how well a given algorithm can perform against a restricted class of opponents. The general properties of an algorithm against any opponent, including game theoretical convergence properties, are deemed less important than the performance results when competing with the opponents that the agent will actually encounter. Maximizing personal reward is the criteria that we also feel should not be forgotten in the storm of newly presented evaluation criteria that MARL algorithms are ranked by. In the end, the only criteria of interest to a purely competitive agent for evaluating its learning algorithm in a specific game is how closely it approaches the highest aggregated reward possible during play for given opponents. Game theoretical notions should however not be ignored as they give a sense of how general the power of a MARL is. The AI agenda however allows for a lively competition possibility by introducing open competition on the extensive list of games generated, for example, in the GAMUT framework [117].

Other Criteria: In the rest of this section we list several miscellaneous evaluation criteria that can play a role in ranking MARL algorithms.

The criterion of **asymptotic stability** was developed in [51]. This provides local dynamic robustness. Two conditions must me met: i) Any solution that is sufficiently close to the equilibrium remains arbitrarily close to it. This condition is called **Liapunov stability**. ii) Any solution that starts close enough to the equilibrium, converges to the equilibrium. These type of criteria recur in several papers as full convergence is a strong concept, but algorithms can be shown to come "close enough" to an equilibrium outcome and stay there.

An example of the above is that Hyper-Q [170]. This algorithm learns the value of joint mixed strategies,instead of joint base actions. In the rock-paper-scissors, the well-known children's game, in self play does not converge to the one third all equilibrium but cycles amongst a small number of grid points, with roughly zero average reward for both players. Quoted: "Conceivably, Hyper-Q could have converged to a cyclic Nash-Equilibrium, which would certainly be a nice outcome of self-play learning in a repeated game." This is an example where the learning algorithm achieves the same average reward as the Nash-Equilibrium, but in a dynamic setting. Note that both outcomes are as desirable from the AI agenda perspective.

Another example is the Extended Replicator Dynamics algorithm of [174]. Here the authors take a dynamical systems approach in which they first design the stable differential equations, reaching an asymptotic stable Nash equilibrium in all types of stateless matrix games. After this they constructed the approximating learning algorithm showing the same behavior as the pre-defined dynamical system, i.e. reaching a stable Nash equilibrium.

[37] introduces the AWESOME algorithm, short for "Adapt When Everybody is Stationary. Otherwise Move to Equilibrium". This algorithm converges to BR against stationary opponents, and otherwise converges to a precomputed Nash-Equilibrium in self play. These two properties are listed as minimal conditions for MARL algorithms.

[24] use the **No-regret-measure** with their GIGA-WOLF algorithm. Regret measures how much worse an algorithm performs compared to the best static strategy, with the goal to guarantee at least zero average regret, i.e. no-regret, in the limit. This is general compares the performance of a learner to the best possible hand-coded opponent that performs the best possible strategy, assuming this is computable, for a given game.

[11] define **Reactivity** that measures how fast a learner can adapt to an unexpected hypothetical change in an opponents policy; how fast can an agent learn a best response to an unexpected worst case switch in the opponent's policy. They show that it approximately predicts the performance of a learner as a function of the parameters of its learning algorithm in the matching pennies game. The criterion of reactivity is special to the MARL domain as it is a measure of how quickly an agent can react to being exploited. This is a relative non-issue in single agent RL and in Game Theory concerned with single stage games, but becomes an important factor in repeated play.

[62] introduce the notion of **Correlated Equilibrium**. Players maintain beliefs about their opponents. They are converged in a Correlated Equilibrium if both believe, based on their beliefs about their opponents, no longer see it as advantageous to adjust their policies.

Lastly, [126] presents and analysis a mathematical model of cuckoo parasitism. This work is of relevance to the MARL as it presents and in depth analysis of the cost of defense mechanisms. The main conclusion of the work is that every defense mechanism has a non-zero cost, and expending time and energy in defending against difficult and unlikely scenarios is not biologically smart. Likewise, an agent in a complex situation with limited computational resources may have to choose to focus on likely opponent strategic behavior, and not cover all bases.

The next section discusses state of the art MARL algorithms not listed above.

Other seminal work. Universal Consistency is a strong concept from game theory. An algorithm with this property approximates the best-response stationary policy against any opponent. [52] and [50] independently show that a multiplicative-weight algorithm exhibits universal consistency. These algorithms however require the strong assumption that an agent know the opponent's policy at each time period, which is intractable in practice.

Nash-Q [76] for general-sum games, has as goal to converge to Nash-Equilibrium. This is accomplished for a limited class of games. Friend or Foe [93] treats other agents as either friend or foe and converges to Nash-Equilibrium with less restrictions than Nash-Q.

The following two papers are well known gradient-ascent type algorithms. The Policy Hill CLimber (PHC) is illustrated in [27]. PHC is a simple adaptive strategy based on its own actions and rewards. It maintains a Q-table of of values for each of its base actions, and at every time step it adjusts its mixed strategy by a small step towards the greedy policy of its current Q-function. In Infinitesimal Gradient Ascent (IGA) [151], an agent uses knowledge of the current strategy pair to make to make a small change in the direction of the gradient of its immediate payoff.

WOLF- Win or Learn Fast by [24, 27] deserves a special mention as it is one of the few, if not the first, MARL algorithm to update its learning parameters with as goal to exploit the opponent. The learning rate is made large if WOLF is losing. Otherwise, the learning rate is kept small as a good strategy has been found. Note that in [34] WOLF is exploited by a bluff and dash hand-tailored algorithm to exploit the small step increment of the latter algorithm.

The leader strategies: Bully and Godfather are introduced in [94]. These two strategies aim to threaten the opponent to play good equilibrium strategies, at least from the viewpoint of the threatening agent. This work shows that many known algorithms, like the gradient descent type, are vulnerable to exploitation by these type of hand-tailored strategies.

Predictive state representations [196] is a recent and growing new line of research. The optimization problem of an individual agent is handled by predicting future states from past observations. This is a step beyond the optimization of a policy by incorporating a link between past and future observations in the decisions on how to update the current policy.

Lastly, we list [188] with the NSCP-learners (Non-Stationary Converging Policies) for n-player general sum stochastic games. This work, as claimed, has a first proof of Convergence in self-play on general sum games. This is achieved by slowly decreasing the area of the state space in which the adaptive policies can "move". This locks in the agents to stationary, possibly mixed, strategies that are, by definition, converged.

More and more complex nested opponent models [77] will probably be the future norm in the MARL agents arms race. Although learning about an opponent while at the same time learning is problematic [113], there is still a need to be "smarter" than your opponents.

5   Contributions of This Book

The previous two sections gave a comprehensive overview of the state-of-the-art research on MASs. This section discusses new contributions of the LAMAS workshop. This event included two prestigious invited talks, which have resulted in two extensive high quality papers included in this book.

The invited talk of Peter Stone, University of Texas at Austin, USA, has been shaped into the paper: Multi-Robot Learning for Continuous Area Sweeping, by Mazda Ahmadi and Peter Stone. In their paper they study the problem of multi-agent continuous area sweeping. In this problem agents are situated in a particular environment in which they have to repeatedly visit every part of it such that they can detect events of interest for their global task and coordinate to minimize the total cost. Events are not uniformly distributed, such that agents need to visit locations non-uniformly. The authors formalize this problem and present an initial algorithm to solve it. Moreover they nicely illustrate their approach with a set of experiments in a routine surveillance task.

The second invited talk of the workshop was by Ann Nowé, professor in computer sciences at the university of Brussels, Belgium, resulting in the paper: Learning Automata as a Basis for Multiagent Reinforcement Learning, by Ann Nowé, Katja Verbeeck and Maarten Peeters. In their work they start with an overview on important theoretical results from the theory of Learning Automata in terms of game theoretic concepts and consider them as a policy iterator in the domain of Reinforcement Learning problems. Doing so they gradually move from the variable structure automaton, mapping to the single stage-single agent case, over learning automata games, mapping to the single stage multi-agent case, to interconnected Learning Automata, considering multi stage-multi agent problems. The authors also show the most interesting connection with the field of Ant Colony Optimization.

The entire program of LAMAS covered a quite wide area in learning and adaption in multi-agent systems, varying from typical application areas as traffic management, rover systems, ant systems and economical systems to more theoretical papers on state space representation, no-regret learning, evolution, exploration-exploitation and noise in cooperative systems.

Starting with the application papers, we have [38, 14, 172, 182]. In [182], the authors introduce a new kind of ant colony optimization algorithm, extending the classical algorithms with multiple types of ants. They use this kind of multi-agent approach for solving the problem of routing and backup trees in optical networks. More precisely, they assign an ant type to each working path and and backup tree.

In [38], the authors identify and explore several interesting opportunities, created by their reservation based mechanism for traffic management, for multi-agent learning. More precisely, their system consists of two kinds of agents, i.e. intersection managers and driver agents, for which they describe the learning opportunities and offer a first-cut solution to each of them. These opportunities, amongst others, include delayed response for the intersection manager, organizing an intersection as a market, agents bidding in this market and autonomous lane changing.

The topic of the paper [14] is coordination in large multi-agent systems, studying effects of guiding the decision process of individual agents. In their work they study this problem in the context of route guidance in traffic management. The guiding information can have different sources and agents are potential players. Simulations of this problem show that it can be beneficial to have a recommendation system for drivers. The authors discuss the different conditions for an optimal performing recommendation system.

Adaptive Multi-Rover Systems are the topic of paper [172]. More precisely, the authors describe how efficient reward methods can be applied to the coordination of multiple agents in a dynamic environment with limited communication possibilities. Difficulties lie in the design of the individual reward functions which need to be aligned with the global reward function and must stay aligned with changes in the reward of each individual agent. Their results show how factored reward functions, in combination with evolutionary computation, can be successful for real world applications.

One of the fundamental problems in RL is the exploration-exploitation dilemma, which is extensively studied in [135]. The authors propose a new algorithm based on meta-heuristics to tune the tradeoff between both and validate it on economic systems. Moreover it is shown to be a promising approach in comparison with other adaptive techniques.

Having a glance at the less application oriented and more theoretical papers, we find five contributions in this book [2, 12, 42, 107, 173].

In [12] the authors present a new multi-agent learning algorithm, which is a modification of the ReDVaLeR algorithm. The new algorithm achieves convergence to near-best response against eventually stationary opponents, no-regret payoff against arbitrary opponents and convergence to the Nash equilibrium in unique mixed equilibria games.

In [2] the authors extend their previous algorithm, which finds Pareto optimal solutions in general sum games, to so-called preferred Pareto Optimal solutions (PPO). A clear definition can be found in their paper. Moreover, they experiment with the opportunity of revelation in two-player two-action conflict games. Their experiments show that their new algorithm is an improvement over previous results.

In [173] the authors give a new direction to research in multi-agent learning by cross-fertilizing the multi-agent learning problem with relational reinforcement learning (RRL). More precisely, they propose to use a relational representation of the state space in multi-agent reinforcement learning as this has many proved benefits over the propositional one, as for instance handling large state spaces, a rich relational language, modeling of other agents without a computational explosion, and generalization over new derived knowledge. Their initial experiments show that the learning rates are quite good and promising when using a relational representation in coordination problems and that they can be increased by using the observations over other agents to learn a relational structure between the agents.

The authors of [42] present their methods for dealing with a noisy environment in cooperative multi-agent learning. More precisely, they introduce an algorithm to cope with perception, communication and position errors for cooperative multi-agent learning tasks. Although this offers interesting possibilities, the improvements are quite expensive seen from a computational perspective.

Tag-mediated interaction has shown to stimulate cooperation in populations of agent playing the Prisoner's Dilemma (PD) game. In [107], the authors try to answer why tags facilitate such cooperation. More precisely, they analyzed the effects of the size of the tag space, mutation rate in the population, on cooperation in a population of agents playing the PD game. Additionally, they empirically analyzed why tags have this influence on this type of systems. The conclusion suggests that tags rather promote mimicry than cooperation.

6   Open Research Issues

Multi-agent learning is a relatively young field and as such its open research issues are still very much in flux. This section singles-out three important open questions that need to be addressed in order to make multi-agent learning more broadly successful as a technique in real world applications. These issues arise from the *multi* in multi-agent learning, and may eventually require new learning methods specifically tailored for multiple agents.

Scalability: Scalability is a problem for many learning techniques, but especially so for multi-agent learning. The dimensionality of the search space grows rapidly with the number of agents, the complexity of their behaviors, and the size of the network of interactions among them. This search space grows so rapidly that one *cannot* learn the entire joint behavior of a large, heterogeneous, strongly inter-communicating multi-agent system. Effective learning in an area this complex requires some degree of sacrifice: either by isolating the learned behaviors among individual agents, by reducing the heterogeneity of the agents, or by reducing the complexity of the agent's capabilities. Techniques such as learning hybrid teams, decomposition, or partially restricting the locality of reinforcement provide promising solutions in this direction.

As problem complexity increases, it gives rise to the spectre of *emergent behavior*, where the global effects of simple agent behaviors cannot be readily predicted. This is an area of considerable study and excitement in artificial life: but it may also be a major problem for machine learning. How does emergence affect the smoothness of the search space? If small perturbations in agent behavior result in radical swings in emergent behavior, can learning methods be expected to scale well at all in this environment?

Adaptive Dynamics and Nash Equilibria: Multi-agent systems are typically dynamic environments, with multiple learning agents vying for resources and tasks. This dynamism presents a unique challenge not normally found in single-agent learning: as the agents learn, their adaptation to one another changes the world scenario. How do agents learn in an environment where the goalposts are constantly and adaptively being moved? In many cases, existing learning methods may converge to suboptimal Nash equilibria. We echo opinions from [90] and express our concern with the use of Nash equilibria in cooperative multi-agent learning: such "rational" convergence to equilibria may well be movement away from globally *team-optimal* solutions [90]. We argue that, in the context of cooperative agents, the requirement of rationality should be secondary to that of optimal team behavior. Mutual trust may be a more useful concept in this context.

Large State Spaces: The state space of a large, joint multi-agent task can be overwhelming. An obvious way to tackle this is to use domain knowledge to simplify the state space, often by providing a smaller set of more "powerful" actions customized for the problem domain. For example, agents may use higher-level descriptions of states and actions [104]. Another alternative has been to reduce complexity by heuristically decomposing the problem, and hence the *joint behavior*, into separate, simpler behaviors for the agents to learn. One approach to such decomposition is to learn basic behaviors first, then set them in stone and learn more complex behaviors based on them. This method is commonly known as *layered learning*, and was successfully applied to robotic soccer [157]. Another approach, *shaping*, gradually changes the reward function from favoring easier behaviors to favoring more complex ones based on those easy behaviors [103, 10].

Less work has been done on formal methods of decomposing tasks (and behaviors) into subtasks (sub-behaviors) appropriate for multi-agent solutions, how agents' sub-behaviors interact, and how and when learning of these sub-behaviors may be parallelized. Guestrin et al note that in many domains the actions of some agents may be independent [65]. Taking advantage of this, they suggest partially decomposing the joint team behavior based on a *coordination graph* that heuristically spells out which agents must interact in order to solve the problem. Ghavamzadeh and Mahadevan suggest a different hierarchical approach to simplifying the inter-agent coordination task, where agents coordinate their high-level behaviors, rather than each primitive action they may perform [59].

An alternative to problem decomposition, is the quest for other representations or formalisms for the state space. One such succesfull method in single-agent learning has been the cross fertilization between reinforcement learning and inductive logic programming [39, 41, 168]. More precisely, in this formalism states are represented in a relational form, that more directly represents the underlying world. Complex tasks as planning or information retrieval on the web can be represented more naturally in relational form than in propositional form, what is usually done in Reinforcement Learning. In [173], the authors are extending this single agent work to multi-agent planning and coordination tasks.

Competitive Agents: Non-cooperative agents [189] for economical and societal settings, or competitive agents for short, are receiving increasing interest in recent years. Such agents have their own, possibly conflicting goals and aim for local optimization. Their owners can e.g. be competing companies or autonomous departments within a bigger organization, where the multi-agent systems should facilitate trading, allocation, or planning between these owners, e.g. by means of negotiation or auctioning.

Due to the advances in the use of Internet technology, providing technology for autonomous or competitive parties has become crucial, both for computer science and for its applications [82, 123]. For competitive agents in a multi-agent system, the continuing question is how such a system can work properly. Here, inspired by economics, competitive games appear to be important.

More and more complex nested opponent models [77] will likely be the future norm in the for agents in the competitive arms race. Although learning about an opponent while at the same time learning is problematic [113], there is still a need to be "smarter" than your opponents. The AI Agenda will play an important role.

References

[1] C. P. A. Byde and N. Jennings. Decision procedures for multiple auctions. In *Proceedings of the 1st Int. Conf. Autonomous Agents and Multi-Agent Systems (AAMAS 2002)*, 2002.

[2] S. Airiau and S. Sen. Towards a pareto-optimal solution in general-sum games, study in 2x2 games. In *LAMAS*, 2005.

[3] A. Alkemade, J. La Poutré, and H. Amman. On social learning and robust evolutionary algorithm design in economic games. In *Proceedings of the 2005 IEEE Congress on Evolutionary Computation (CEC 2005)*, pages 2445–2452. IEEE Press, 2005.

[4] F. Alkemade and J. La Poutré. Heterogeneous, boundedly rational agents in the cournot duopoly. In *In: R. Cowan and N. Jonard (eds.), Heterogenous Agents, Interactions and Economic Performance, Springer Lecture Notes in Economics and Mathematical Systems (LNEMS) 521*, pages 3–17. Springer Verlag, 2002.

[5] P. Anthony and N. Jennings. Developing a bidding agent for multiple heterogeneous auctions. In *ACM Transactions on Internet Technology (ACM TOIT) 3*, pages 185–217, 2003.

[6] W. Arthur. Inductive reasoning and bounded rationality. *American Economic Review 84*, pages 406–411, 1994.

[7] R. Axelrod. *The evolution of cooperation*. Basic Books, New York, NY, 1984.

[8] T. Balch. Learning roles: Behavioral diversity in robot teams. Technical Report GIT-CC-97-12, Georgia Institute of Technology, 1997.

[9] T. Balch. *Behavioral Diversity in Learning Robot Teams*. PhD thesis, College of Computing, Georgia Institute of Technology, 1998.

[10] T. Balch. Reward and diversity in multirobot foraging. In *IJCAI-99 Workshop on Agents Learning About, From and With other Agents*, pages 92–99, 1999.

[11] B. Banerjee and J. Peng. The role of reactivity in multiagent learning. In *Third International Joint Conference on Autonomous Agents and Multiagent Systems*, pages 538–545, 2004.

[12] B. Banerjee and J. Peng. Convergence of no-regret learning in multiagent systems. In *LAMAS*, 2005.

[13] A. Barto and S. Mahadevan. Recent advances in hierarchical reinforcement learning. *Discrete-Event Systems journal*, 13:41–77, 2003.

[14] A. L. C. Bazzan, M. Fehler, and F. Klugl. Learning to coordinate in a network of social drivers: the role of information. In *LAMAS*, 2005.

[15] H. Berenji and D. Vengerov. Advantages of cooperation between reinforcement learning agents in difficult stochastic problems. In *Proceedings of 9th IEEE International Conference on Fuzzy Systems*, 2000.

[16] D. Bernhardt and D. Scoones. A note on sequential auctions. *The American Economic Review*, 84(3):653–657, 1994.

[17] D. Bernstein, S. Zilberstein, and N. Immerman. The complexity of decentralized control of MDPs. In *Proceedings of UAI-2000: The Sixteenth Conference on Uncertainty in Artificial Intelligence*, pages 819–840, 2000.

[18] K. Binmore. *Fun and Games*. D.C. Heath and Company, Lexington, MA, 1992.

[19] K. Binmore and N. Vulkan. Applying game theory to automated negotiation. *Netnomics*, 1:1–9, 1999.

[20] A. Biso, F. Rossi, and A. Sperdutti. Experimental results on learning soft constraints. In *A. G. Cohn, F. Giunchiglia, and B. Selman (eds.), Proceedings of KR2000: Principles of Knowledge Representation and Reasoning*, pages 435–444, 2000.

[21] S. Bohté, E. Gerding, and J. La Poutré. Market-based recommendation: Agents that compete for consumer attention. *ACM Transactions on Internet Technology (ACM TOIT), (Special Issue on Machine Learning on the Internet)*, 4(4):420–448, 2004.

[22] E. Bonabeau, M. Dorigo, and G. Theraulaz. *Swarm Intelligence: From Natural to Artificial Systems*. SFI Studies in the Sciences of Complexity. Oxford University Press, 1999.

[23] C. Boutilier, M. Goldszmidt, , and B. Sabata. Sequential auctions for the allocation of resources with complementaries. In *Proceedings of the 16th International Joint Conference on Artificial Intelligence (IJCAI 99)*, pages 527–534, 1999.

[24] M. Bowling. Convergence and no-regret in multiagent learning. In *Advances in Neural Information Processing Systems*, volume 17, pages 209–216, 2004.

[25] M. Bowling and M. Velose. Rational and convergent learning in stochastic games. In *Proceedings of the Seventh International Joint Conference on Artificial Intelligence (IJCAI)*, pages 1021–1026, 2001.

[26] M. Bowling and M. Veloso. An analysis of stochastic game theory for multiagent reinforcement learning. Technical Report CMU-CS-00-165, Computer Science Department, Carnegie Mellon University, 2000.

[27] M. Bowling and M. Veloso. Multiagent learning using a variable learning rate. *Artificial Intelligence*, 136(2):215–250, 2002.

[28] C. Brooks, S. Fay, R. Das, J. MacKie-Mason, J. Kephart, and E. Durfee. Automated strategy searches in an electronic goods market: Learning complex price schedules. In *Proceedings of the ACM Conference on Electronic Commerce (ACM-EC)*, pages 31–41. ACM Press, 1999.

[29] G. W. Brown. Iterative solution of games by Fictitious Play, 1951. In Activity Analysis of Production and Allocation (T.C. Koopmans, Ed.), pp. 374-376, Wiley: New York.

[30] L. Bull and T. C. Fogarty. Evolving cooperative communicating classifier systems. In A. V. Sebald and L. J. Fogel, editors, *Proceedings of the Fourth Annual Conference on Evolutionary Programming (EP94)*, pages 308–315, 1994.

[31] A. Byde. Applying evolutionary game theory to auction mechanism design. In *ACM Conference on E-Commerce (ACM-EC'03)*, 2003.

[32] G. Chalkiadakis and C. Boutilier. Coordination in multiagent reinforcement learning: A Bayesian approach. In *Proceedings of The Second International Joint Conference on Autonomous Agents & Multiagent Systems (AAMAS 2003)*, pages 709–716. ACM, 2003.

[33] Y.-H. Chang, T. Ho, and L. Kaelbling. All learning is local: Multi-agent learning in global reward games. In *Proceedings of Neural Information Processing Systems (NIPS-03)*, 2003.

[34] Y.-H. Chang and L. P. Kaelbling. Playing is believing: the role of beliefs in multi-agent learning. In *Advances in Neural Information Processing Systems-(NIPS)*, volume 14, 2002.

[35] S.-F. Cheng, E. Leung, K. Lochner, K. O'Malley, D. Reeves, L. Schvartzman, and M. Wellman. Walverine: A Walrasian trading agent. *Decision Support Systems*, 39:169–184, 2005.

[36] S. Clearwater. *Market based Control of Distributed Systems*. World Scientific Press, Singapore, 1995.

[37] V. Conitzer and T. Sandholm. AWESOME: A general multiagent learning algorithm that converges in self-play and learns a best response against stationary opponents. In *20th International Conference on Machine Learning (ICML)*, pages 83–90, 2003.

[38] K. Dresner and P. Stone. Multiagent traffic management: Opportunities for multiagent learning. In *LAMAS*, 2005.

[39] K. Driessens and S. Dzeroski. Integrating guidance into relational reinforcement learning. *Machine Learning*, 57(3):271–304, Dec. 2004.

[40] E. Durfee, V. Lesser, and D. Corkill. Coherent cooperation among communicating problem solvers. *IEEE Transactions on Computers*, C-36(11):1275–1291, 1987.

[41] S. Dzeroski, L. D. Raedt, and K. Driessens. Relational reinforcement learning. *Machine Learning*, 43:7–52, 2001.

[42] C. O. e Sousa and L. Custodio. Dealing with errors in a cooperative multi-agent learning system. In *LAMAS*, 2005.

[43] W. Elmaghraby. The importance of ordering in sequential auctions. *Management Science*, 49(5):673–682, 2003.

[44] P. Faratin, C. Sierra, and N. Jennings. Negotiation decision functions for autonomous agents. *International Journal of Robotics and Autonomous Systems*, 34(24):159–182, 1998.

[45] P. Faratin, C. Sierra, and N. Jennings. Using similarity criteria to make issue trade-offs. *Artificial Intelligence*, 142:205–237, 2002.

[46] S. Fatima, M. Wooldridge, and N. Jennings. Comparing equilibria for game theoretic and evolutionary bargaining models. In *Proceedings of the 5th International Workshop on Agent-Mediated Electronic Commerce (AMEC V)*, pages 70–77, 2003.

[47] S. Ficici, O. Melnik, and J. Pollack. *Selection in Coevolutionary Algorithms and the Inverse Problem*, pages 277–294. Springer, 2004.

[48] S. Ficici and J. Pollack. A game-theoretic approach to the simple coevolutionary algorithm. In *Proceedings of the Sixth International Conference on Parallel Problem Solving from Nature (PPSN VI)*. Springer Verlag, 2000.

[49] D. P. Foster and H. P. Young. On the impossibility of predicting behavior of rational agents. In *PNAS (Proceedings of the National Academy of Sciences of the USA) 98 (22)*, 2001.

[50] Y. Freund and R. E. Schapire. Adaptive game playing using multiplicative weights. *Games and Economic Behavior*, 29:79–103, 1999.

[51] M. Frisch and S. Smale. *Differential Equations, Dynamical Systems and Linear Algebra*. Academic Press, Inc, 1974.

[52] D. Fudenberg and D. Levine. Consistency and cautious fictitious play. *Journal of Economic Dynamics and Control*, 19:1065–1089, 1995.

[53] D. Fudenberg and D. K. Levine. *The Theory of Learning in Games*. Cambridge, Massachusetts: MIT Press, 1999.

[54] D. Fudenberg and J. Tirole. *Game Theory*. MIT Press, 1991.

[55] E. Gerding and J. La Poutré. Bargaining with posterior opportunities: An evolutionary social simulation. In *M. Gallegati and A.P. Kirman and M. Marsili (eds.), The Complex Dynamics of Economic Interactions, Springer Lecture Notes in Economics and Mathematical Systems (LNEMS) 531*, pages 241–256, 2003.

[56] E. Gerding, K. Somefun, and H. La Poutré. Automated bilateral bargaining about multiple attributes in a one-to-many setting. In *Proceedings of the Sixth International Conference on Electronic Commerce (ICEC04)*, pages 105–112. ACM Press, 2004.

[57] E. Gerding, K. Somefun, and H. La Poutré. Bilateral bargaining in a one-to-many bargaining setting. In *Agent Mediated Electronic Commerce VI (AMEC-VI), Springer Lecture Notes in Artificial Intelligence (LNAI), Springer Verlag, (invited for publication)*, 2004. to appear.

[58] E. Gerding, D. van Bragt, and J. La Poutré. Multi-issue negotiation processes by evolutionary simulation: Validation and social extensions. *Computational Economics*, 22:39–63, 2003.

[59] M. Ghavamzadeh and S. Mahadevan. Learning to communicate and act using hierarchical reinforcement learning. In *AAMAS-2004 — Proceedings of the Third International Joint Conference on Autonomous Agents and Multi Agent Systems*, pages 1114–1121, 2004.

[60] C. Gintis. *Game Theory Evolving*. University Press, Princeton, 2000.

[61] A. Greenwald and J. Boyan. Bidding under uncertainty: Theory and experiments. In *Twentieth Conference on Uncertainty in Artificial Intelligence*, pages 209–216, 2004.

[62] A. Greenwald and K. Hall. Correlated Q-learning. In *Proceedings of the Twentieth International Conference on Machine Learning, ICML*, pages 242–249, 2003.

[63] A. Greenwald and J. Kephart. Shopbots and pricebots. In *Proceedings of the 16th International Joint Conference on Artificial Intelligence (IJCAI 99)*, pages 506–511, 1999.

[64] J. Grefenstette and R. Daley. Methods for competitive and cooperative coevolution. In *Adaptation, Coevolution and Learning in Multiagent Systems: Papers from the 1996 AAAI Spring Symposium*, pages 45–50. AAAI Press., 1996. Technical Report SS-96-01.

[65] C. Guestrin, M. Lagoudakis, and R. Parr. Coordinated reinforcement learning. In *Proceedings of the 2002 AAAI Symposium Series: Collaborative Learning Agents*, pages 227 – 234, 2002.

[66] Y. Guo, J. Muller, and C. Weinhardt. Learning user preferences for multiattribute negotiation: An evolutionary approach. In *In. J. Muller, V. Marik, and M. Pechoucek (eds.), Multi-Agent Systems and Applications III, Springer Lecture Notes in Artificial Intelligence, Vol. 2691*, pages 303–313. Springer-Verlag, 2003.

[67] A. Hara and T. Nagao. Emergence of cooperative behavior using ADG; Automatically Defined Groups. In *Proceedings of the 1999 Genetic and Evolutionary Computation Conference (GECCO-99)*, pages 1038–1046, 1999.

[68] T. Haynes and S. Sen. Evolving behavioral strategies in predators and prey. In G. Weiß and S. Sen, editors, *Adaptation and Learning in Multiagent Systems*, Lecture Notes in Artificial Intelligence. Springer Verlag, Berlin, Germany, 1995.

[69] T. D. Haynes and S. Sen. Co-adaptation in a team. *International Journal of Computational Intelligence and Organizations (IJCIO)*, 1(4), 1997.

[70] M. He and N. R. Jennings. Southampton TAC: An adaptive autonomous trading agent. *ACM Transactions on Internet Technology*, 3:218–235, 2003.

[71] M. He, N. R. Jennings, and A. Prgel-Bennett. A heuristic bidding strategy for buying multiple goods in multiple english auctions. *ACM Transactions on Internet Technology*, 2006. to appear.

[72] M. He, H. Leung, and N. R. Jennings. A fuzzy logic based bidding strategy for autonomous agents in continuous double auctions. *IEEE Trans. on Knowledge and Data Engineering*, 15:1345–1363, 2003.

[73] J. Hofbauer and K. Sigmund. *Evolutionary Games and Population Dynamics*. Cambridge University Press, 1998.

[74] R. Hoffman and N. Shadbolt. Eliciting knowledge from experts: A methodological analysis. *Organizational and Human Decision Process*, 62(2):129–158, 1995.

[75] B. Hölldobler and E. O. Wilson. *The Ants*. Harvard University Press, 1990.

[76] J. Hu and M. Wellman. Multiagent reinforcement learning: theoretical framework and an algorithm. In *Proceedings of the Fifteenth International Conference on Machine Learning*, pages 242–250. Morgan Kaufmann, San Francisco, CA, 1998.

[77] J. Hu and M. Wellman. Online learning about other agents in a dynamic multiagent system. In K. P. Sycara and M. Wooldridge, editors, *Proceedings of the Second International Conference on Autonomous Agents (Agents'98)*, pages 239–246, New York, 1998. ACM Press.

[78] B. Hudson and T. Sandholm. Effectiveness of preference elicitation in combinatorial auctions. In *J. Padget, O. Shehory, D. Parkes, N. Sadeh, and W.E. Walsh (eds.), Agent-Mediated Electronic Commerce IV (AMEC IV): Designing Mechanisms and Systems, Springer Lecture Notes in Computer Science, Vol. 2531*, pages 69–86. Springer-Verlag, 2002.

[79] H. Iba. Evolutionary learning of communicating agents. *Information Sciences*, 108:181–206, 1998.

[80] H. Iba. Evolving multiple agents by genetic programming. In L. Spector, W. Langdon, U.-M. O'Reilly, and P. Angeline, editors, *Advances in Genetic Programming 3*, pages 447–466. The MIT Press, Cambridge, MA, 1999.

[81] T. Jansen and R. P. Wiegand. Exploring the explorative advantage of the cooperative coevolutionary (1+1) EA. In E. Cantu-Paz *et al*, editor, *Prooceedings of the Genetic and Evolutionary Computation Conference (GECCO)*. Springer-Verlag, 2003.

[82] N. Jennings, P. Faratin, A. Lomuscio, S. Parsons, C. Sierra, and M. Wooldrigde. Automated negotiation: prospects, methods, and challenges. *International Journal of Group Decision and Negotiation*, 10:199–215, 2001.

[83] K.-C. Jim and C. L. Giles. Talking helps: Evolving communicating agents for the predator-prey pursuit problem. *Artificial Life*, 6(3):237–254, 2000.

[84] L. P. Kaelbling, M. L. Littman, and A. P. Moore. Reinforcement learning: A survey. *Journal of Artificial Intelligence Research*, 4:237–285, 1996.

[85] S. Kapetanakis and D. Kudenko. Reinforcement learning of coordination in cooperative multi-agent systems. In *Proceedings of the Nineteenth National Conference on Artificial Intelligence (AAAI02)*, 2002.

[86] J. Kephart, C. Brooks, and R. Das. Pricing information bundles in a dynamic environment. In *Proceedings of the 3rd ACM Conference on Electronic Commerce (ACMEC)*, pages 180–190. ACM Press, 2001.

[87] J. Kephart, J. Hanson, , and A. Greenwald. Dynamic pricing by software agents. *Computer Networks*, 36(6):731–752, 2000.

[88] M. Klein, P. Faratin, H. Sayama, and Y. Bar-Yam. Negotiating complex contracts. *Group Decision and Negotiation*, 12:111–125, 2003.

[89] V. Krishna. *Auction Theory*. Academic Press, 2002.

[90] M. I. Lichbach. *The cooperator's dilemma*. University of Michigan Press, 1996.

[91] R. Lin. Bilateral multi-issue contract negotiation for task redistribution using a mediation service. In *Proceedings Agent Mediated Electronic Commerce VI*, 2004. to appear.

[92] M. Littman. Markov games as a framework for multi-agent reinforcement learning. In *Proceedings of the 11th International Conference on Machine Learning (ML-94)*, pages 157–163, New Brunswick, NJ, 1994. Morgan Kaufmann.

[93] M. Littman. Friend-or-foe Q-learning in general-sum games. In *Proceedings of the Eighteenth International Conference on Machine Learning*, pages 322–328. Morgan Kaufmann Publishers Inc., 2001.

[94] M. Littman and P. Stone. Leading best-response strategies in repeated games. In *Seventeenth International Joint Conference on Artificial Intelligence (IJCAI) workshop on Economic Agents, Models, and Mechanisms*, 2001.

[95] M. L. Littman and S. M. Majercik. Large-scale planning under uncertainty: A survey. In *Workshop on Planning and Scheduling for Space*, 1997.

[96] M. L. Littman and P. Stone. A polynomial-time nash equilibrium algorithm for repeated games. In *Proceedings of the 4th ACM conference on Electronic commerce*, 2003. also appeared in *Decision Support Systems,39:55–66,2005.*

[97] S. Luke. Genetic programming produced competitive soccer softbot teams for RoboCup97. In J. R. Koza *et al*, editor, *Genetic Programming 1998: Proceedings of the Third Annual Conference*, pages 214–222. Morgan Kaufmann, 1998.

[98] S. Luke and L. Spector. Evolving teamwork and coordination with genetic programming. In J. R. Koza, D. E. Goldberg, D. B. Fogel, and R. L. Riolo, editors, *Genetic Programming 1996: Proceedings of the First Annual Conference*, pages 150–156, Stanford University, CA, USA, 28–31 1996. MIT Press.

[99] X. Luo, N. R. Jennings, and N. Shadbolt. Acquiring tradeoff preferences for automated negotiations: A case study. In *proceedings of the 5th International Workshop on Agent-Mediated Electronic Commerce (AMEC V)*, pages 37–55, 2003.

[100] X. Luo, N. R. Jennings, N. Shadbolt, H. Leung, and J. H. Lee. A fuzzy constraint based model for bilateral multi-issue negotiations in semi-competitive environments. *Artificial Intelligence Journal*, 148(1-2):53–102, 2003.

[101] J. K. MacKie-Mason, A. Osepayshvili, D. M. Reeves, and M. P. Wellman. Price prediction strategies for market-based scheduling. In *Fourteenth International Conference on Automated Planning and Scheduling*, pages 244–252, 2004.

[102] A. Mas-Collel, M. Whinston, and J. Green. *Microeconomic Theory*. Oxford University Press, 1995.

[103] M. Mataric. Reinforcement learning in the multi-robot domain. *Autonomous Robots*, 4(1):73–83, 1997.

[104] M. Mataric. Using communication to reduce locality in distributed multi-agent learning. *Joint Special Issue on Learning in Autonomous Robots, Machine Learning, 31(1-3), 141-167, and Autonomous Robots, 5(3-4), Jul/Aug 1998, 335-354*, 1998.

[105] J. Maynard-Smith. *Evolution and the Theory of Games*. Cambridge University Press, 1982.

[106] J. Maynard Smith and J. Price. The logic of animal conflict. *Nature*, 146:15–18, 1973.

[107] A. McDonald and S. Sen. The success and failure of tag-mediated evolution of cooperation. In *LAMAS*, 2005.

[108] T. Miconi. When evolving populations is better than coevolving individuals: The blind mice problem. In *Proceedings of the Eighteenth International Joint Conference on Artificial Intelligence (IJCAI-03)*, pages 647–652, 2003.

[109] M. Mitchell, J. Crutchfield, and R. Das. Evolving cellular automata with genetic algorithms: A review of recent work. In *Proceedings of the First International Conference on Evolutionary Computation and its Applications (EvCA'96)*, 1996.

[110] N. D. Monekosso and P. Remagnino. Phe-Q: A pheromone based Q-learning. In *Australian Joint Conference on Artificial Intelligence*, pages 345–355, 2001.

[111] R. B. Myerson. *Game Theory. Analysis of Conflict*. Harvard University Press, 1991.

[112] J. Nachbar. Prediction, optimization, and learning in repeated games. *Econometrica*, 65(2):275–309, 1997.

[113] J. H. Nachbar and W. R. Zame. Non-computable strategies and discounted repeated games. *Economic Theory*, 8:103–122, 1996.

[114] R. Nair, D. Pynadath, M. Yokoo, M. Tambe, and S. Marsella. Taming decentralized POMDPs: Towards efficient policy computation for multiagent settings. In *Proceedings of the Eighteenth International Joint Conference on Artificial Intelligence (IJCAI-03)*, 2003.

[115] J. Nash. Non-cooperative games. *Annals of Mathematics*, 54:286–295, 1951.

[116] T. Nguyen and N. Jennings. Coordinating multiple concurrent negotiations. In *Proceedings of the Third International Joint Conference on Autonomous Agents and Multi Agent Systems (AAMAS 2004)*. ACM Press, 2004.

[117] E. Nudelman, J. Wortman, Y. Shoham, and K. Leyton-Brown. Run the GAMUT: A comprehensive approach to evaluating game-theoretic algorithms. In *Third International Joint Conference on Autonomous Agents and Multiagent Systems*, 2004.

[118] M. Osborne and A. Rubinstein. *Bargaining and Markets*. Academic Press, 1990.

[119] M. Osborne and A. Rubinstein. *A Course in Game Theory*. MIT Press, 1994.

[120] A. Osepayshvili, M. P. Wellman, D. M. Reeves, and J. K. MacKie-Mason. Self-confirming price prediction for bidding in simultaneous ascending auctions. In *Twenty First Conference on Uncertainty in Artificial Intelligence*, pages 441–449, 2005.

[121] L. Panait, R. P. Wiegand, and S. Luke. A visual demonstration of convergence properties of cooperative coevolution. In *Parallel Problem Solving from Nature — PPSN-2004*, pages 892–901. Springer, 2004.

[122] L. A. Panait, R. P. Wiegand, and S. Luke. Improving coevolutionary search for optimal multiagent behaviors. In *Proceedings of the Eighteenth International Joint Conference on Artificial Intelligence (IJCAI-03)*, 2003.

[123] C. Papadimitriou. Algorithms, games, and the internet. In *Proceedings of the ACM Symposium on Theory of Computing (STOC 2001)*, pages 749–753. ACM Press, 2001.

[124] C. Papadimitriou and J. Tsitsiklis. Complexity of markov decision processes. *Mathematics of Operations Research*, 12(3):441–450, 1987.

[125] L. Peshkin, K.-E. Kim, N. Meuleau, and L. Kaelbling. Learning to cooperate via policy search. In *Sixteenth Conference on Uncertainty in Artificial Intelligence*, pages 307–314. Morgan Kaufmann, 2000.

[126] R. Planqué, N. Britton, N. Franks, and M. A. Peletier. The adaptiveness of defense strategies against cuckoo parasitism. *Bull. Math. Biol.*, 64:1045–1068, 2001.

[127] M. Potter, L. Meeden, and A. Schultz. Heterogeneity in the coevolved behaviors of mobile robots: The emergence of specialists. In *Proceedings of The Seventeenth International Conference on Artificial Intelligence (IJCAI-2001)*, 2001.

[128] R. Powers and Y. Shoham. New criteria and a new algorithm for learning in multi-agent systems. In *Neural Information Processing Systems (NIPS)*, 2004.

[129] R. Powers and Y. Shoham. Learning against opponents with bounded memory. In *International Joint Conference on Artificial Intelligence (IJCAI)*, 2005.

[130] C. Preist, A. Byde, , and C. Bartolini. Economic dynamics of agents in multiple autions. In *Proceedings of the fifth International Conference on Autonomous Agents*, pages 545–551, 2001.

[131] M. Quinn. Evolving communication without dedicated communication channels. In *Advances in Artificial Life: Sixth European Conference on Artificial Life (ECAL01)*, 2001.

[132] A. Rapoport, M. Guyer, , and D. Gordon. *The 2x2 Game*. MI: University of Michigan Press, 1976.

[133] F. Redondo. *Game Theory and Economics*. Cambridge University Press, 2001.

[134] D. M. Reeves, M. P. Wellman, J. K. MacKie-Mason, and A. Osepayshvili. Exploring bidding strategies for market-based scheduling. *Decision Support Systems*, 39:67–85, 2005.

[135] L. Rejeb, Z. Guessoum, and R. MHallah. An adaptive approach for the exploration-exploitation dilemma and its application to economic systems. In *LAMAS*, 2005.

[136] V. Robu and J. La Poutré. Learning the structure of utility graphs used in multi-issue negotiation through collaborative filtering. In *Proceedings of the Pacific Rim International Workshop on Multi-Agents (PRIMA'05), Springer Lecture Notes in Artificial Intelligence (LNCS / LNAI)*, 2005. to appear.

[137] V. Robu, K. Somefun, and J. La Poutré. Modeling complex multi-issue negotiations using utility graphs. In *Proceedings of the Fourth International Joint Conference on Autonomous Agents and Multi Agent Systems (AAMAS 2005)*. ACM Press, 2005.

[138] J. Rosenschein and G. Zlotkin. *Rules of Encounter*. MIT Press, 1994.

[139] A. Rubinstein. *Modeling Bounded Rationality*. MIT Press, Cambridge, MA, 1998.

[140] R. Salustowicz, M. Wiering, and J. Schmidhuber. Learning team strategies with multiple policy-sharing agents: A soccer case study. Technical report, ISDIA, Corso Elvezia 36, 6900 Lugano, Switzerland, 1997.

[141] L. Samuelson. *Evolutionary Games and Equilibrium Selection*. MIT Press, Cambridge, MA, 1997.

[142] T. Sandholm and S. Suri. BOB: Improved winner determination in combinatorial auctions and generalizations. *Artificial Intelligence*, 145:33–58, 2003.

[143] T. W. Sandholm and R. H. Crites. On multiagent Q-learning in a semi-competitive domain. In *G. Weiss and S. Sen, editors, Adaptation and Learning in Multiagent Systems*, pages 191–205. Springer Verlag, 1996.

[144] H. Scarf and T. Hansen. *The Computation of Economic Equilibria*. Yale University Press, 1973.

[145] S. Sen and M. Sekaran. Multiagent coordination with learning classifier systems. In G. Weiß and S. Sen, editors, *Proceedings of the IJCAI Workshop on Adaption and Learning in Multi-Agent Systems*, volume 1042, pages 218–233. Springer Verlag, 1996.

[146] S. Sen and M. Sekaran. Individual learning of coordination knowledge. *Journal of Experimental and Theoretical Artificial Intelligence*, 10(3):333–356, 1998.

[147] S. Sen and G. Weiss. *Learning in Multiagent Systems*, chapter 6. MIT Press, Cambridge MA, 1999.

[148] Y. Shoham, R. Powers, and T. Grenager. Multi-agent reinforcement learning: a critical survey. In *AAAI Fall Symposium on Artificial Multi-Agent Learning*, 2004.

[149] C. Sierra. Agent-mediated electronic commerce. *Autonomous Agents and MultiAgent Systems*, 9(3):285–301, 2004.

[150] H. Simon. *Models of Bounded Rationality, volume 2*. MIT Press, 1982.

[151] S. P. Singh, M. J. Kearns, and Y. Mansour. Nash convergence of gradient dynamics in general-sum games. In *UAI '00: Proceedings of the 16th Conference on Uncertainty in Artificial Intelligence*, pages 541–548, San Francisco, CA, USA, 2000. Morgan Kaufmann Publishers Inc.

[152] K. Somefun, E. Gerding, S. Bohté, and J. La Poutré. Automated negotiation and bundling of information goods. In *In: Agent Mediated Electronic Commerce V (AMECV), Springer Lecture Notes in Artificial Intelligence (LNAI), 3048*, pages 1–17, 2004.

[153] K. Somefun, E. Gerding, S. Bohté, and J. La Poutré. Efficient methods for automated multi-issue negotiation: Negotiating over a two-part tariff. *International Journal of Intelligent Systems (special issue on Learning Approaches for Negotiation Agents and Automated Negotiation)*, 2006. to appear.

[154] K. Somefun, T. Klos, and H. La Poutré. Negotiating over bundles and prices using aggregate knowledge. In *Proceedings of the 5th International Conference on Electronic Commerce and Web Technologies (EC-Web), Springer Lecture Notes in Computer Science (LNCS), 3182*, pages 218–227, 2004.

[155] K. Somefun, T. Klos, and H. La Poutré. Online learning of aggregate knowledge about nonlinear preferences applied to negotiating prices and bundles. In *Proceedings of the Sixth International Conference on Electronic Commerce (ICEC04)*, pages 361–370. ACM Press, 2005.

[156] K. Somefun and J. La Poutré. Bundling and pricing for information brokerage: Customer satisfaction as a means to profit optimization. In *Proceedings of the IEEE/WIC International Conference on Web Intellingence (WI2003)*, pages 182–189. IEEE Computer Society press, 2003.

[157] P. Stone. *Layered Learning in Multi-Agent Systems*. PhD thesis, Carnegie Mellon University, 1998.

[158] P. Stone and M. Littman. Implicit negotiation in repeated games. In *In: J.-J. Meyer and M. Tambe (eds.), Proceedings of The Eighth International Workshop on Agent Theories, Architectures, and Languages (ATAL-2001)*, pages 393–404, 2001.

[159] P. Stone, R. S. P., M. L. Littman, J. A. Csirik, and D. McAllester. Decision-theoretic bidding based on learned density models in simultaneous, interacting auctions. *Journal of Artificial Intelligence Research*, 19:209–242, 2003.

[160] P. Stone and M. M. Veloso. Multiagent systems: A survey from a machine learning perspective. *Autonomous Robots*, 8(3):345–383, 2000.

[161] N. Suematsu and A. Hayashi. A multiagent reinforcement learning algorithm using extended optimal response. In *Proceedings of First International Joint Conference on Autonomous Agents and Multi-Agent Systems (AAMAS-02)*, pages 370–377, 2002.

[162] D. Suryadi and P. J. Gmytrasiewicz. Learning models of other agents using influence diagrams. In *Preceedings of the 1999 International Conference on User Modeling*, pages 223–232, 1999.

[163] R. Sutton and A. Barto. *Reinforcement Learning: An introduction*. Cambridge, MA: MIT Press, 1998.

[164] P. 't Hoen and J. La Poutré. A decommitment strategy in a competitive multiagent transportation setting. In *Agent Mediated Electronic Commerce V (AMEC-V), Springer Lecture Notes in Artificial Intelligence (LNAI), 3048*, pages 56–72, 2004.

[165] P. 't Hoen and J. La Poutré. Repeated auctions with complementarities. In *Proceedings of the 7th International Workshop on Agent-Mediated Electronic Commerce (AMEC VII), Springer Lecture Note in Artificial Intelligence*, 2006. to appear.

[166] P. 't Hoen and K. Tuyls. Analyzing multi-agent reinforcement learning using evolutionary dynamics. In *Proceedings of the 15th European Conference on Machine Learning (ECML)*, 2004.

[167] tac dev@sics.se. Trading agent competitition (tac): Tac classic and TAC supply chain management (scm), http://www.sics.se/tac, 2006.

[168] P. Tadepalli, R. Givan, and K. Driessens. Relational reinforcement learning: An overview. In P. Tadepalli, R. Givan, and K. Driessens, editors, *Proceedings of the ICML'04 Workshop on Relational Reinforcement Learning*, pages 1–9, 2004.

[169] M. Tan. Multi-agent reinforcement learning: Independent vs. cooperative learning. In M. N. Huhns and M. P. Singh, editors, *Readings in Agents*, pages 487–494. Morgan Kaufmann, San Francisco, CA, USA, 1993.

[170] G. Tesauro. Extending Q-learning to general adaptive multi-agent systems. In *Neural Information Processing Systems (NIPS)*, 2003.

[171] L. Tesfatsion. Introduction to the special issue on agent-based computational economics. *Journal of Economic Dynamics and Control*, 25:281–293, 2001.

[172] K. Tumer and A. Agogino. Efficient reward functions for adaptive multi-rover systems. In *LAMAS*, 2005.

[173] K. Tuyls, T. Croonenborghs, J. Ramon, R. Goetschalckx, and M. Bruynooghe. Multi-agent relational reinforcement learning. In *LAMAS*, 2005.

[174] K. Tuyls, D. Heytens, A. Now, and B. Manderick. Extended replicator dynamics as a key to reinforcement learning in multi-agent systems. In *14th European Conference on Machine Learning, Cavtat-Dubrovnik, Croatia, September 22-26, 2003*, volume Lecture Notes in Computer Science 2837, pages 421–431, 2003.

[175] K. Tuyls and A. Nowé. Evolutionary game theory and multi-agent reinforcement learning. *The Knowledge Engineering Review*, 20(01):63–90, 2006.

[176] K. Tuyls, K. Verbeeck, and T. Lenaerts. A selection-mutation model for Q-learning in Multi-Agent Systems. In *The second International Joint Conference on Autonomous Agents and Multi-Agent Systems*. ACM Press, Melbourne, Australia, 2003.

[177] D. van Bragt and J. La Poutré. Co-evolving automata negotiate with a variety of opponents. In *Proceedings of the IEEE Congress on Evolutionary Computation 2002 (CEC 2002)*, volume 2, pages 1426–1431. IEEE Press, 2002.

[178] D. van Bragt and J. La Poutré. Why agents for automated negotiation should be adaptive. *Netnomics*, 5:101–118, 2003.

[179] S. van Otterloo. The value of privacy. In *AAMAS*, 2005.

[180] I. Vermeulen, K. Somefun, and H. La Poutré. An efficient turnkey agent for repeated trading with overall budget and preferences. In *Proceedings of the 2004 IEEE Conference on Cybernetics and Intelligent Systems (CIS 2004)*, pages 1072–1077. IEEE Press, 2004.

[181] J. Vidal and E. Durfee. The impact of nested agent models in an information economy. In *Proceedings Of the 2nd Intern. Conf. On Multiagent Systems*, pages 377–384. AAAI press, 1996.

[182] P. Vrancx, A. Nowé, and K. Steenhaut. Multi-type ACO for light path protection. In *LAMAS*, 2005.

[183] K. Wagner. Cooperative strategies and the evolution of communication. *Artificial Life*, 6(2):149–179, Spring 2000.

[184] W. Walsh, R. Das, G. Tesauro, , and J. Kephart. Analyzing complex strategic interactions in multi-agent games. In *Proceedings of the The Eighteenth National Conference on Artificial Intelligence (AAAI-02) Workshop on Game Theoretic and Decision Theoretic Agents*, pages 109–118, 2002.

[185] X. Wang and T. Sandholm. Reinforcement learning to play an optimal Nash equilibrium in team Markov games. In *Advances in Neural Information Processing Systems (NIPS-2002)*, 2002.

[186] C. J. C. H. Watkins. *Learning from Delayed Rewards*. PhD thesis, University of Cambridge, 1989.

[187] J. Weibull. *Evolutionary Game Theory*. MIT Press, 1996.

[188] M. Weinberg and J. S. Rosenschein. Best-response multiagent learning in non-stationary environments. In *The Third International Joint Conference on Autonomous Agents and Multiagent Systems*, New York, July 2004.

[189] G. Weiss. *Multi-agent Systems: A Modern Approach to Distributed Artificial Intelligence*. MIT Press, Cambridge, 1999.

[190] M. Wellman. A market-oriented programming environment and its application to distributed multicommodity flow problems. *Journal of Artificial Intelligence Research*, 1:1–23, 1993.

[191] M. Wellman, A. Greenwald, P. Stone, and P. Wurman. The 2001 Trading Agent Competition. *Electronic Markets*, 13:4–12, 2003.

[192] M. Wellman and J. Hu. Conjectural equilibrium in multiagent learning. *Machine Learning*, 33(2-3):179–200, 1998.

[193] M. Wellman, D. Reeves, and a. Y. V. K. Lochner. Price prediction in a trading agent competition. *Journal of Artificial Intelligence Research*, 21:19–36, 2004.

[194] M. Wellman, P. Wurman, K. O'Malley, R. Bangera, S. d. Lin, D. Reeves, and W. Walsh. Designing the market game for the trading agent competition. *IEEE Internet Computing*, 5:43–51, 2001.

[195] R. P. Wiegand. *Analysis of Cooperative Coevolutionary Algorithms*. PhD thesis, Department of Computer Science, George Mason University, 2003.

[196] B. Wolfe, M. R. James, and S. Singh. Learning predictive state representations in dynamical systems without resct. In *Proceedings of the 2005 International Conference on Machine Learning*, 2005.

[197] D. H. Wolpert and K. Tumer. Optimal payoff functions for members of collectives. *Advances in Complex Systems*, 4(2/3):265–279, 2001.

A   Introductory Notions from (Evolutionary) Game Theory

In this section, as an Appendix, we introduce elementary concepts from Game Theory (GT) and Evolutionary Game Theory (EGT) necessary to understand Sections 3 and 4 of this paper. Game Theory is an economical theory that models interactions between agents as games of two or more players. More precisely, the agents participating in such a game can choose from a set of strategies to play, according to their own preferences. Game Theory is the mathematical study of interactive decision making in the sense that the agents involved in the decisions take into account their own choices and those of others. Choices are determined by stable preferences concerning the outcomes of their possible decisions, and by the relation between their own choices and those of others.

After the stagnation of GT for many years, John Maynard Smith applied Game Theory to Biology, which made him relax the strong premises behind GT. Under these biological circumstances, it becomes impossible to judge what choices are the most rational ones. The question now becomes how a player can learn to optimize its behavior and maximize its return. This learning process is analogous to the concept of evolution in Biology. These new ideas have led to the development of the concept of Evolutionary Stable Strategies (ESS), a special case of the Nash condition. In contrast to GT, EGT is descriptive and starts from more realistic views of the game and its players. Here the game is no longer played exactly once by rational players who know all the details of the game. Details of the game include each others preferences over outcomes. Instead EGT assumes that the game is played repeatedly by players randomly drawn from large populations, uninformed of the preferences of the opponent players.

We provide definitions of strategic games, as well zero sum as general sum, and introduce concepts as Nash equilibrium, Pareto optimality, Pareto Dominance, Evolutionary Stable Strategies and Population Dynamics. For the connection between these concepts we refer the interested reader to [175, 133, 187].

A.1   Strategic Games

In this section we define n-player normal form games as a conflict situation involving gains and losses between n players. In such a game n players repeatedly interact with each other by all choosing an action (or strategy) to play. All players choose their strategy at the same time. For reasons of simplicity, we limit the pure strategy set of the players to 2 strategies. A strategy is defined as a probability distribution over all possible actions. In the 2-pure strategies case, we have: $s_1 = (1, 0)$ and $s_2 = (0, 1)$. A mixed strategy s_m is then defined by $s_m = (x_1, x_2)$ with $x_1, x_2 \neq 0$ and $x_1 + x_2 = 1$.

Defining a game more formally we restrict ourselves to the 2-player 2-action game. Nevertheless, an extension to n-players n-actions games is straightforward, but examples in the n-player case do not show the same illustrative strength as in the 2-player case. A game $G = (S_1, S_2, P_1, P_2)$ is defined by the payoff functions P_1, P_2 and their strategy sets S_1 for the first player and S_2 for the second player. In the 2-player 2-strategies case, the payoff functions $P_1 : S_1 \times S_2 \to \Re$ and $P_2 : S_1 \times S_2 \to \Re$ are defined by the payoff matrices, A for the first player and B for the second player, see Table 8. The payoff tables A, B define the instantaneous rewards. Element a_{ij} is the reward the row-player (player 1) receives for choosing pure strategy s_i from set S_1 when the column-player (player 2) chooses the pure strategy s_j from set S_2. Element b_{ij} is the reward for the column-player for choosing the pure strategy s_j from set S_2 when the row-player chooses pure strategy s_i from set S_1.

If now $a_{ij} + b_{ij} = 0$ for all i and j, we call the game a *zero sum game*. This means that the sum of what is won by one agent (positive) and lost by another (negative) equals zero. This corresponds to a situation of *pure competition*. In case that $a_{ij} + b_{ij} \neq 0$ for all i and j we call the game a *general sum game*. In this situation it might be very beneficial for the different agents to cooperate with one another.

The family of 2×2 games is usually classified in three subclasses, as follows [133],

Subclass 1: if $(a_{11} - a_{21})(a_{12} - a_{22}) > 0$ or $(b_{11} - b_{12})(b_{21} - b_{22}) > 0$, at least one of the 2 players has a dominant strategy, therefore there is just 1 strict equilibrium.

Table 8. The left matrix (A) defines the payoff for the row player, the right matrix (B) defines the payoff for the column player

$$A = \begin{pmatrix} a_{11} & a_{12} \\ a_{21} & a_{22} \end{pmatrix} B = \begin{pmatrix} b_{11} & b_{12} \\ b_{21} & b_{22} \end{pmatrix}$$

Subclass 2: if $(a_{11} - a_{21})(a_{12} - a_{22}) < 0, (b_{11} - b_{12})(b_{21} - b_{22}) < 0$, and $(a_{11} - a_{21})(b_{11} - b_{12}) > 0$, there are 2 pure equilibria and 1 mixed equilibrium.
Subclass 3: if $(a_{11} - a_{21})(a_{12} - a_{22}) < 0, (b_{11} - b_{12})(b_{21} - b_{22}) < 0$, and $(a_{11} - a_{21})(b_{11} - b_{12}) < 0$, there is just 1 mixed equilibrium.

The first subclass includes those type of games where each player has a dominant strategy[8], as for instance the prisoner's dilemma. However it includes a larger collection of games since only one of the players needs to have a dominant strategy. In the second subclass none of the players has a dominated strategy (e.g. battle of the sexes). But both players receive the highest payoff by both playing their first or second strategy. This is expressed in the condition $(a_{11} - a_{21})(b_{11} - b_{12}) > 0$. The third subclass only differs from the second in the fact that the players do not receive their highest payoff by both playing the first or the second strategy (e.g. matching pennies game). This is expressed by the condition $(a_{11} - a_{21})(b_{11} - b_{12}) < 0$.

A.2   Nash Equilibrium

In traditional game theory it is assumed that the players are rational, meaning that every player will choose the action that is best for him, given his beliefs about the other players' actions. A basic definition of a Nash equilibrium is stated as follows. If there is a set of strategies for a game with the property that no player can increase its payoff by changing his strategy while the other players keep their strategies unchanged, then that set of strategies and the corresponding payoffs constitute a Nash equilibrium.

Formally, a Nash equilibrium is defined as follows. When 2 players play the strategy profile $s = (s_i, s_j)$ belonging to the product set $S_1 \times S_2$ then s is a Nash equilibrium if $P_1(s_i, s_j) \geq P_1(s_x, s_j) \ \forall x \in \{1, ..., n\}$ and $P_2(s_i, s_j) \geq P_2(s_i, s_x)$ $\forall x \in \{1, ..., m\}$ [9].

A.3   Minimax and Maximin

In the context of zero-sum games two specific value are of particular interest, i.e. *minimax* and *maximin*. More precisely, recall from Section A.1 that in case of zero-sum games we have, $a_{ij} + b_{ij} = 0$ or $a_{ij} = -b_{ij}$. Player one will try to maximize this value and player two will try to minimize it. Intuitively, *maximin* is

---

[8] A strategy is dominant if it is always better than any other strategy, regardless of what the opponent may do.
[9] For a definition in terms of best reply or best response functions we refer the reader to [187].

the maximum payoff that player one will receive if player two responds optimally to every strategy of player one by minimizing one's payoff. Formally, we have

$$maximin = \max_{s_i \in S_1} \min_{s_j \in S_2} P(s_i, s_j) \tag{4}$$

$$\max_{s_i \in S_1} \min_{s_j \in S_2} s_i A s_j^T \tag{5}$$

Note that s_i and s_j need to be interpreted as probability distributions with $s_i = (x_1, x_2)$ where $x_1, x_2 \geq 0$ and $x_1 + x_2 = 1$.

Analogously, *minimax* is defined as follows for the second player,

$$minimax = \min_{s_j \in S_2} \max_{s_i \in S_1} s_i A s_j^T \tag{6}$$

Von Neumann proved that for any zero sum game there exists a $v \in R$ such that $minimax = maximin = v$. This means that for any 2-player finite zero sum game *maximin* and *minimax* always coincide. Moreover, for every Nash equilibrium (s_i^*, s_j^*) holds: $s_i^* A s_j^* = v$. The interested reader can find the proofs in [133].

A.4 Pareto Optimality

The concept of Pareto optimality is named after the Italian economist Vilfredo Pareto(1848-1923). Intuitively a Pareto optimal solution of a game can be defined as follows: a combination of actions of agents in a game is Pareto optimal if there is no other solution for which all players do at least as well and at least one agent is strictly better off.

More formally we have: a strategy combination $s = (s_1, ..., s_n)$ for n agents in a game is Pareto optimal if there does not exist another strategy combination s' for which each player receives at least the same payoff P_i and at least one player j receives a strictly higher payoff than P_j.

Another related concept is that of Pareto Dominance: An outcome of a game is Pareto dominated if some other outcome would make at least one player better off without hurting any other player. That is, some other outcome is weakly preferred by all players and strictly preferred by at least one player. If an outcome is not Pareto dominated by any other, than it is Pareto optimal.

A.5 Evolutionary Stable Strategies

The core equilibrium concept of Evolutionary Game Theory is that of an Evolutionary Stable Strategy (ESS). The idea of an evolutionarily stable strategy was introduced by John Maynard Smith and Price in 1973 [106]. Imagine a population of agents playing the same strategy. Assume that this population is invaded by a different strategy, which is initially played by a small number of the total population. If the reproductive success of the new strategy is smaller than the original one, it will not overrule the original strategy and will eventually disappear. In this case we say that the strategy is evolutionary stable against this new appearing strategy. More generally, we say a strategy is an Evolutionary Stable strategy if it is robust against evolutionary pressure from any appearing mutant strategy.

Formally an ESS is defined as follows. Suppose that a large population of agents is programmed to play the (mixed) strategy s, and suppose that this population is invaded by a small number of agents playing strategy s'. The population share of agents playing this mutant strategy is $\epsilon \in]0,1[$. When an individual is playing the game against a random chosen agent, chances that he is playing against a mutant are ϵ and against a non-mutant are $1 - \epsilon$. The payoff for the first player, being a non mutant is:

$$P(s, (1 - \epsilon)s + \epsilon s')$$

and being a mutant is,

$$P(s', (1 - \epsilon)s + \epsilon s')$$

Now we can state that a strategy s is an ESS if $\forall \, s' \neq s$ there exists some $\delta \in]0,1[$ such that $\forall \, \epsilon : \, 0 < \epsilon < \delta$,

$$P(s, (1 - \epsilon)s + \epsilon s') > P(s', (1 - \epsilon)s + \epsilon s')$$

holds. The condition $\forall \, \epsilon : \, 0 < \epsilon < \delta$ expresses that the share of mutants needs to be sufficiently small.

A.6   Population Dynamics

In this section we discuss the Replicator Dynamics in a single population setting. For a discussion on the multi-population setting we refer the reader to [60, 133, 187].

The basic concepts and techniques developed in EGT were initially formulated in the context of evolutionary biology [105, 187, 141]. In this context, the strategies of all the players are genetically encoded (called genotype). Each genotype refers to a particular behavior which is used to calculate the payoff of the player. The payoff of each player's genotype is determined by the frequency of other player types in the environment.

One way in which EGT proceeds is by constructing a dynamic process in which the proportions of various strategies in a population evolve. Examining the expected value of this process gives an approximation which is called the RD. An abstraction of an evolutionary process usually combines two basic elements: **selection** and **mutation**. Selection favors some varieties over others, while mutation provides variety in the population. The replicator dynamics highlight the role of selection, it describes how systems consisting of different strategies change over time. They are formalized as a system of differential equations. Each replicator (or genotype) represents one (pure) strategy s_i. This strategy is inherited by all the offspring of the replicator. The general form of a replicator dynamic is the following:

$$\frac{dx_i}{dt} = [(Ax)_i - \mathbf{x} \cdot Ax]x_i \tag{7}$$

In equation (7), x_i represents the density of strategy s_i in the population, A is the payoff matrix which describes the different payoff values each individual replicator receives when interacting with other replicators in the population. The state of the population ($\mathbf{x}$) can be described as a probability vector $\mathbf{x} = (x_1, x_2, ..., x_J)$ which expresses the different densities of all the different types of replicators in the population. Hence $(A\mathbf{x})_i$ is the payoff which replicator s_i receives in a population with state x and $\mathbf{x} \cdot A\mathbf{x}$ describes the average payoff in the population. The growth rate $\frac{\frac{dx_i}{dt}}{x_i}$ of the population share using strategy s_i equals the difference between the strategy's current payoff and the average payoff in the population. For further details we refer the reader to [73, 187].

Multi-robot Learning for Continuous Area Sweeping

Mazda Ahmadi and Peter Stone

Learning Agent Research Group (LARG),
Department of Computer Science
{mazda, pstone}@cs.utexas.edu
http://www.cs.utexas.edu/~{mazda,pstone}

Abstract. As mobile robots become increasingly autonomous over extended periods of time, opportunities arise for their use on repetitive tasks. We define and implement behaviors for a class of such tasks that we call *continuous area sweeping* tasks. A continuous area sweeping task is one in which a group of robots must repeatedly visit all points in a fixed area, possibly with non-uniform frequency, as specified by a task-dependent cost function. Examples of problems that need continuous area sweeping are trash removal in a large building and routine surveillance. We present a formulation for this problem and an initial algorithm to address it. The approach is analyzed analytically and is fully implemented and tested, both in simulation and on physical robots.

1 Introduction

Consider a group of robots whose goal is to keep the floors clean in a large office building. This task requires continual execution: by the time the robots have cleaned the entire building once, some parts have become dirty again. A first-cut approach might lead the robots to simply clean the building from top to bottom and then start over again. However, if the rate at which areas of the building become dirty is non-uniform and possibly even non-stationary, a more sophisticated solution is called for. In particular, the robots should ensure that they clean highly-trafficked areas, such as the main entrance and the restrooms, much more frequently than, say, the closets.

We define such a task as an example of *continuous area sweeping* tasks. More generally, a continuous area sweeping task is one in which a group of robots must repeatedly visit all points in a fixed area, possibly with non-uniform frequency, as specified by a task-dependent cost function.

Additional examples of continuous area sweeping tasks include trash removal and the task we consider in this paper, routine surveillance. When performing surveillance, a robot needs to continually traverse its environment in an effort to detect some events of interest, such as gas leaks, water dripping, lights on, open doors, etc. In the surveillance task, a location can be "visited" by observing, rather than by occupying it physically.

K. Tuyls et al. (Eds.): LAMAS 2005, LNAI 3898, pp. 47–70, 2006.

The goal of a continuous area sweeping task is not just to sweep the area in minimum time, but to sweep the area in such a way as to minimize the average event detection time, possibly weighted by the importance of different events. *Event detection time* is the time-period between event occurrence and its detection. The definition of *event importance* is problem-dependent. For example, in the trash collection task, the importance of collecting food trash may be higher than that of collecting paper goods. Minimizing the weighted average event detection time will result in the sensible behavior of visiting kitchens and other public areas more often than (most) individual offices. Similarly, for the surveillance task, one may define the importance of identifying gas leaks as being higher than finding lights on.

We tackle continuous area sweeping by dividing it into two sub-problems:

1. Enabling a *single* robot to autonomously perform a continuous area sweeping task in a sub-region.
2. Partitioning the overall area among the *multiple* robots.

Once the area is partitioned among the robots, each one of them sweeps its part of the environment using the single-robot area sweeping method.

The remainder of the paper is organized as follows. Section 2 surveys the previous work most related to our own. In Section 3 we formalize the class of continuous area sweeping tasks. Section 4 introduces the algorithmic solution to single robot continuous area sweeping tasks (subproblem 1). In Section 5 the negotiation method for adaptive area partitioning is introduced (subproblem 2). In the next two sections, we instantiate the formalism and algorithms on the robot surveillance domain. In Section 6 single robot experiments are presented, multi-robot experiments are presented in Section 7. Our methods are fully implemented and tested both in simulation and on a physical robot, the Sony AIBO ERS-7 4-legged robot. Section 8 discusses future work and concludes.

2   Related Work

Continuous area sweeping tasks are closely related to the *security sweep* [1], or *sweeping* [2] task. In the security sweep or sweeping task, the goal is to make the robot(s) visit the whole environment *just once* in minimum time. Continuous area sweeping is also related to *coverage path-planning* [3], which "is a new path planning approach that determines a path for a robot to pass over all points in its free space." [3] The relevant differences are that in continuous area sweeping, the sweep must be performed i) repeatedly (continuously), and ii) non-uniformly, that is with more frequent attention given to some areas than to others. As surveyed by Parker [4], most previous approaches to surveillance assume ideal sensors and no computational bounds. In contrast, in this paper we consider solutions that are fully implementable (and implemented) on physical robots.

Most of the methods for area partitioning use fully centralized and static approaches. For example Hert et. al. [5] tries to partition the environment into n equal size parts. Bern et. al. [6] also try to partition the environment into equal size parts but with the additional condition that the parts do not have any acute angles.

Notice that these works assume a heuristic for the notion of best partitioning, such as equal size parts, or parts without acute angles. But in our work, the goal is to minimize the average detection time, and the algorithms will directly try to achieve that goal. In our experimental results section, we will provide an example in which the partitions do not follow any of these heuristics (Figure 12(b)).

There are some other methods that address dynamic area partitioning in different ways, but that are not suitable for continuous area sweeping. For example Min and Kin [7] propose a dynamic area partitioning method in which the robots start with an initial static partitioned area. When a robot finishes its assigned task, it negotiates for more parts of the environment. Since they do not partition the environment permanently, although it is suitable for their one sweep of the environment, it is not good for our continuous sweeping task. For example in Figure 1(a) the robot "a" is responsible for part A and robot "b" is responsible of parts B and C. If by the time that robot "a" finishes part A, robot "b" is still sweeping part B, then robot "a" will be responsible for part C. But a better partition, which our algorithm will achieve is the one in Figure 1(b), where robot "a" gets a little more area close to its original responsibility area. Additionally, Min and Yin assume full and error-free communication, whereas we do not assume full communication between all robots.

Jager and Nebel [8] partition the environment into polygons such that each robot requests to clean a polygon and the others respond if they have cleaned it. This will result in an unpredictable area partitioning, because while a robot is requesting a polygon, it does not consider the whole region that it has and will sweep. Thus, this method is also most suitable for single sweep applications.

Schneider and Mataric [9] propose a dynamic method in which all the robots have full knowledge of the positions of the other robots. The only dynamic factor that they can respond to is the addition of a new robot. In addition to the fact that our algorithm handles different dynamic factors (e.g. robots with changing speeds), it does not rely on knowledge of other robots' positions at any given time.

In contrast to these previous approaches, in our proposed method, the robots start with an arbitrary partition, and use negotiation to transfer the parts of the environment between themselves. The negotiation method is designed to

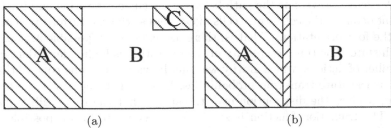

(a)   (b)

Fig. 1. (a) Partitioning using Min and Kin algorithm [7]. (b) Partitioning using our method.

adaptively partition the environment with the goal that average event-detection time is minimized for all parts of the environment. If *robot a* can sustain a better detection time for a part of the environment that belongs to *robot b*, *robot a* will take over responsibility for that part. With this method, the partition is adaptive to heterogeneous robots, robot malfunctions, addition of robots to the system, and also dynamically changing event patterns. For example if a robot slows down due to a malfunction, the average detection time that it can sustain for the parts that it is responsible for is increased and other robots will take over responsibility for some of its partition.

3   Continuous Area Sweeping Formulation

In this section we specify our task in detail. In a continuous area sweeping task, the robot must repeatedly visit all the points in its environment in an effort to detect or react to different types of events $e \in E$. The events can in general have varying degrees of importance, imp_e, and each event may occur in different places with varying frequencies. In the case that all points are equally likely locations for an event of interest, the events are equally important, and the robot needs to be physically present at the point to "visit" it, the problem reduces to the traveling salesman problem. Thus, in general, continuous area sweeping is NP-Hard, and we must rely on approximate solutions.

We begin by dividing the robot's environment into disjoint grid G, with each event occurring in one grid cell. We consider time as a sequence of discrete steps. The orientation $\theta \in O = \{North, South, East, West\}$ of the robot is also considered as being one of 4 disjoint values. We track the time a robot has *last visited* each cell $g \in G$ in an array $LV[G]$ by setting $LV[g] =$ current-time whenever the robot visits cell g.

The problem is defined as a tuple $(S, A, T_{sa}, P_{eg}, CF)$, where:

- $S = G \times O \times LV[G]$ is a set of *states*, representing the position and orientation of the robot as well as the array of last-visit times to each cell.
- A is the set of possible actions. The actions in this formulation are specified as going to a point in the environment. In particular, the environment is divided into a *coarse grid* called CG (CG need not be related to G in any way, though in general we expect it to be coarser than G). Each action $a \in A$ is defined as traversing the path between the current position and the center point of one of the coarse grid cells in CG and at the end turning to reach one of the four orientations. That is, there are $|CG| \times |O|$ possible actions from each state. The time complexity of the algorithm is highly dependent on the number of actions, which is why we usually want CG to be coarser than G.
- T_{sa} is the state transition probabilities. Based on the current state and action, it gives the distribution over the states that the robot will transition to. The transition function is stochastic, because based on possible robot localization errors and non-determinism in its movement, the robot may end up in grid cell g_j when aiming for grid cell g_i.

- P_{eg} is the probability of appearance of event e in cell g per cycle. For example, if $P_{eg} = 0.1$, there is the expectation of event e occurring every 10 cycles in cell g. P_{eg} is a property of the environment and is not observable by the robots.
- CF is the *cost function* of the *policy*. The cost function that we define for the continuous area sweeping problem is the average time elapsed from appearance to detection of the events, weighted by the importance of the event (imp_e). Since the robots should collectively observe the environment in order to detect all the events in minimum time, this criterion is for the whole multi-robot system.

The goal of each robot is to find a *policy* $\pi : S \mapsto A$ such that the joint policy of all robots minimizes the cost function. For each robot, the policy determines which action is chosen by the robot in each state.

Since the robots do not observe the times of event appearances (e.g. when a robot finds a piece of trash, it has no way of knowing how long it has been there), they are unable to calculate the cost function (CF) of their executed policies. Thus direct methods to minimize CF even in the single-robot case will not work. A heuristic single-robot algorithm will be presented in the next section.

4   Single Robot Continuous Area Sweeping

In this section, we present a detailed description of our single-robot approach to continuous area sweeping tasks. We begin by assuming that time is discretized into *cycles* representing the times at which the robot can make action decisions. For the purposes of our algorithm, we define an *expected reward* of each grid-cell g at time t as the expected sum of *importance values* of the events present in grid g at time t.

The algorithm consists of two main modules:

Learning: Learn the expected accumulation rate of event importance values in each cell (*potential reward*). The *expected reward* of visiting a cell at any given time depends on this rate and the time at which the cell was last visited.

Planning: Given these expected rewards and knowledge of the robot's (possibly stochastic) transition function, compute a sequence of actions for the robot (*policy*) with minimum cost.

The details of these two modules of the algorithm are presented in Sections 4.1 and 4.2. In Section 4.3 we show that this approach approximately minimizes the cost function defined in Section 3, which is the goal in the problem formulation.

4.1   Learning the Expected Reward

The aim of learning is to approximate the *expected reward* for visiting a cell at any given time. Expected reward is defined as the expected sum of importance values of the events present in grid g at time t. In Section 4.3 we show how minimizing the estimated cost (average expected reward) will result in minimizing the average *detection time* (i.e. maximizing the policy's value). A greedy approach to minimizing the expected reward is presented in Section 4.2.

Formally expected reward is defined as:

$$exp\_reward_{gt} = \sum_{all\ e} (t - LV[g]) \times P_{eg} \times imp_e \qquad (1)$$

where $LV[g]$ is the last time that cell g has been visited before time t. Notice that the value of $(t - LV[g])$ is known to the robot and is independent of the rest of the equation. Thus, it is only needed to approximate the value of $\sum_{all\ e}(P_{eg} \times imp_e)$. We refer to this quantity as the *potential reward* of cell g. Note that the potential reward of cell g is independent of time: it is the sum of the importance values of the expected events for cell g per second, or the *rate* of reward accumulation.

The high-level pseudocode of the algorithm which estimates potential reward for cell g is given in Algorithm 1. For each grid-cell g, the reward potential pot_reward_g is initialized to $\epsilon > 0$, which in our case $\epsilon = 1$ (see lines 2-4 of Algorithm 1). By initializing the pot_reward_g's to a non-zero constant value, we are assuming that all grid-cells have an equal positive probability of all events occurring. That is, we start with the assumption that $\forall e, g, g', P_{eg} = P_{eg'} > 0$. If we have prior knowledge that some grid-cells have a higher importance event possibility than others, potential reward for those grid-cells can be initialized to a higher value.

Algorithm 1. High level pseudocode for learning the reward potential.

1: $\alpha = 0.9$; {learning rate}
2: **for all** grid-cells 'g' **do**
3:     $pot\_reward_g := 1$; {initialize}
4: **end for**
5: **for each** cycle **do**
6:     t[g] := current-time - LV[g];
7:     **for each** detected event e in grid g do **do**
8:         $pot\_reward_g := (1 - \alpha) \times pot\_reward_g + \alpha \times imp_e/\text{t}[g]$;
9:     **end for**
10:     **for each** visited g with no event **do**
11:         $pot\_reward_g := pot\_reward_g \times 0.99$;
12:     **end for**
13: **end for**

It is assumed that after an appearance of a rewarding event in grid-cell g, the event will remain there until the robot visits g. Thus, if grid-cell g is visited after t_g time-units and the robot visits the events with sum of importance values of *IMP*, it can be assumed that with a higher probability every $\sim t_g$ time-units, an event with the importance value of *IMP* appears in grid-cell g. Whenever a non-empty set of events with sum of *event importance* values of *IMP* are visited in grid-cell g, the following update happens (lines 7-9 of Algorithm 1):

$$pot\_reward_g \leftarrow (1 - \alpha) * pot\_reward_g + \alpha * \frac{IMP}{t - LV[g]}$$

where, α is a learning rate, which in our experiments is set to 0.9. The update rule presented above, changes the estimation of *potential_reward$_g$* to be closer to $\frac{IMP}{t_g}$, which is the assumed sum of events importance values per time for grid-cell g. The estimation of reward potential for g will become more accurate after more visits to grid-cell g.

Since the frequency of event appearance may not be constant over time, there is also a need to unlearn the reward potentials. Thus, every time that the robot visits grid-cell g with no event, it will perform the following update on reward potential *pot_reward$_g$* (lines 10-12 of Algorithm 1):

$$pot\_reward_g \leftarrow pot\_reward_g * f$$

where f is an unlearn factor and in our experiments is set to 0.99. This update rule enables the robot to gradually unlearn the one-time events. Notice that the learning of potential reward for grid g happens only when there is an event in g. If no event is detected while visiting grid g, the above unlearning update will be performed. Since a lasting influence of a detected event is desired, the rate of learning is much faster than unlearning

Expected reward is defined as the expected sum of the importance values of the events present in grid g at time t. We compute it incrementally by adding potential reward (expected reward per second) in each cycle. The pseudocode for computing the expected reward for each grid-cell is shown in Algorithm 2. In each cycle, if a grid-cell is being visited, the expected reward for that grid-cell will be set to zero (see lines 6-7 of Algorithm 2), otherwise it will be incremented by the amount of the potential reward of that grid-cell (lines 8-9 of Algorithm 2). As a result, the expected reward for cell g will be equal to the potential reward of g multiplied by the amount of time that g has not been visited.

Algorithm 2. High level pseudocode for computing expected reward for grid-cells in each cycle. The pot_reward is computed in the Algorithm 1.

```
 1: for all grid-cells 'g' do
 2:     exp_reward_g := 0;
 3: end for
 4: for each cycle do
 5:     for all grid-cells 'g' do
 6:         if g is being visited then
 7:             exp_reward_g := 0;
 8:         else
 9:             exp_reward_g += pot_reward_g;
10:         end if
11:     end for
12: end for
```

4.2 Choosing Actions

When choosing an action, the robot can move to the center point of any cell in the coarse grid CG, and after reaching the destination turn to face one of the four orientations {*North, South, East, West*}. We assume that the map of the environment is already known and that the robot has a model of its own (stochastic) motion. As an initial approach, we use a form of greedy action selection.

The pseudocode to choose the action is given in Algorithm 3. For each action of going to point *cg*, the robot computes the trajectory of going to that point (see line 11 of Algorithm 3). For computing this trajectory, the shortest path between all pairs of center grid cells is found using the Floyd-Warshall algorithm [10]. Let P be the shortest path from the center of the cell that robot is in, to its final destination. The trajectory starts from where the robot is, to the center of the next grid cell on P, and continues on the center grid cells of P. Each trajectory is divided into discrete points, one point for each cell of G, which is the center of the line segment that passes through G. For each one of the discrete points of the trajectory, the grid-cells that will be seen from that point are computed as follows. We assume a 180-degree field of view for the robot, and the robot computes 181 rays with origin at its position and with angles ranging from -90 to 90 degrees from the robot's orientation. For each one of the lines, the cells that the line passes through before hitting a wall are considered "visited".

The expected reward of these visited grid-cells will be summed up for all the points in the trajectory and the result will be the *expected received reward* of

---

Algorithm 3. High level pseudocode for choosing the best action in one cycle.

1: s: state of the robot
2: A: possible actions in the state s
3: obs[g]: temp array to avoid double counting
4: max_reward := minimum_value;
5: **for** each action $a \in A$ **do**
6:     a_reward := 0;
7:     time_a : time to perform a
8:     **for all** g **do**
9:         obs[g] := false;
10:     **end for**
11:     compute the trajectory T for a
12:     **for** each point $t \in T$ **do**
13:         **for** each g visited from t **do**
14:             **if** not obs[g] **then**
15:                 a_reward := a_reward + exp_reward_g;
16:                 obs[g] := true;
17:             **end if**
18:         **end for**
19:     **end for**
20:     **if** a_reward / time_a > max_reward **then**
21:         max_reward := a_reward/time_a;
22:         best_action := a;
23:     **end if**
24: **end for**
25: **perform** best_action;

---

performing the action (lines 12-19 of Algorithm 3). After computing the expected reward values, the algorithm greedily chooses the action with the maximum expected reward per time (lines 20-23 of Algorithm 3).

The intuition behind this approach is that after the grid-cells with high expected reward are visited, their expected reward is set to zero, thus the estimated cost (average expected reward) decreases. By choosing the action with maximum expected received reward per time, for *one* action, we will have the maximum possible decrease in the estimated cost. It is possible to use more complex planning approaches to achieve closer to optimal solutions for this formulation, but the greedy approach is sufficient to achieve a good result in this environment.

4.3   Correctness of the Approach

In this subsection, we provide a proof that minimizing the estimated cost (average expected reward) will result in minimizing the cost function of the problem formulation. For the sake of analysis, we assume a finite horizon, with finite time and events.

The cost function in the formulation is the average detection time multiplied by the importance of the event. The goal is to minimize the cost function:

$$minimize(\sum_{e=1}^{E}(detect\_time_e \times imp_e)) \tag{2}$$

where E is the number of events in our finite horizon, $detect\_time_e$ is the detection time of event e and imp_e is the importance value of event e.

The goal in the presented approach is to minimize the estimated cost over time. That is:

$$minimize((\sum_{t=1}^{C}\sum_{g=1}^{|G|}exp\_reward_{gt})) \tag{3}$$

where, $|G|$ is the number of grids, C is the number of cycles in our horizon and exp_reward_{gt} is the expected reward of grid-cell g at time t.

By the definition of expected reward (Eq. 1), in the finite horizon we have:

$$exp\_reward_{gt} = \sum_{e=1}^{E}(t - LV[g]) \times P_{eg} \times imp_e \tag{4}$$

where $LV[g]$ is the last time that grid-cell g has been visited before time t and P_{eg} is the probability of appearance of event e in grid-cell g.

Based on equations 3 and 4, the goal of the proposed approach is to minimize the following equation:

$$\sum_{e=1}^{E}\sum_{t=1}^{C}\sum_{g=1}^{|G|}((t - LV[g]) \times P_{eg} \times imp_e) \tag{5}$$

The average value of $(t - LV[g])$ over time (average detection time) is equal to $0.5T_g$, where T_g is the average time between two visits of the robot to grid-cell g. Thus minimizing the Eq. 5 results in minimizing this equation:

$$\sum_{e=1}^{E}\sum_{g=1}^{|G|}(T_g \times P_{eg} \times imp_e) \tag{6}$$

Notice $\sum_{g=1}^{|G|}(T_g \times P_{eg})$ is the *expected detection time* of grid-cell g and since imp_e is independent of g, minimizing the above equation will result in minimizing the cost function (Eq. 2).

In this section, we showed that by achieving the goal of the proposed approach (i.e. minimizing the estimated cost over time) the cost function of the problem formulation will be minimized (which is the goal of the optimal policy). We are using a greedy approach to minimize the estimated cost over time, which is not necessarily optimal, but given the proven fact that minimizing estimated cost will result in minimizing the cost function, it is a reasonable approach.

5   Multi-robot Continuous Area Sweeping

In Section 4 we considered a single robot engaged in continuous area sweeping. Recall from Section 1 that our overall algorithm can be decomposed into that and a partitioning algorithm. We achieve cooperative behavior by partitioning the environment among robots. Partitions are assigned to different robots, and the robots do the exploration autonomously (using single-robot algorithm presented in Section 4) in their assigned partitions. In this section, we present a partitioning algorithm that is robust to heterogeneous robots, robot malfunctions, unexpected additions of robots to the system, and dynamic changes of event appearance patterns. Note that restricting robots to partitions may not necessarily lead to the optimal behavior for multi-robot continuous area sweeping, but doing so allows for a convenient and efficient task decomposition.

A naïve first approach is to statically partition the environment among the robots. However in our environment, with the probability of event appearances changing dynamically plus the possibility of the addition and removal of robots from the environment, static partitioning is not suitable.

Instead, we propose a negotiation model for partitioning the environment among robots. We define RG_x as the set of grid cells that robot x is responsible for. The basic idea behind the negotiation method is: Considering two robots, a and b, if there is a $g \in RG_a$ that robot b can visit — following its own exploration algorithm — more often than robot a, then g should be added to RG_b and removed from RG_a.

The high-level negotiation procedure is shown in Fig 2. Assuming each robot is already responsible for a partition, the negotiation structure is as follows. The algorithm for assigning initial partitions will be specified later in the section.

First: in fixed periods each robot (as shown in step *1* of Figure 2),

(a) labels the grid cells on the border of its RG (RG_a for robot a) as *candidates*. These grid cells are the ones that the robot is considering giving up

1) **(Robot 1): send** $S_1 = \{border\ line\ grid\ cells\}$ *of message type 1.*

2) **(Robot 2):** *Upon receiving* S_1 *of message type 1:*

$t := big\ negative\ number;$

$for\ all\ g \in S_1$

    $t_1 := possible\ time\ between\ visits\ for\ g\ (by\ Robot\ 2)$

    $t_2 := available\ time\ between\ visits\ for\ g\ (by\ Robot\ 1)$

    $if\ (t_2 - t_1) > t\ do$

      $t := t_2 - t_1;$

      $g_{max} := g;$

$G^* := cells\ that\ will\ be\ visited\ because\ of\ addition\ responsibility\ of\ g_{max}.$

send $S_2 = \{G^*\}$ *of message type 2 as an offer.*

3) **Robot 2** *upon receiving message type 2, accepts the best offer, and sends an acknowledgement (message type 3).*

4) **Robot 1** *Upon receiving acknowledgement, the transfer will be complete.*

Fig. 2. High level negotiation procedure

responsibility for. Note that all the grid cells on the border of a robot's responsibility area, but not on the border of the whole environment are considered candidates.

(b) Broadcasts a message consisting of information about the candidate grid cells. The message format is as follows:

$$(g, avg\_time, pot\_reward)$$

where, g is the grid cell id and avg_time is the robot's current average detection time for that grid cell. pot_reward is potential reward which is the learned expected accumulation rate of event importance values in cell g. pot_reward is used to compute *expected* reward and is sent to other robots for use in the robots' single-robot exploration algorithm (because they have no first-hand experience about the rate of event appearance in other robots' grid cells). These messages are called *type 1 messages*.

Second: Upon receiving type 1 messages, the robot stores them in a list. At fixed intervals, each robot processes its stored messages as follows (step 2 in Figure 2):

(a) For each grid cell g in the stored messages, the robot pretends that it is responsible for it (in addition to its whole current partition), and using the single-robot algorithm finds a new hypothetical path. With that path, it computes *time between visits* for g, and stores it in $time_g$.

(b) For each grid cell g in stored messages, using $time_g$ and imp_e the robot computes the weighted detection time ($new\_avg\_time_g$) for that grid cell under the assumption that the robot adds g to its partition.

(c) From among all the grid cells mentioned in type 1 messages, each robot finds the cell with the maximum difference between the computed event detection time ($new\_avg\_time_g$) and the average detection time that the message sender could provide (avg_time_g from the message). That is it finds the cell $maxg$ such that ($new\_avg\_time_g - avg\_time_g$) is maximized. From the local information that the robot has, from among all the candidate cells in type 1 messages, $maxg$ is the best one to add to the robot's partition, because it is the one for which its addition to the partition will most decrease the cost function. Notice that transfer of any cell between two robots may change cells' time between visits for both robots. Since the robots do not have information on those changes, the decisions based on time between visits for transferring more than a single cell could lead to unpredictable transfers, and likely oscillations.

(d) $maxg$ which was computed in the previous step, is the cell that the robot will offer to take into its partition. In the new path that the robot has to take in order to visit $maxg$, possibly some additional cells from other partitions will be visited. The robot stores these cells in V_{maxg}. The cells in V_{maxg} will be visited without any further effort, thus the robot offers to take over responsibility for them as well. In particular, it sends a message to take over all the cells in V_{maxg} to the robots currently responsible for them. The message format is as follows:

$$(num, (g_0, avg\_time_0), (g_1, avg\_time_1), ...)$$

where, num is the number of offered grid cells, while g_i and avg_time_i, for $0 \leq i < num$, are grid cell ids and average detection times for each offered grid cell respectively. These messages are called *type 2 messages*.

Third: Each robot accumulates its received type 2 messages, and then processes them at fixed intervals (step *3* in Figure 2).

(a) The robot has the chance to accept one of the offers, that is, it can give away a set of its cells to one of the robots that has made an offer for them. For this purpose, it assigns a value to each offer. For offer o, its value will be equal to:

$$\sum_{i=0, g_i \in RG}^{i=num-1} avg\_time_i - my\_avg\_time_{g_i}$$

where num is the number of cells in offer o, avg_time_i is the average time between visits for grid g_i in offer o and $my\_avg\_time_{g_i}$ is the robot's average time between visits for that same grid cell. By accepting cell g_i, avg_time_i will decrease to $my\_avg\_time_{g_i}$. Thus, the offers that decrease the cost function the most have the most value. If the highest value is positive, the offer associated with it is accepted.

In other words, from all the offered grid cells, it finds the set (received from a single robot and in the robot's own RG) such that the sum of the difference between the offered detection time and the current average detection time is maximized.

(b) The robot then gives up the responsibility for the cells in the accepted offer.

(c) Finally, if the robot has accepted an offer it sends an acknowledgement to the robot willing to take responsibility for them (message type 3).

Fourth: When a robot receives an acknowledgement for a set of grid cells (message type 3), it assumes the responsibility of that set of grid cells and the negotiation is considered finished (step *4* in Figure 2). Each robot then resumes its single-robot sweeping within its (possibly changed) partition.

Notice that the only message type of the three that can cause inconsistency if it is not delivered, is the acknowledgement message (message type 3). If any other message does not get delivered, no change of responsibility will occur. But if the acknowledgement message does not get delivered no robot will assume the responsibility for a set of grid cells and if there is no recovery mechanism, the inconsistency can be permanent. In our current system, we send the acknowledgement message 5 times to reduce the possibility of that inconsistency. In our experiments the maximum of consecutive message losses was 2, and thus no inconsistency occurred.

When a new robot is added to the environment, it sends out a message declaring its presence, and the robots who are close enough to hear its message send out their position information to it. It then takes responsibility for half of the partition of the closest robot to it. The negotiation then continues, and appropriate adjustments are made. Similarly, when a robot is removed from the environment, it sends out a signal notifying others that it is being removed, or if it crashes, other robots will detect its removal after not hearing from it for an extended period of time. After that, the closest robot to it takes charge of its responsibility area, and further negotiations will split the area appropriately.

6   Single Robot Results

To test our approach, we have implemented and evaluated our algorithm on a physical robot in a representation of the routine surveillance task. As our robot, we use a Sony ERS-7 four-legged AIBO robot (Figure 3). The robot's sensor device for "visiting" locations in its environment is a camera mounted on the head of the robot. It can capture 208×160 frames of pixels at roughly 30Hz. Due to the computational intensity of image processing, our robots typically make decisions at roughly 25Hz, thus the cycle defined in Section 4 is set to 0.04 second. By turning its head, the robot can gain a 180-degree field of view. It has 20 degrees of freedom and a 576Mhz on-board processor.

As baseline software, we use the UT Austin Villa code base [11], which provides robust color-based vision, fast locomotion, and reasonably accurate localization within a 2.9m $\times$ 4.4m area[1] via a particle filtering approach. Even so, the robot is not, in general, perfectly localized, as a result of both noisy sensations and noisy actions. The robot also has limited processing power, which limits the algorithms that can be designed for it. G is equal to a 18×15 grid, that is we

---

[1] The field is as specified in the 2004 rules of the RoboCup Four-Legged Robot League: http://www.tzi.de/4legged

Fig. 3. ERS-7 Sony AIBO robot

discretize the robot's environment into an 18 × 15 grid. CG, which defines the available actions, is set to a 6 × 5 grid. There is just one type of event in the environment, which is the appearance of an orange ball that the robot can recognize from anywhere on the field provided that it has an unobstructed view. We test two different configurations of the world with the real robot. One other configuration is tested in a custom-built AIBO simulator [11]. The simulator, though abstract with respect to locomotion, provides a reasonable representation of the Aibo's visual and localization capabilities, and allows for a more thorough experimentation, particularly with regards to testing different distributions of ball appearances.

6.1   Single-Robot Configuration I with a Real Robot

As an initial experiment, we configured the robot's environment as shown in Figure 4(a). A picture of the actual environment with the robot is shown in Figure 5. The robot knows the locations of the walls in the environment, but must decide for itself how to move so as to perform surveillance.

Before appearance of the balls, the path that the robot found is *path 1* in Figure 4(b). It is the minimal path for uniformly visiting the whole environment.

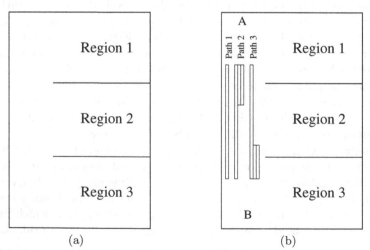

(a)   (b)

Fig. 4. (a) Representation of configuration I. (b) The path the robot traverses in configuration I.

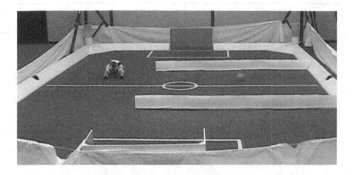

Fig. 5. Picture of configuration I with the real robot

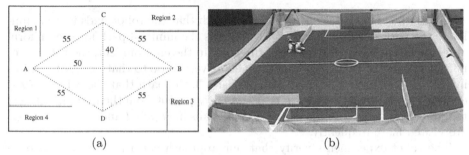

(a)   (b)

Fig. 6. (a) Representation of configuration II (b) Configuration II with a real robot

After that, we started to show the balls to the robot in region 1 and 2, but not region 3. In this new situation the robot found *path 2* in Figure 4(b). By traversing this path, robot visits region 1 and 2 more often than 3 and that is a desirable result[2].

Later in the experiment we stopped showing any balls to the robot. As a result of the forgetting parameter, the robot gradually went back to uniform exploration (*path 1* in Figure 4(b)). Finally, we again started to show the ball, this time in regions 2 and 3. The path that the robot found in this new situation is *path 3* in Figure 4(b)[3].

6.2   Single-Robot Configuration II with a Real Robot

As a follow-up to this initial experiment, we created a more complex environment as is illustrated in Figure 6(a) and pictured in Figure 6(b).

---

[2] Videos of the robot in action in this environment are available from http://www. scs.utexas.edu/~AustinVilla/?p=research/surveillance, named configuration I part 1.

[3] A video of the robot forgetting what it has learned before and re-learning the new distribution of the ball appearances is available at http://www.cs.utexas. edu/~AustinVilla/?p=research/surveillance, named configuration I part 2.

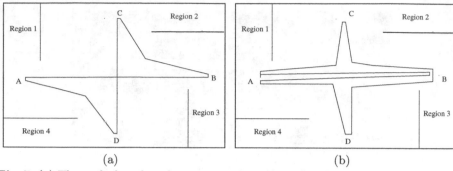

(a)   (b)

Fig. 7. (a) The path that the robot traverses in uniform distribution of the appearance of the ball. (b) The path that the robot finds when there is several appearances of the ball in region 1 and 3.

Before the appearance of the balls, the path that the robot finds is very similar to the path shown in Figure 7(a), which is the minimal path for the uniform appearance of the balls. Because of the noise in the environment, the robot does not exactly follow that path, but the path is very close to that one. After showing the ball for several times in regions 1 and 3, the path that the robot finds is close to the one shown in Figure 7(b) [4]. As is apparent from the path, because of the higher probability of appearance of the balls in *region 1* and *3*, those regions are visited more frequently.

The robot experiments verify that our approach can run in real time on a computationally limited platform, and that the robot can operate using the same algorithm in multiple environments. However, due to the time-consuming nature of running experiments in the real world, we further validate our approach in simulation.

6.3   Single-Robot Simulation

We use an extended version of our group's custom-built AIBO simulator[5] to test our approach. The architecture of our AIBO code is designed in two layers. The lower layer is responsible for managing the visual sensor and translating high-level commands to robot motor commands, while the upper layer reasons about the visual inputs and issues high-level motion commands. Our simulator is designed to take the place of the environment and the lower layer, providing abstract visual input to the control code, and simulating robot motions. Full details of the code organization and simulator interface can be found in our technical report [11].

With this simulator platform, we are able to run identical upper-level code both on the robot and on the simulator. Using the simulator, we are able to control precisely the distribution of locations at which the ball appears, and we are able to run experiments much more quickly.

---

[4] A video of this experiment is available at `http://www.cs.utexas.edu/AustinVilla/?p=research/surveillance.`, named configuration *II*.

[5] The original simulator was created by Gregory Kuhlmann.

In our simulation experiments, we test four different distributions of ball appearances in configuration II from the real robot experiments (Figure 6(a)). In all the distributions, the ball appears in each cell g with probability $P_{eg} * 50$ every 50 seconds. In particular, this means that a ball can appear in more than one cell before the robot sees any of them, and that there can be more than one ball in the same place by the time the robot visits that place. P_{eg} is different in each one of the experiments.

In the same Figure 6(a), the approximate time needed (in seconds) for walking between each pair of points, as measured on the physical robot, is given beside the dotted lines. Notice that the time it takes to walk straight across the field — even the long way from A to B — is less than the time it takes to move between adjacent points such as B and D. The reason for the difference is that the robot takes significant time to turn.

In the following subsections, we discuss the results in each of four distributions: a uniform distribution; a distribution in which the ball only appears in one place; a biased distribution; and a non-stationary distribution.

Uniform Distribution. In our first experiment, the ball appears with identical probability in each of the four regions. Notice that were the ball to appear anywhere else in the environment, the optimal policy would not be affected significantly, since almost all of the actions visit the center part of the environment. The path that the robot finds after learning is approximately the path shown in figure Figure 7(a).

In order for the robot to visit all the regions it at least needs to go through the points A, B, C and D or a small area around them. Based on the travel times in Figure 6(a), the solution shown in Figure 7(a) is optimal, which we can check by exhaustive search.

While following the path that the robot found, each ball was approximately visited after 106 ± 2.1 seconds. In the experiment, 100 balls were shown to the robot. The optimum average detection time is 100 seconds, which is the result of traversing the path in Figure 7(a). The whole traversing time for that path is $55 + 40 + 55 + 50 = 200$. Thus, it takes between 0 and 200 seconds to detect each event, and the average detection time is 100 seconds. As a result, our approach is in 4% margin of error, which is quite close to optimal, with the error coming mainly from action noise. The path that the robot found is not exactly the one in Figure 7(a), since for example the robot does not always go to the exact grid-cell of point A. Rather, to visit region 1, it goes to one of the grid-cells close to A. The exact motion of the robot is visible in our on-line videos.

This initial experiment verifies that our greedy algorithm can produce the optimal solution in the most benign case.

Always in One Region Distribution. As a second test, we created a distribution such that the ball only appeared in region 2. The path that the robot finds is approximately the one shown in Figure 8(a). It took the robot only one pass through the field to approximately follow the path in Figure 8(a).

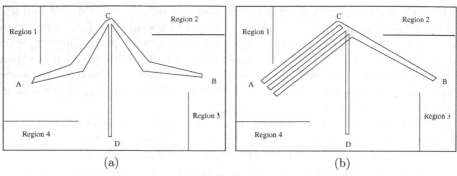

Fig. 8. (a) The path the robot traverses when the ball always appears in region 2. (b) The path that the robot traverses in the face of a biased distribution, where the chance of the ball appearance is 60% in region 2, 30% in region 1 and 5% in regions 3 and 4.

On average, every ball is noticed 47 ± 1.3 seconds after its appearance. In the experiment 100 balls were shown to the robot. Of course, the optimum solution here is for the robot to stay close to region 2 and visit the balls right after it appears, but our algorithm enforces the constraint that the robot should continually visit the whole environment at least periodically in case new events occur. With the condition that we want to visit the whole environment *continually*, 47 seconds is reasonable. In particular, learning the distribution has gained us a 50% performance improvement: without learning the robot would traverse the environment uniformly, resulting in an average detection time of 106 seconds or ideally 100 seconds. Notice that the average detection time in uniformly traversing the environment and visiting each cell once in the full traverse of the environment is independent of the distribution of event appearances. Because whatever the distribution, the average detection time for each event is constant and equal to the half of the whole traversing time.

Biased Distribution. In our next experiment we tested the robustness of our approach in a scenario such that the balls appear in all the regions but with different probabilities. In the biased distribution, with probability 60% the ball appears in region 2, with probability 30% it appears in region 1, with probability 5% in 3, and with probability 5% in 4 ($P_{eg} = .6/50, .3/50, .05/50,$ and $.05/50$ respectively). The path that the robot traverses is approximately the one in Figure 8(b).

The time needed for the robot to change its path from the uniform case to the path shown in Figure 8(b) is based on how fast it can learn the distribution, which itself is based on frequency of ball appearances. In our experiment, every 50 seconds an average of 1 ball appeared. In this setting, the robot took 9 complete traverses (1734 seconds or 35 ball appearances) to start traversing the shown path.

After the 1734 seconds, when the robot learned the distribution, on average every ball was visited 79 ± 1.2 seconds after its appearance. In the experiment, 200 balls were shown to the robot. This result is significantly better than uniform traversal which results in average detection time of 106 or ideally 100 seconds.

Changing Distributions. In our final experiment we tested the robustness of the approach to changing distributions. In particular, we consider a scenario in which at some unknown point in time the probability of appearance of the balls changes abruptly. The initial distribution of the ball appearance was the same as the biased case discussed in previous section, that is 60% in region 2, 30% in region 1, 5% in region 3, and 5% in 4. After 100 ball appearances, the distribution changes to the uniform appearance of the ball.

The path that the robot found with the starting distribution is the same as the one in Figure 8(b). It took the robot about 1820 seconds or 36 ball appearances to adapt to the second distribution and approximately follow the path in Figure 7(a).

7 Multi-robot Results

The experiments in Section 6 verified the single-robot algorithms. In this section the partitioning algorithms will be evaluated. Together single-robot and partitioning algorithms build the full multi-robot system for continuous area sweeping.

We have tested two different configurations of the world in a custom-built simulator, and one configuration on real robots. The specification of the robots and the simulator is the same as the one described in the previous section. In this section, the focus of the experiments is on the negotiation and the adaptive area partitioning.

7.1 Multi-robot Configuration *I* in Simulation

The configuration of the environment in the first experiment, is shown in Figure 9(a). For this experiment, we divide the world (4.4m × 2.9m) into a 45 × 54 grid (*G*). The coarse grid (*CG*) is a 15×18 grid. The reported results are averaged over at least 10 trials.

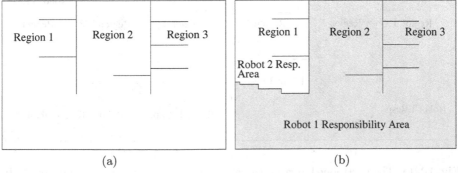

(a)   (b)

Fig. 9. (a) Representation of configuration *I*. (b) The partitioned area between two homogeneous robots in configuration *I*.

Two homogeneous robots. We start with having two homogeneous robots on the field. In the initial partitioning, each robot gets half of the area (divided vertically). The partitioned area, which is achieved after reaching equilibrium is shown in Figure 9(b). Notice that when robot 2 traverses the path between regions 2 and 3, it automatically visits the bottom cells, thus it takes the responsibility for all of the bottom grid cells. They reached this assignment with only one negotiation in which 683 cells were transferred from robot 2 to robot 1.

Conventional area partitioning algorithms will try to divide the area equally between the two robots, which is less efficient than the equilibrium that our robots reached. If the area is divided equally between robots, the average event detection time would be 33.9 ± 0.7 seconds, while with our partitioned area, it is 32.2 ± 0.6 seconds. Since there are just two homogeneous robots in a simple environment, a minor performance enhancement (in this case %5) is all we can expect.

Three homogeneous robots. Later in the experiment we added a new robot in the middle of the field. While usual non-adaptive area partitioning methods cannot adapt to the addition of the new robot, our robots reached a new equilibrium which is showed in Figure 10(a). It took the robots two negotiations to reach this partitioning. 421 cells were transferred from robot 3 to robot 2 and 283 cells from robot 2 to robot 1.

A conventional static partitioning for three robots could achieve a similar partitioning. The average event detection time in this case was 28.3 ± 0.6 seconds.

Three heterogeneous robots. Following the previous experiment, we slowed down robot 3 to half of its original speed. That condition can happen in the real world as the result of a joint failure. It took the robots one negotiation with 457 cells transfered to reach the new partitioning which is shown in Figure 10(b).

If no new negotiation were performed after slowing down robot 3, the average event detection time would have been 30.1 ± 0.4 seconds. However, after the negotiation and the resulting new partitioning, the average event detection time

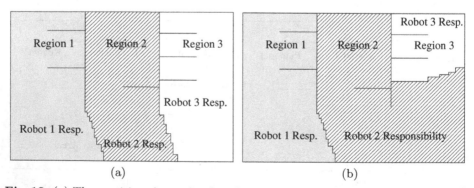

(a)   (b)

Fig. 10. (a) The partitioned area for three homogeneous robots in configuration I. (b) The partitioned area for three heterogeneous robots in configuration I. The robot 3 has half the speed of the other two robots.

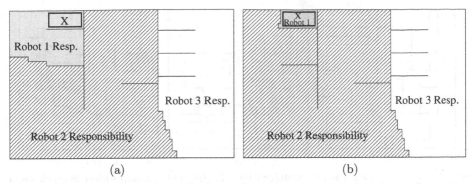

Fig. 11. (a) The partitioned area between three homogeneous robots in configuration I, when the chance of ball appearance in area X is 10 times the other cells. (b) The partitioned area between three homogeneous robots in configuration I, when the chance of event appearance is 1000 times more in area X.

was 29.3 ± 0.2 seconds. Notice that here we only have 3 robots, and only one of them slows down. If there are more robots, the speedup will be more significant. To our knowledge, previous work in the area could not adapt to this new situation.

Non uniform distribution of event occurrences. Continuing with three homogeneous robots, we next consider the case in which the chance of event appearance in area X (Figure 11(a)), which consists of 45 grid cells, increases by a factor of 10. The robot can learn the distribution based on the event occurrence by itself, though it requires time to notice the change. In this case, to speed up the experiment, we manually increased the potential reward value in the robot's internal algorithm to represent the new distribution. With only one negotiation and 497 cell transfer, the new partitioning is formed, which is shown in Figure 11(a). The average event detection time with the original partitioned area, (shown in Figure 10(a)) was 34.7 ± 0.8 seconds, while with the new partitioning it reduces to 29.4 ± 0.5 seconds.

If the chance of the ball appearance in area X is multiplied by 1000, one of the robots ends up constantly staying and watching area X, while the other two robots divide the environment as shown in Figure 11(b). With the original partitioned area (Figure 10(a)), the average detection time would be 45.3 ± 0.2 seconds, but with the new partitioning it reduces to to 0.2 ± 0.0 seconds. Notice that with the new partitioning, one of the robots constantly watches area X and thus most of the events are observed in no time.

7.2   Multi-robot Configuration II in Simulation

The aim of this experiment is to show that the cooperation algorithm can scale up to more complex situations. The environment in this experiment is shown in Figure 12(a). It is 8m × 8m and is divided into a 80×80 grid G. CG is a 20×20 grid.

There are 8 robots with different speeds, as shown in Table 1. The partitioned area after negotiation is shown in Figure 12(b). It took the robots 67 negotia-

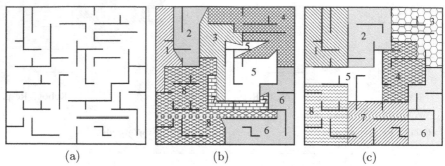

Fig. 12. (a) Representation of configuration II. (b) Task decomposition of 8 robots in configuration II, which is achieved by our partitioning algorithm. (c) A typical and reasonable task decomposition in configuration II.

Table 1. Speed of robots for configuration II experiment

Robots	1	2	3	4	5	6	7	8
Speed (cm/s)	10	20	10	30	40	40	20	50

tions and in total 24535 cell transfers to reach this partitioning. Although some of the shapes looks irregular, each robot can observe its whole partition while following a simple path. Using a perfectly space-equivalent partition (as some approaches do), leads to average event detection time of 15.3 ± 1.0 seconds. In Figures 12(c) we show a heuristic partition chosen so as to roughly equalize space, but in a way that follows borders and appears to be reasonable. The average detection time in the heuristic reasonable partition (Figure 12(c)) is 9.0 ± 0.8, while with our partitioning (Figure 12(b)), it decreases to 6.1 ± 0.5. This data is averaged over 10 trials. This significant improvement over the static

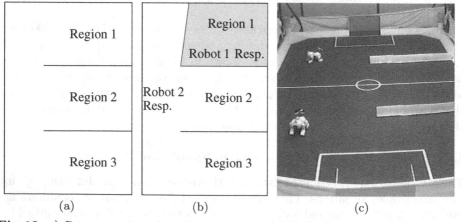

Fig. 13. a) Representation of configuration III. (b) Task division for real robots in configuration III. (c) Picture of configuration III with two robots.

area partitioning suggests that with higher number of robots, the advantage of our method is more significant.

7.3 Multi-robot Configuration *III* with Real Robots

To show that the system also works on real robots, we present an experiment with real robots in a simple environment. An overview of the configuration is shown in Figure 13(a) and the picture of the actual environment with the robot is shown in Figure 13(c). The robots know the locations of the walls in the environment, but must decide for themselves how to move so as to perform surveillance.

In this case, the grid G was 15×18, and CG was a 5×6 grid. The resulting task division between the robots is shown in Figure 13(b). For the same reason as discussed in Section 7.1, this is the optimal task division. For a movie of this experiment, please visit `http://www.cs.utexas.edu/~AustinVilla/?p=research/surveillance`.

8   Conclusions

In this paper, the problem of *multi-robot continuous area sweeping* is examined. The problem is defined as one in which robots must repeatedly visit every part of the environment in order to detect a set of events of interest. The frequency of the events can possibly be non-uniform. Thus the robots should visit the points with non-uniform frequency. Examples of continuous area sweeping tasks are surveillance and cleaning.

In this paper, we formalize the problem and introduce an initial single-robot approach that non-uniformly visits the environment to minimize the estimated cost. The approach is analyzed analytically and is tested both in simulation and on real robots. The single-robot approach is extended to multi-robot cases, with a help of a dynamic area partitioning method. Each robot will continue with its single-robot algorithm in its assigned partition. The area partitioning is done by a negotiation method, which is adaptive to dynamic environments. The adaptive area partitioning is especially important if the rate of event appearance is non-uniform in the environment, or if the robots are heterogeneous in their capabilities.

Our on-going research agenda includes expanding the robot behavior to include non-greedy planning and to find an optimality bound for the area partitioning method. Also we are working on designing recovery mechanisms for the cases where unbounded consecutive messages get lost, and an inconsistency occurs.

Acknowledgment

The authors would like to thank the members of the UT Austin Villa team for their efforts in developing the software used as a basis for the work reported in this paper. Special thanks to Greg Kuhlmann for developing the simulator. We also want to thank Bikramjit Banerjee, Roozbeh Mottaghi, Ali Nouri and Mohan

Sridharan for their comments on earlier versions of this paper. This research was supported in part by NSF CAREER award IIS-0237699 and ONR YIP award N00014-04-1-0545.

References

1. Kalra, N., Stentz, A.T., Ferguson, D.: Hoplites: A market framework for complex tight coordination in multi-agent teams. Technical Report CMU-RI-TR-04-41, Robotics Institute, Carnegie Mellon University, Pittsburgh, PA (2004)
2. Kurabayashi, D. Ota, J.A.T.Y.E.: Cooperative sweeping by multiple mobile robots. In: Proc. of IEEE International Conference on Robotics & Automation (ICRA). (1996)
3. Choset, H.: Coverage for robotics; a survey of recent results. Annals of Mathematics and Artificial Intelligence **31** (2001) 113–126
4. Parker, L.E.: Distributed algorithms for multi-robot observation of multiple moving targets. Autonomous Robots **12** (2002) 231–255
5. Hert, S., Lumelsky, V.: Polygon area decomposition for multiple-robot workspace division. Special Issue of International Journal of Computational Geometry & Applications on Applied Computational Geometry **8** (1998) 437–466
6. Bast, H., Hert, S.: The area partitioning problem. In: Proceedings of the 12th Canadian Conference on Computational Geometry. (1995)
7. Min, T.W., Yin, H.K.: A decentralized approach for cooperative sweeping by multiple mobile robots. In: International Conference on Intelligent Robots and Systems (IROS). (1998)
8. Jager, M., Nebel, B.: Dynamic decentralized area partitioning for cooperating cleaning robots. In: ICRA. (2002)
9. Schneider-Fontan, M., Mataric, M.: Territorial multi-robot task division. IEEE Transactions on Robotics and Automation **15** (1998)
10. Cormen, T., Leiserson, C., Rivest, R., Stein, C.: Introduction to Algorithms. 2nd edn. The MIT Press (2001)
11. Stone, P., Dresner, K., Fidelman, P., Jong, N.K., Kohl, N., Kuhlmann, G., Sridharan, M., Stronger, D.: The UT Austin Villa 2004 RoboCup four-legged team: Coming of age. Technical Report UT-AI-TR-04-313, The University of Texas at Austin, Department of Computer Sciences, AI Laboratory (2004)

Learning Automata as a Basis for Multi Agent Reinforcement Learning

Ann Nowé, Katja Verbeeck, and Maarten Peeters*

Computational Modeling Lab, Vrije Universiteit Brussel,
Pleinlaan 2, Brussel 1050, Belgium
ann.nowe@vub.ac.be, kaverbee@vub.ac.be, mjpeeter@vub.ac.be

Abstract. In this paper we summarize some important theoretical results from the domain of Learning Automata. We start with single stage, single agent learning schema's, and gradually extend the setting to multi-stage multi agent systems. We argue that the theory of Learning Automata is an ideal basis to build multi agent learning algorithms.

1 Introduction

Learning Automata (LA) are adaptive decision making devices suited for operation in unknown environments [12]. Originally they were developed in the area of mathematical psychology and used for modeling observed behavior. In its current form, LA are closely related to Reinforcement Learning (RL) approaches and most popular in the area of engineering. LA combine fast and accurate convergence with low computational complexity, and have been applied to a broad range of modeling and control problems. However, the intuitive, yet analytically tractable concept of learning automata makes them also very suitable as a theoretical framework for Multi agent Reinforcement Learning (MARL).

Reinforcement Learning (RL) is already an established and profound theoretical framework for learning in stand-alone or single-agent systems. Yet, extending RL to multi-agent systems (MAS) does not guarantee the same theoretical grounding. As long as the environment an agent is experiencing is Markov, and the agent can experiment sufficiently, RL guarantees convergence to the optimal strategy. In a MAS however, the reinforcement an agent receives, may depend on the actions taken by the other agents acting in the same environment. Hence, the Markov property no longer holds. And as such, guarantees of convergence are lost. In the light of the above problem it is important to fully understand the dynamics of multi-agent reinforcement learning.

Although, they are not fully recognized as such, LA are valuable tools for current MARL research. LA are updated strictly on the basis of the response of the environment, and not on the basis of any knowledge regarding other

---

* Research funded by a Ph.D grant of the Institute for the Promotion of Innovation through Science and Technology in Flanders (IWT Vlaanderen).

K. Tuyls et al. (Eds.): LAMAS 2005, LNAI 3898, pp. 71–85, 2006.

automata, i.e. nor their strategies, nor their feedback. As such LA agents are very simple. Moreover, LA can be treated analytically. Convergence proofs do exist for a variety of settings ranging from a single automaton model acting in a simple stationary random environment to a distributed automata model interacting in a complex environment.

In this paper we introduce the Learning Automaton as a Policy Iterator and discuss some convergence issues. Then we move to collections of learning automata, that can independently converge to interesting solution concepts. We study the single stage setting, including the analytical results. Then we generalize to interconnected learning automata, that can deal with multi agent multistage problems. We also show how Ant Colony Optimization can be mapped to the interconnected Learning Automata setting.

2   Variable Structure: Single Stage, Single Agent

Learning Automata (LA) are adaptive decision making devices suited for operation in unknown stochastic environments. Originally, they were developed in the area of mathematical psychology [4], and used by psychologists and biologists to describe the human behavior from psychological and biological viewpoints. Nowadays, they are most popular in the domain of engineering. Since LA combine fast and accurate convergence with low computational complexity, they can be applied to a broad range of modeling and control problems. For instance, in [17] an intelligent controller is designed, using learning automata theory, for an automated vehicle that plans its own trajectory based on sensor and communication data. In [14] a learning-automata based solution to the capacity assignment problem of communication networks is proposed.

The study of learning automata started in the 1960's by Tsetlin and his co-workers [16]. The early models were examples of fixed-structure stochastic automata. In its current form, a LA corresponds to a variable structure stochastic learning automaton.

2.1   Basic LA Schemes

A variable structure LA is closely related to a Reinforcement Learner of the policy iteration type. In this section we introduce the basic case of a stateless LA, corresponding to the single stage, single agent setting.

At each point in time the LA has a probability distribution over it's actions, denoted by $p(t) = (p_1(t), \ldots, p_l(t))$ where $p_i(t)$ represents the probability for selecting the ith action at time t and l denotes the number of actions. These probabilities are adjusted in time based on a reinforcement signal coming from the environment after an action has been performed by the automaton. Below we introduce the most commonly used update schemes. First, we assume that the reinforcement signal is binary, i.e. the action was a success or a failure. Then we move to a more general setting.

Reward-Penalty with binary feedback. In case of success we have:

$$\begin{cases} p_i(t+1) = p_i(t) + a(1 - p_i(t)) \\ \qquad \text{if action i was taken at time step t} \\ p_j(t+1) = (1 - a)p_j(t) \\ \qquad \forall j \neq i \end{cases}$$

where a belongs to the interval $]0, 1[$.

In case of failure this becomes:

$$\begin{cases} p_i(t+1) = p_i(t) - bp_i(t) \\ \qquad \text{if action i was taken at time step t} \\ \\ p_j(t+1) = p_j(t) + b[(l-1)^{-1} - p_j(t)] \\ \qquad \forall j \neq i \end{cases}$$

with $b \in]0, 1[$ and l the number of actions in the action set of the automaton. The constants a and b are the reward and penalty parameters respectively.

When we set $a = b$, the algorithm is referred to as *linear reward-penalty* (L_{R-P}). When b is taken to be zero, so only reward is taken into account, it is referred to as *linear reward inaction* (L_{R-I}). When a is small compared to b the schema is called *linear reward-ϵ-penalty* $(L_{R-\epsilon P})$.

The schema given above, applies to the binary feedback case, also referred to as the *P-model*. More general schema's allow the feedback signal to be drawn form a set of discrete values, in this case we talk about a *Q-model*, and in case the feedback is allowed to take a continuous range of values, the model is referred to as an *S-model*. The update schema for the more general S-model is given below.

Reward-Penalty with continuous valued feedback. In the general setting of continuous values reward, the update is given by:

$$\begin{cases} p_i(t+1) = p_i(t) + a\, r(t)(1 - p_i(t)) - b(1 - r(t))p_i(t) \\ \qquad \text{if action i was taken at time step } t \\ \\ p_j(t+1) = p_j(t) - a\, r(t)p_j(t) + b(1 - r(t))[(l-1)^{-1} - p_j(t)] \\ \qquad \forall j \neq i \end{cases}$$

with $a \in]0, 1[$, $b \in]0, 1[$, and l the number of actions of the action set of the automaton. Again the constants a and b are the reward and penalty parameters respectively. As mentioned above, depending on the ratio of a over b we get (L_{R-P}) if $a = b$, (L_{R-I}) if $b = 0$ and $(L_{R-\epsilon P})$ if $b << a$.

In the above schema's it is assumed that the action set of the automaton is finite. These automata are called *Finite Action Learning Automata* or for short FALA. More general schema's allow continuous actions sets, in these cases the automata are *Continuous Action Learning Automata* or CALA. In this paper we will only consider the FALA.

2.2   Illustration of LA Behavior

In Figure 1 we show the behavior of a 2-action reward penalty automaton with reward probabilities 0.6 and 0.2 respectively, and illustrate the role of the parameters a and b. It should be noted that, in the context of LA, it is common to use a linear, i.e. a proportional action selection mechanism.

In case of an (L_{R-I}) schema with $a = 0.1$ the probability of the automaton's best action (i.e. action 1) converges rather smoothly to 1, see Figure 1 (Top Left). We get a pure policy where all probability mass is given to the best action. When we also take punishment into account, i.e. $b > 0$, then we no longer get a pure policy. Figure 1 (Top Right) depicts the behavior of an ($L_{R-\epsilon P}$) schema with $a = 0.1$ and $b = 0.05$. This is a schema with a small penalty parameter compared to the reward parameter. The policy approaches a pure policy, but not quite. Note that the plot now shows 500 updates. The *drop* around update 450 is due to the fact that with some non-zero probability action 2 is selected

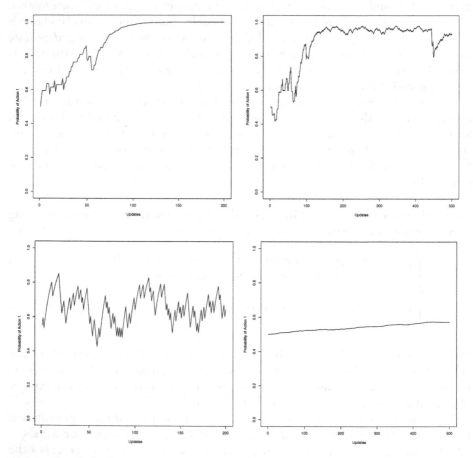

Fig. 1. Top Left: L_{R-I} a=0.1, Top Right: L_{R-P} a=0.1 b=0.05, Bottom Left: L_{R-P} a=b=0.1,Bottom Right: L_{R-I} with a = b = 0.001

which receives with probability 0.2, a reward, this is what happened at this point.

In Figure 1 (Top Right) we plot the behavior of an (L_{R-P}) schema with $a = b = 0.1$. The behavior is much more oscillatory for these settings of a and b. However the oscillations tend to become smaller with the number of updates. If we further reduce a and b we get a smoother behavior. In Figure 1 (Bottom left) we further reduce a and b to 0.001. We observe on the one hand that the oscillations become much smaller and on the other hand the learning process slows down significantly. The figure now shows 500 update steps. It should be noted that the LA in figures Figure 1 (Bottom left) and Figure 1 (Bottom right) no longer converge to a pure policy but to a mixed policy. In general we observe that if the ratio between a and b, i.e. $\gamma = \frac{a}{b}$ approaches 1, the more the action probabilities approach the reward probabilities, and express the quality of the action like the Q-values in value iteration RL [15].

In the sequel of our discussion we will in particular be interested in the convergence to pure policies. Therefore we plotted the behavior of the (L_{R-I}) schema on the same problem, with $b = 0$ and for different settings of the parameter a, i.e. $a = 0.1$, $a = 0.5$ and $a = 0.8$. The plots in Figure 2 show that the bigger we set a, the faster the convergence, so the parameter a in an (L_{R-I}) schema can be considered as a learning rate. However, the bigger we set a the higher the probability of convergence to a suboptimal action, this is due to the fact that an L_{R-I} schema is only guaranteed to be ϵ-optimal (see following section). So we should expect that with some probability the action probability of action 1 converges to zero, if parameter a is set too close to 1. This is illustrated in Table 1, which gives the percentage of runs over which action 1 converges to 0 as a function of a. From Table 1 it is clear that if one were to tolerate a 5% error, a suitable value for the step size parameter a would be 0.3, which would substantially increase the speed of convergence.

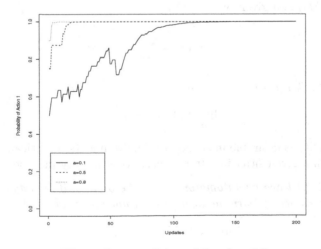

Fig. 2. L_{R-I} a=0.1, a=0.5 and a=0.8

Table 1. Table taken from [12]

a	% of wrong convergence
0.9	22
0.5	12
0.3	5
0.1	0
0.01	0
0.001	0

In the following section we state some formal convergence properties of Learning automata in stationary environments.

2.3   Some Convergence Properties More Formally

In the above, it is assumed that the reward probability for a particular action is constant. This implies that the environment is stationary and that the optimal action a_m can be identified. The goal of the learning automaton is to find this optimal action, without knowing the environments' reward or penalty probabilities. The penalty parameter[1] c_m for the optimal action has the property that $c_m = \min_i\{c_i\}$. Optimality of the learning automaton can then be defined using quantity $M(t)$ which is the average penalty for a given action probability vector and which can be written as:

$$M(t) = E[r(t) = 0|p(t)] = \sum_{i=1}^{l} c_i p_i(t)$$

Consider for instance a pure-chance automaton, i.e. the action probability vector $p(n)$ is given by: $p_i(n) = \frac{1}{l}$ for all $i : 1, \ldots, l$. Then $M(t)$ is a constant (denoted by M_0) and given by:

$$M_0 = \frac{1}{l} \sum_{i=1}^{l} c_i$$

Definition 1. *A learning automaton is called optimal if*

$$\lim_{t \to \infty} E[M(t)] = c_m$$

While optimality is desirable in stationary environments, practically it may not be achieved in a given situation. In this case, ϵ-optimality may be reached:

Definition 2. *A learning automaton is called ϵ-optimal if for any arbitrary $\epsilon >$ 0, and proper choice of learning algorithm parameters holds that*

$$lim_{t \to \infty} E[M(t)] < c_m + \epsilon$$

---
[1] $c_m = 1 - r_m$, with r_m the reward parameter.

Put differently, the objective of the learning scheme is to maximize the expected value of reinforcement received from the environment, i.e. $E[r(t)|p(t) = p]$ by searching the space of all possible action probability vectors. Stated as above, a learning automata algorithm can be viewed as a policy iteration approach.

In arbitrary environments and for arbitrary initial conditions, optimality or ϵ-optimality may be hard to reach. Some form of desired behavior in these cases can be specified by expediency and absolute expediency.

Definition 3. *A learning automaton is called expedient if it performs better than a pure-chance automaton, i.e.* $lim_{t\to\infty}M(t) < M_0$

Definition 4. *A learning automaton is said to be absolutely expedient if*

$$E[M(t+1)|p(t)] < M(t)$$

Absolute expediency imposes an inequality on the conditional expectation of $M(t)$ at each instant. In [12] it is shown that in stationary environments absolute expediency implies ϵ-optimality.

The reinforcement learning algorithms given above, i.e the (L_{R-P}), (L_{R-I}) and $(L_{R-\epsilon P})$ schemes show the following asymptotic behavior: the (L_{R-I}) schema is proved to be absolutely expedient and thus ϵ-optimal in stationary environments. The (L_{R-P}) schema is found to be expedient, while the $(L_{R-\epsilon P})$ schema is also ϵ-optimal, [12].

3   Automata Games Games: Single Stage, Multi-agent

So far we have assumed that only one single automaton was acting in the environment. In this section we consider the more interesting case of Automata games. In Automata games multiple LA are placed in the same environment and select their actions independently. This setting corresponds to the single stage multi agent learning case. Clearly, the learning problem is more challenging, since in general the feedback received by a single LA depends not only on the action taken by that LA, but also on the actions taken by the other LA. In the context of LA, this effect of non stationarity is referred to as the *state dependent non stationarity*.

With respect to learning in multi agent systems, the following theorem of Narendra and Wheeler, apparently as yet still not know in the multi agent learning community, is of great value.

Theorem 1. *(Narendra and Wheeler, 1989) Players in an n-person non-zero sum game who use independently a reward-inaction update scheme with an arbitrarily small step size will always converge to a pure equilibrium point. If the game has a NE, the equilibrium point will be one of the NE.*

Important to note is that the players are independent automata each applying a (L_{R-I}) update scheme. The fact that they are independent allows each LA to update the probability vector over its actions based on private information only, i.e. its own action taken, and its own reward received from the environment. The automaton gets no information of the other automata whatsoever. It is not informed on the actions taken by the other automata, nor their reward received. In the context of multi agent systems, where communication is usually assumed to come with some cost, this is a very important feature. Further, this result also applies to games with stochastic rewards. In these games repeated sampling is necessary to find out the expected reward of an action.

3.1 The Solution Concept

Theorem 1 guarantees convergence to a pure equilibrium point. If the game has a pure Nash Equilibrium, the team of LA will converge to one of the NE. In case multiple NE are present in the game, what NE will be reached depends on the initial setting of the action probabilities, and the region of attraction of each of the NE. Nevertheless a NE is often proposed as an interesting solution of a game, there might be other solution concepts of interest depending on the type of the game.

In a common interest game the individual interest coincides with the group interest. An example of a common interest game is the penalty game given in Figure 3. This game has 3 NE, of which 2 are Pareto optimal[2]. From a

	a_{21}	a_{22}	a_{23}
a_{11}	$(10, 10)$	$(0, 0)$	(k, k)
a_{12}	$(0, 0)$	$(2, 2)$	$(0, 0)$
a_{13}	(k, k)	$(0, 0)$	$(10, 10)$

Fig. 3. The penalty game from [5]. Mis-coordination at the Pareto optimal Nash equilibria (a_{11}, a_{21}) and (a_{13}, a_{23}) is penalized with k, where $k < 0$.

learning point of view, when the payoff matrix is not known to the agents and rewards are stochastic, coordinating on one of the NE is not obvious. Since two NE yield the same reward to both agents, the agents are faced with a difficult coordination problem. Mis-coordination leads to severe punishments. However LA have no problem with this. LA are guaranteed to converge, without any form of communication[3] to a pure NE in the game. Convergence to Pareto Optimal (Nash) Equilibrium is however not guaranteed. To which NE the LA team will converge depends on the initial settings of the action probabilities and the strength of attraction of each of the NE.

How to make independent LA converge to a Pareto optimal NE? The theorem stated above only assures the convergence to a NE, however the NE converged to is not necessarily the best one present in the game. As shown in [19, 18], it is

---

[2] A solution is called Pareto optimal if there is no other solution in which all players simultaneously do better and at least one player is doing strictly better.

[3] Meaning that actions taken and rewards received by other agents are not communicated.

possible to force the LA to search for other, possibly better, NE by excluding one or more actions involved in the NE currently converged to. Excluding actions forces the LA to explore other regions of the game and converge to other NE. In case of a two agent games, the exclusion of the actions of both agents involved in the NE will not remove any strictly better NE form the game, only the one just converged to. In the case of 3 agents or more, more careful exclusions and random restarts are necessary in order not to miss interesting NE. The strength of the approach is that the LA will only visit points of attraction, where the potential interesting NE are located. Exhaustive visit of all joint actions is not required.

In case of a conflicting interest, the theorem of Narendra and Wheeler also guarantees convergence to some NE, but what do we aim for here? In conflicting interest (i.e. non common interest) the solution concept is not always clear, and depends on the relationship between the individual rewards given to the agents and the goal of the overall systems. NE, correlated equilibria but also Pareto optimal solutions can be reached by a team of LA using the idea of repeatedly exclusion one or more actions of the attractors [18]. Therefore LA are ideal building blocks for multi agent learning and this for a variety of learning objectives.

4 Interconnected LA for MDPs or Multi-stage, Multi-LA But Still Single Agent

In this section we further generalize the setting, and move to multistage problems of the Markovian decision problem(MDP) type. We get a system of interconnected LA by putting in each of the action states of the MDP a single LA. These LA are activated sequentially. When a LA is active in a certain state, the probability that a particular LA will be the next active LA, is determined by the action taken by the currently active LA and the current active state only. In other words, these probabilities are the state transition probabilities of the MDP. Again Wheeler and Narendra offer an important theoretical result on which we can build upon for multi agent learning.

4.1 Update Rule for Interconnected LA

As stated above, only one LA is active at each time step and the transition to the next state triggers the LA from that state to become active and take some action. The updates follow a Monte Carlo approach. This means that the learning automaton LA_i active in state i is not immediately informed of the one-step reward resulting from taking its action a_k, and leading to state j. When the state i is visited again, the LA_i receives two pieces of data: 1) the cumulative reward generated by the process up to the current time step and 2) the current global time. From these, LA_i computes the incremental reward generated since this last visit at time t and the corresponding elapsed global time Δt. The environment response or the input to LA_i is then taken to be:

$$r(t+m) = \frac{R_k^i(t, t+m)}{n} \tag{1}$$

where $R_k^i(t, t+m)$ is the cumulative total reward generated for action a_k in state i and n the cumulative total time elapsed[4]. The authors in [20] denote updating rules (2.1) with the environment response of equation (1) as learning scheme T1. They prove that this interconnected LA-model is capable of solving the MDP.

Theorem 2 (Wheeler and Narendra, 1986). *Associate with every action state i of an N state Markov chain, an automaton LA_i using learning scheme T1 and having l_i actions be associated with. Assume that the Markov Chain corresponding to each policy π is ergodic[5] . Then, the group of learning algorithms is ϵ optimal in the controlled Markov chain.*

5   Interconnected LA and Their Relationship to Ant Colony Optimization

There is an apparent relationship between the updating of action probabilities in interconnected LA, and the way ant algorithms update the pheromone trails and as such the probabilities of selecting an action.

Ant Colony Optimization, ACO, [8, 7] is a relatively new meta heuristic based on the observation that real ants are capable of finding the shortest path between 2 locations. To do this, ants rely on a system of indirect communication through pheromones. An ant leaves a trail of pheromones while it walks. Other ants that encounter this trail have a high probability of following it, and reinforcing it with their own pheromones. When faced with multiple possible paths this system allows an ant colony to converge on a single path. In addition, since shorter paths allow faster travel, they accumulate pheromones faster and are more likely to be selected by the colony.

Based on this mechanism Colorni et al [9, 6] proposed the first algorithm of the ant colony meta heuristic. The meta heuristic consists of a number of algorithms that mimic the pheromone communication of real ants in order to solve a wide range of optimization problems. In ACO algorithms a number of ant like agents construct solutions by adding (problem specific) solution components to a partial solution. In our particular case these solution components are network links that are added to an ant's path. The decision of which component to add is made probabilistically, based on an artificial pheromone associated with each component. The original Ant System [9] assigned the following probability to each possible next component c:

$$P(c) = \frac{[\tau(c)]^\alpha [\eta(c)]^\beta}{\sum_a [\tau(a)]^\alpha [\eta(a)]^\beta} \tag{2}$$

The probability of adding a solution component depends on the pheromone τ that is associated with it as well as a problem specific heuristic value η. The

---

[4] The one step reward is normalized so that r remains in $[0, 1]$.
[5] A Markov Chain $x(n)_n$ is said to be ergodic when the distribution of the chain converges to a limiting distribution as $n \to \infty$.

powers α and β are algorithm parameters that determine an ant's sensitivity toward both factors. The probability is normalized by taking the sum over all possible next components a.

When an ant agent completes its solution, it updates the pheromones concentrations for each of the solution components it used. The update for each component depends on the global quality of the solution the agent produced. Pheromone updates consist of two parts: an evaporation and a pheromone deposit.

$$\tau \leftarrow \rho\tau + \Delta\tau \tag{3}$$

Pheromone evaporation is simulated by multiplying the current amount of pheromones with a factor $0 \leq \rho < 1$. Evaporation is needed to bound the increase in pheromone concentrations and prevent early stagnation of the algorithm [1, 10]. Pheromone evaporation can be global (all pheromones are evaporated at regular intervals) or can be performed only when a component receives a pheromone deposit.

The pheromone deposit adds additional pheromones $\Delta\tau(c)$ to the components that were used in an ant's solution. In Ant Cycle, a basic ACO algorithm, the amount of pheromone contributed by a single ant depends on the quality of the solution found by ant k, here represented by r_k.

$$\Delta\tau_{ij}(t, t+n) = \Sigma_{k=1}^{m} \Delta\tau_{ij}^{k}(t, t+n) \tag{4}$$

$\Delta\tau_{ij}^{k}(t, t+n)$ is the total amount of pheromone added to the link ij in the interval $[t, t+n]$ and consists of individual contributions of all ants ($k : 1 \ldots m$), i.e.

$$\Delta\tau_{ij}^{k}(t, t+n) = \begin{cases} r_k & \text{if } k\text{-th ant used edge } (i, j) \text{ in its solution} \\ 0 & \text{otherwise.} \end{cases} \tag{5}$$

To make the mapping to the interconnected network of LA used for controlling a MDP, one should notice that an ant can be viewed as a dummy mobile agent, that walks around in the graph of interconnected LA, makes states/LA active and brings information so that the LA involved can update their local state. The main difference is that in the ant algorithms several ants are walking around simultaneously, and thus several LA can be active at the same time. In the model of Wheeler and Narendra given in Theorem 2 above, there is only one LA active at a time.

If we translate the pheromone updates into action probability updates, and hereby omitting the heuristic component, i.e. putting $\beta = 0$, we get

$$P_{ij}(t+n) \leftarrow P_{ij}(t) + r_k\left(\frac{[\Delta\tau_{ij}]}{[\Sigma_j \Delta\tau_{ij}]} - P_{ij}(t)\right) \tag{6}$$

And if we single out the contribution of a single ant k we get:

$$P_{ij}(t+n) \leftarrow P_{ij}(t) + r_k(1 - P_{ij}(t)) \tag{7}$$

For the case the single ant included edge ij in its solution,

$$P_{ij}(t+1) \leftarrow P_{ij}(t) + r_k(0 - P_{ij}(t)) \tag{8}$$

with $r_k = \frac{R_k}{\rho[\Sigma_j \tau_{ij}] + R_k}$, where R_k represents the total reward collect by ant k on its path. This matches a L_{R-I} scheme with real valued reward, and $a = 1$.

In section 2.3 it was assumed that a was strictly smaller than 1, this is important for the theoretical results to hold. In conclusion, ant algorithms apply a L_{R-I} schema with an extreme setting for a. However the heuristic component in the action selection formula, provided it is chosen in an appropriate manner, helps to drive the system in the right direction, and as such avoids premature convergence to a suboptimal solution.

6   Markov Games: Multi-stage, Multi Agent

A Markov game can be seen as a extension of a MDP by putting in each state a team of agents playing a game against each other. In the special case where the agents have the same payoff function, a Markov game has also been referred to as a Multi-agent Markov Decision Processes [11]. Formally, a MMDP is a tuple $(\mathbb{S}, n, (A_i)_{i:1...n}, Pr, R)$ where $\mathbb{S}$ is a set of states, n the number of agents, A_i a finite set of actions available to agent i, $Pr : \mathbb{S} \times A_1 \times \ldots \times A_n \times \mathbb{S} \to [0,1]$ a transition function and $R : \mathbb{S} \to \mathbb{R}$ the (expected) global reward function.

In order to solve an MMDP , Boutilier [2], decomposes the MMDP into local (single stage) state games and the agents search for coordinated joint actions at the individual state games instead of trying to find a coordinated sequential policy. It is assumed that every agent knows the structure of the game and therefore is able to compute the optimal value function for the joint MDP. In [3], the agents reason explicitly about specific coordination mechanisms. In our view, the MMDP is a sequence of one stage games as in [2], however, our agents are independent. The only assumption made is that the MMDP has a tree structure, i.e. there are no loops in the state diagram of the MMDP and the paths are disjunct. For now we assume that the transitions are deterministic, but unlike [2], we allow that the rewards of the stage games are stochastic. In Figure reffigure:mmdp2 we show a two stage two player game, where each agent has in each stage 2 actions to choose from.

This situation can be mapped into a hierarchy of LA as follows :

LA theory guarantees convergence to a Nash Path in case the LA are using a L_{R-I} schema, and the multistage game is a common interest game with absorbing states without loops, i.e. a game tree. Indeed, in [13], it was shown that hierarchical learning automata systems were particularly suited for representing systems in which decisions are made at multiple levels using decentralized decision makers. A simple problem of consistently labeling images was given. At a first stage, the object had to be recognized and in a second stage the background of the image was determined.

The following behavior is proved for a collective of n L_{R-I} hierarchical learning automata involved in L levels [13]:

Theorem 3. *If for a collective of n hierarchical learning automata involved in L levels of identical payoff games, the following assumptions hold:*

- *all automata use the S-model reward-inaction scheme,*
- *at any stage t and for every hierarchical agent j all the L automata of agent j involved in the play are aware of the outcomes of the L games played at each of the L levels, and*
- *the reward parameter of the level l + 1 automaton chosen at stage t varies with time as:*

$$\alpha^{l+1}_{reward}(t) = \frac{\alpha^{l}_{reward}(t)}{p^{l}_{i}(t+1)}$$

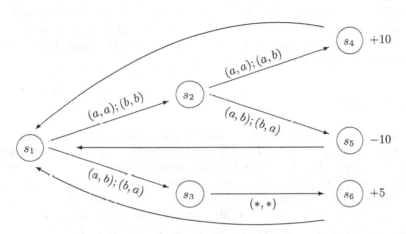

Fig. 4. A simple MMDP with a possible coordination problem in both stages

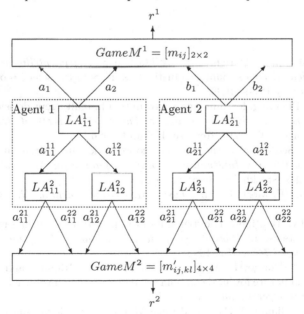

Fig. 5. An interaction of two hierarchies of learning automata at 2 stages [13]

where i is the action taken by this automaton during the previous game iteration, and $p_i^l(t+1)$ is the probability that the previous level automaton has on action i that leads to the current level l automaton.

then the overall system is proved absolutely expedient.

Stated differently, this means that the overall performance of the system will improve at each time step and convergence is assured toward an local optimal path. By applying again the idea of sequential exclusions of actions, we can make the hierarchical LA converge to the optimal Nash path, which is well defined in a common interest Markov game. [19, 18] The research challenge is to provide a proof of convergence to a Nash path in the more general setting of conflicting interest games. This combined with a method for bootstrapping, would be a major contribution in multi agent learning.

7   Conclusion

In this paper we have argued that LA are very interesting building blocks for learning in multi agent systems. The LA can be viewed as policy iterators, who update their action probabilities based on private information only. This is a very attractive property in applications where communication is expensive. LA are in particular appealing in games with stochastic payoffs. They allow to design multi agent learning algorithms with different learning objectives. Further, LA have also proved to be able to work in asynchronous settings, where the actions of the LA are not taken simultaneously and where reward comes with delay.

References

1. Eric Bonabeau, Marco Dorigo, and Guy Theraulaz. *Swarm Intelligence, From Natural to Artificial Systems*. Santa Fe Institute studies in the sciences of complexity. Oxford University Press, 1999.
2. C. Boutilier. Planning, learning and coordination in multiagent decision processes. In *Proceedings of the 6th Conference on Theoretical Aspects of Rationality and Knowledge*, pages 195 – 210, Renesse, Holland, 1996.
3. C. Boutilier. Sequential optimality and coordination in multiagent systems. In *Proceedings of the 16th International Joint Conference on Artificial Intelligence*, pages 478 – 485, Stockholm, Sweden, 1999.
4. R.R. Bush and F. Mosteller. *Stochastic Models for Learning*. Wiley, New York, 1958.
5. C. Claus and C. Boutilier. The dynamics of reinforcement learning in cooperative multiagent systems. In *Proceedings of the 15th National Conference on Artificial Intelligence*, pages 746 – 752, 1998.
6. A. Colorni, M. Dorigo, F. Maffioli, V. Maniezzo, G. Righini, and M. Trubian. Heuristics from nature for hard combinatorial optimization problems. *International Transactions in Operational Research*, 1996.
7. Marco Dorigo, Gianni Di Caro, and Luca Maria Gambardella. Ant algorithms for discrete optimization. *Artificial Life 5*, pages 137–172, 1999.

8. Marco Dorigo and Gianno Di Caro. The ant colony optimization meta-heuristic. *D.Corne, M.Dorigo and F.Glover (Eds.), New Ideas In Optimization, Maidenhaid, UK: McGraw-Hill*, 1999.

9. Marco Dorigo, Vittorio Maniezzo, and Alberto Colorni. The ant system: Optimization by a colony of cooperating agents. *IEE Transactions on Systems, Man, and Cybernetics*, 1996.

10. Marco Dorigo and Thomas Stützle. *Ant Colony Optimization*. The MIT Press, 2004.

11. M. Littman. Markov games as a framework for multi-agent reinforcement learning. In *Proceedings of the 11th International Conference on Machine Learning*, pages 322 – 328, 1994.

12. K. Narendra and M. Thathachar. *Learning Automata: An Introduction*. Prentice-Hall International, Inc, 1989.

13. K.S. Narendra and K. Parthasarathy. Learning automata approach to hierarchical multiobjective analysis. Technical Report Report No. 8811, Electrical Engineering Yale University, New Haven, Connecticut, 1988.

14. B.J. Oommen and T.D. Roberts. Continuous learning automata solutions to the capacity assignment problem. *IEEE Transactions on Computations*, 49:608 – 620, 2000.

15. R. Sutton and A. Barto. *Reinforcement Learning: An Introduction*. MIT Press, Cambridge, MA, 1998.

16. M.L. Tsotlin. Automaton theory and modelling of biological systems. *Mathematics in Science and Engineering*, 102, 1973.

17. C. Unsal, P. Kachroo, and J.S. Bay. Multiple stochastic learning automata for vehicle path control in an automated highway system. *IEEE Transactions on Systems, Man, and Cybernetics, Part A*, 29:120 – 128, 1999.

18. K. Verbeeck. *Coordinated Exploration in Multi-Agent Reinforcement Learning*. PhD thesis, Computational Modeling Lab, Vrije Universiteit Brussel, Belgium, 2004.

19. K. Verbeeck, A. Nowé, K. Tuyls, and M.Peeters. Multi-agent reinforcement learning in stochastic single and multi-stage games. In *Kudenko et al (Eds): Adaptive Agents and Multi-Agent Systems II*, pages 275–294. Springer LNAI 3394, 2005.

20. R.M. Wheeler and K.S. Narendra. Decentralized learning in finite markov chains. *IEEE Transactions on Automatic Control*, AC-31:519 – 526, 1986.

Learning Pareto-optimal Solutions in 2x2 Conflict Games

Stéphane Airiau and Sandip Sen

Department of Mathematical & Computer Sciences,
The University of Tulsa, USA
{stephane, sandip}@utulsa.edu

Abstract. Multiagent learning literature has investigated iterated two-player games to develop mechanisms that allow agents to learn to converge on Nash Equilibrium strategy profiles. Such equilibrium configurations imply that no player has the motivation to unilaterally change its strategy. Often, in general sum games, a higher payoff can be obtained by both players if one chooses not to respond myopically to the other player. By developing mutual trust, agents can avoid immediate best responses that will lead to a Nash Equilibrium with lesser payoff. In this paper we experiment with agents who select actions based on expected utility calculations that incorporate the observed frequencies of the actions of the opponent(s). We augment these stochastically greedy agents with an interesting action revelation strategy that involves strategic declaration of one's commitment to an action to avoid worst-case, pessimistic moves. We argue that in certain situations, such apparently risky action revelation can indeed produce better payoffs than a non-revealing approach. In particular, it is possible to obtain Pareto-optimal Nash Equilibrium outcomes. We improve on the outcome efficiency of a previous algorithm and present results over the set of structurally distinct two-person two-action conflict games where the players' preferences form a total order over the possible outcomes. We also present results on a large number of randomly generated payoff matrices of varying sizes and compare the payoffs of strategically revealing learners to payoffs at Nash equilibrium.

1 Introduction

The goal of a rational learner, repeatedly playing a stage game against an opponent, is to maximize its expected utility. In a two-player, general-sum game, this means that the players need to systematically explore the joint action space before settling on an efficient action combination[1]. Both agents can make concessions from greedy strategies to improve their individual payoffs in the long run [1]. Reinforcement learning schemes, and in particular, Q-learning [2] have

---

[1] Though the general motivation behind our work and the proposed algorithms generalize to n-person games, we restrict our discussion in this paper to two-person games.

K. Tuyls et al. (Eds.): LAMAS 2005, LNAI 3898, pp. 86–99, 2006.
© Springer-Verlag Berlin Heidelberg 2006

been widely used in single-agent learning situations. In the context of two-player games, if one agent plays a stationary strategy, the stochastic game becomes a Markov Decision Process and techniques like Q-learning can be used to learn to play an optimal response against such a static opponent. When two agents learn to play concurrently, however, the stationary environment assumption does not hold any longer, and Q-learning is not guaranteed to converge in self-play. In such cases, researchers have used the goal of convergence to Nash equilibrium in self-play, where each player is playing a best response to the opponent strategy and does not have any incentive to deviate from its strategy. This emphasis on convergence of learning to Nash equilibrium is rooted in the literature in game theory [3] where techniques like fictitious play and its variants lead to Nash equilibrium convergence under certain conditions.

Convergence can be a desirable property in multiagent systems, but converging to just any Nash equilibrium is not necessarily the preferred outcome. A Nash equilibrium of the single shot,i.e., stage game is not guaranteed to be Pareto optimal[2]. For example, the widely studied Prisoner's dilemma (PD in Table 1(b)) game has a single pure strategy Nash equilibrium that is defect-defect, which is

Table 1. Prisoner's dilemma and Battle of Sexes games

(a) Battle of the Sexes

	C	D
C	1,1	3,4
D	4,3	2,2

(b) Prisoners' dilemma

	C	D
C	3,3	1,4
D	4,1	2,2

dominated by the cooperate-cooperate outcome. On the other hand, a strategy that is Pareto Optimal is not necessarily a Nash equilibrium, i.e., there might be incentives for one agent to deviate and obtain higher payoff. For example, each of the agents has the incentive to deviate from the cooperate-cooperate Pareto optima in PD. In the context of learning in games, it is assumed that the players are likely to play the game over and over again. This opens the possibility for such defections to be deterred or curtailed in repeated games by using disincentives. Actually, in the context of repeated games, the Folks Theorems ensure that any payoffs pair that dominates the security value[3] can be sustained by a Nash equilibrium. This means that in the context of the repeated games, Pareto optimal outcome can be the outcome of a Nash equilibrium. In [4], Littman and

---

[2] A Pareto optimal outcome is one such that there is no other outcome where some agent's utility can be increased without decreasing the utility of some other agent. An outcome X *strongly dominates* another outcome B if all agents receive a higher utility in X compared to Y. An outcome X *weakly dominates* (or simply *dominates*) another outcome B if at least one agent receives a higher utility in X and no agent receives a lesser utility compared to outcome Y. A non-dominated outcome is Pareto optimal.

[3] The security value is the minimax outcome of the game: it is the outcome that a player can guarantee itself even when its opponent tries to minimize its payoff.

Stone present an algorithm that converges to a particular Pareto Optimal Nash equilibrium in the repeated game.

It is evident that the primary goal of a rational agent, learning or otherwise, is to maximize utility. Though we, as system designers, want convergence and corresponding system stability, those considerations are necessarily secondary for a rational agent. The question then is what kind of outcomes are preferable for agents engaged in repeated interactions with an uncertain horizon, i.e., without knowledge of how many future interactions will happen. Several current multi-agent learning approaches [4, 5, 6] assume that convergence to Nash equilibrium in self-play is the desired goal, and we concur since it is required to obtain a stable equilibrium. We additionally claim that any Nash equilibrium that is also Pareto optimal should be preferred over other Pareto optimal outcomes. This is because both the goals of utility maximization and stability can be met in such cases. But we find no rational for preferring convergence to a dominated Nash equilibria. Based on these considerations we now posit the following goal for rational learners in self-play:

> **Learning goal in repeated play:** The goal of learning agents in repeated self-play with an uncertain horizon is to reach a Pareto-optimal Nash equilibria (PONE) of the repeated game.

We are interested in developing mechanisms by which agents can produce PONE outcomes. In this paper, we experiment with two-person, general-sum games where each agent only gets to observe its own payoff and the action played by the opponent, but not the payoff received by the opponent. The knowledge of this payoff would allow the players to compute PONE equilibria and to bargain about the equilibrium. For example the algorithm in [4] assumes the game is played under complete information, and the players compute and execute the strategy to reach a particular equilibrium (the Nash bargaining equilibrium). However, the payoff represents a utility that is private to the player. The player may not want to share this information. Moreover, sharing one's payoff structure requires trust: deceptive information can be used to take advantage of the opponent. The ignorance of the opponent's payoff requires the player to estimate the preference of its opponent by its actions rather than by what could be communicated. By observing the actions played, our goal is to make players discover outcomes that are beneficial for both players and provide incentive to make these outcomes stable. This is challenging since agents cannot realize whether or not the equilibrium reached is Pareto Optimal.

We had previously proposed a modification of the simultaneous-move game playing protocol that allowed an agent to communicate to the opponent its irrevocable commitment to an action [7]. If an agent makes such a commitment, the opponent can choose any action in response, essentially mirroring a sequential play situation. At each iteration of the play, then, agents can choose to play a simultaneous move game or a sequential move game. The motivation behind this augmented protocol is for agents to build trust by committing up front to a "cooperating" move, e.g., a cooperate move in PD. If the opponent myopically chooses an exploitative action, e.g., a defect move in PD, the initiating agent would be less likely to repeat such cooperation commitments, leading to outcomes that are less desirable to both parties than mutual cooperation. But if the opponent resists the temptation to exploit and responds cooperatively, then such mutually beneficial cooperation can be sustained.

We view the outcome of a Nash equilibrium of the one shot game as an outcome reached by two players that do not want to try to build trust in search of an efficient outcome. Though our ultimate goal is to develop augmented learning algorithms that provably converge to PONE outcomes of the repeated game, in this paper we highlight the advantage of outcomes from our augmented learning schemes over Nash equilibrium outcomes of the single shot, stage game. In the rest of the paper, by Nash equilibrium, we refer to the Nash equilibrium of the stage game, which is a subset of the set of Nash equilibria of the repeated version of the stage game.

We have empirically shown, over a large number of two-player games of varying sizes, that our proposed revelation protocol, that is motivated by considerations of developing trusted behavior, produces higher average utility outcome than Nash equilibrium outcomes of the single-shot games[7]. For a more systematic evaluation of the performance of our proposed protocol, we study, in more detail, all two-player, two-action conflict games to develop more insight about these results and to improve on our previous approach. A *conflict game* is a game where both players do not view the same outcome as most profitable. We are not interested in no-conflict games as the single outcome preferred by both players is easily learned. We use the testbed proposed by Brams in [8] and consisting of all 2x2 structurally distinct conflict games. In these games, each agent rank orders each of the four possible outcomes. On closer inspection of the results from our previous work, we identified enhancement possibilities over our previous approaches. In this paper, we present the updated learners, the corresponding testbed results and the challenges highlighted by those experiments.

2 Related Work

Over the past few years, multiagent learning researchers have adopted convergence to Nash equilibrium of the repeated game as the desired goal for a rational learner [4, 5, 6]. By modeling its opponent, Joint-Action Learners [9] converge to a Nash equilibrium in cooperative domains. By using a variable rate, WoLF [6] is guaranteed to converge to a Nash equilibrium in a two-person, two-actions iterated general-sum game, and converges empirically on a number of single-state, multiple state, zero-sum, general-sum, two-player and multi-player stochastic games. Finally, in any repeated game AWESOME [5] is guaranteed to learn to play optimally against stationary opponents and to converge to a Nash equilibrium in self-play.

Some multiagent learning researchers have investigated other non-Nash equilibrium concepts like *coordination equilibrium* [10] and *correlated equilibrium* [11]. If no communication is allowed during the play of the game, the players choose their strategies independently. When players use mixed strategies, some bad outcome can occur. The concept of correlated equilibrium [12] permits dependencies between the strategies: for example, before the play, the players can adopt a strategy according to the joint observation of a public random variable. [11] introduces algorithms which empirically converge to a correlated equilibrium in a testbed of Markov game.

Consider the example of a Battle of Sexes game represented in Table 1(a). The game models the dilemma of a couple deciding on the next date: they are interested to go in different places, but both prefer to be be together than alone. In this game, defecting is following one's own interest whereas cooperating is following the other's interest. If both defect, they will be on their own, but enjoy the activity they individually preferred, with a payoff of 2. If they both cooperate, they will also be on their own, and will be worse off, with the lowest payoff of 1, as they are now participating in the activity preferred by their partner. The best (and fair) solution would consists in alternating between (Coordinate, Defect) and (Defect, Coordinate) to obtain an average payoff of 3.5. The Nash equilibrium of the game is to play each action with probability 0.5, which yields an average payoff of 2.5. Only if the players observe a public random variable can they avoid the worst outcomes.

The commitment that one player makes to an action in our revelation protocol can also be understood as a signal that can be used to reach a correlated equilibrium [11]. For example, in the Battle of Sexes game, if a player commits to cooperate, the other player can exploit the situation by playing defect, which is beneficial for both players. When both players try to commit, they obtain 3.5 on average.

3   Game Protocol and Learners

In this paper, we build on the simultaneous revelation protocol [7]. Agents play an nxn bimatrix game. At each iteration of the game, each player first announces whether it wants to commit to an action or not (we will also use reveal an action or not). If both players want to commit at the same time, one is chosen randomly with equal probability. If none decides to commit, then both players simultaneously announce their action. When one player commits an action, the other player plays its best response to this action. Note that for now, the answer to the committed action is myopic, we do not consider yet a strategic answer to the revealed action. Each agent can observe whether the opponent wanted to commit, which agent actually committed, and which action the opponent played. Only the payoff of the opponent remains unknown, since its preferences are considered private.

Let us use as an example matrix #27 of the testbed (Table 2(a)). The only Nash equilibrium of the stage game is when both players play action 0, but this state is dominated by the state where both agents play action 1. If the row player commits to play action 1, the column player plays its best response that is action 1: the row player gets 3, and the column player gets 4, which improves on the payoff of the Nash equilibrium where row gets 2 and column gets 3. The

Table 2. Representative games where proposed strategy enhancement leads to improvement

(a) Game 27

	0	1
0	2, 3	4, 1
1	1, 2	3, 4

(b) Game 29

	0	1
0	3, 2	2, 1
1	4, 3	1, 4

(c) Game 48

	0	1
0	3, 3	2, 1
1	4, 2	1, 4

column player could ensure a payoff of 3 (the payoff of the Nash equilibrium) by revealing action 0, since the row player would play the best response, i.e. action 0. However, by choosing not to commit, the column player let the row player commit: thus the column player obtains its most preferred outcome of 4. If the row player learns to reveal action 1 and the column learns not to reveal in this game matrix, the two learners can converge to a Pareto optimal state that dominates Nash equilibrium.

3.1 Learners

The agents used are expected utility based probabilistic (EUP) learners. An agent estimates the expected utility of each of its action and plays by sampling a probability distribution based on the expected utilities. First, the agent must decide whether to reveal or not. We will use the following notation:

- $Q(a,b)$ is the payoff of the agent when it plays a and the opponent plays b.
- $BR(b)$ denotes the best response to action b.
- p_{OR} is the probability that the opponent wants to reveal.
- $p_{BR}(b|a)$ is the probability that the opponent plays action b when the agent reveals action a.
- $p_R(b)$ is the probability that the opponent reveals b given that it reveals.
- $p_{NR}(b)$ is the probability that the opponent plays action b in simultaneous play, i.e., when no agent reveals.

In [7], the expected utility to reveal an action is

$$EU_r(a) = \sum_{b \in B} p_{BR}(b|a)Q(a,b)$$

and the expected utility of not revealing is

$$EU_{nr}(a) = \sum_{b \in B} p_{NR}(b)Q(a,b),$$

where B is the opponent's action set. Back to our example of game #27 (Table 2(a)), the row player quickly learns to reveal action 1, providing it a payoff of 3 and allowing the column player to get its most preferred outcome. However, the expected utility of the column player to reveal action 0 is 3, and the expected utility of not revealing an action should be 4, and not 3 as computed from the above equations used in our previous work. This difference is because a utility-maximizing opponent will prefer to always reveal in this game. Hence, we need to take into account the possibility of the opponent revealing in the computation of the expected utility. Our augmented expressions for computing the expected utilities to reveal action a is

$$EU_r(a) = \begin{matrix} (1 - p_{OR}) \sum_{b \in \mathcal{B}} p_{BR}(b|a)Q(a,b) \\ + \\ \frac{p_{OR}}{2} \sum_{b \in \mathcal{B}} (p_R(b)Q(BR(b),b) + p_{BR}(b|a)Q(a,b)). \end{matrix}$$

Two cases can occur. Either the opponent does not want to reveal, in which case the opponent will reply to the agent's revelation, or the opponent also wants to reveal, and with equal probability the opponent and the agent will get to reveal its action. We also have the same cases when computing the expected utility of playing action a, but not revealing. If the opponent reveals, the agent will have to play the best response to the revealed action. If the opponent does not reveal, both agents will announce their actions simultaneously. Hence the expected utility is:

$$EU_{nr}(a) = \begin{matrix} p_{OR} \sum_{b \in \mathcal{B}} p_R(b)Q(BR(b),b) \\ + \\ (1 - p_{OR}) \sum_{b \in \mathcal{B}} p_{NR}(b)Q(a,b) \end{matrix}$$

To choose an action from the expected utilities computed, the agent samples the Boltzmann probability distribution with temperature T and decides to reveal action a with probability :

$$p(\text{reveal } a) = \frac{e^{\frac{EU_r(a)}{T}}}{\sum_{x \in \mathcal{A}} \left(e^{\frac{EU_r(x)}{T}} + e^{\frac{EU_{nr}(x)}{T}} \right)}$$

and it decides not to reveal with probability

$$p(\text{not reveal}) = \frac{\sum_{x \in \mathcal{A}} e^{\frac{EU_{nr}(x)}{T}}}{\sum_{x \in \mathcal{A}} \left(e^{\frac{EU(x)}{T}} + e^{\frac{EU_{nr}(x)}{T}} \right)},$$

where $\mathcal{A}$ is the agent's action set.

If the agent reveals but not the opponent, the agent is done. If the opponent reveals action b, the agent plays its best response: $\text{argmax}_a Q(a,b)$. If no agent has decided to reveal, the agent computes the expected utility to play each action:

$$EU(a) = \sum_{b \in \mathcal{B}} p_{NR}(b)Q(a,b).$$

The agent chooses its action a sampling the corresponding Boltzmann probability distribution

$$p(a) = \frac{e^{\frac{EU(a)}{T}}}{\sum_{b \in \mathcal{B}} e^{\frac{EU(b)}{T}}}.$$

The temperature parameter, T, controls the exploration versus exploitation tradeoff. At the beginning of the game, the temperature is set to a high value, which ensures exploration. At each iteration, the temperature is reduced until the temperature reaches a preset minimum threshold (the threshold is used to prevent exponent overflow computation errors). The use of the Boltzmann probability distribution with a decreasing temperature means that the players converge to play pure strategies. If both agents learn to reveal, however, the equilibrium reached is a restricted mixed strategy (at most two states of the games will be played with equal probability).

4   Experimental Results

In the stage game, the players cannot build any trust required to find a mutually beneficial outcome of the game. The goal of our experiments is to study whether the learners using our augmented revelation protocol and by repeatedly playing a game can improve performance compared to Nash equilibrium payoffs of the stage game. In the following, by Nash equilibrium we refer to the Nash equilibrium of the single shot, stage game.

The testbed, introduced by Brams in [8] consists of all 2x2 conflicting games with ordinal payoff. Each player has a total preference order over the 4 different outcomes. We use the numbers 1, 2, 3 and 4 as the preference of an agent, with 4 being the most preferred. We do not consider games where both agents have the highest preference for the same outcome. Hence games in our testbed contain all possible conflicting situations with ordinal payoffs and two choices per agent. There are 57 structurally different, i.e., no two games are identical by renaming the actions or the players, 2x2 conflict games.

In order to estimate the probabilities presented in the previous section, we used frequency counts over the history of the play. We start with a temperature of 10, and we decrease the temperature with a decay of .5% at each iteration. We are first presenting results on a set of interesting matrices and then provide results on the entire testbed.

4.1   Results on the Testbed

Benefits of the Augmented Protocol. We compared the results over the testbed to evaluate the effectiveness of the augmentation. We found out that in the three games of Table 2, the equilibrium found strictly dominates the equilibrium found with the non-augmented algorithm. The payoffs, averaged over 100 runs are presented in Table 3. In the three games, one player needs to realize that it is better off by letting the opponent reveal its action, which is the purpose of the augmentation. Note that even without the augmentation, the

Table 3. Comparison of the average payoff between the augmented and the non augmented Expected Utility calculations

	Nash Payoff	Not augmented		Augmented	
		average payoff	strategy	average payoff	strategy
Game 27	(2,2)	(2.5, 3.5)	row: reveal 1 col: reveal 0	(3.0, 4.0)	row: reveal 1 col: no rev
Game 29	(2.5, 2.5)	(3.5, 2.5)	row: no rev 0 col: no rev 0	(4.0, 3.0)	row: no rev col: reveal 0
Game 48	(2,3)	(2.5, 3.5)	row: reveal 1 col: reveal 0	(3.0, 4.0)	row: reveal 1 col: no rev
Game 50	(2,4)	(2.3, 3.3)	row: mix col: mix	(2.5, 3.0)	row: reveal 1 col: reveal 0

opportunity of revealing the action brings an advantage since the equilibrium found dominates the Nash equilibrium of the single stage game.

We provide in Figures 1 and 2 the learning curves of the augmented and the non-augmented players, respectively, for game #27 of the testbed (see Table 2(a)). The figures present the dynamics of the expected values of the different actions and the probability distributions for both players when they learn to play. With the augmentation, we see that the row player first learns to play its Nash equilibrium component, before realizing that revealing its action 1 is a better option. The column player first learns to either reveal action 0 or not reveal and then play action 0. But as soon as the column player starts to reveal

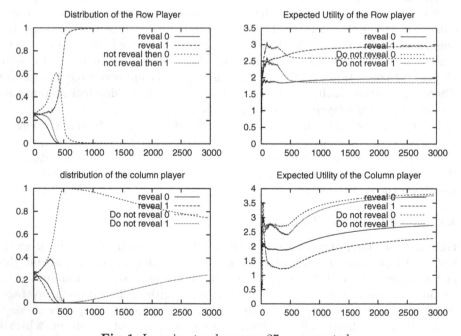

Fig. 1. Learning to play game 27 - augmented

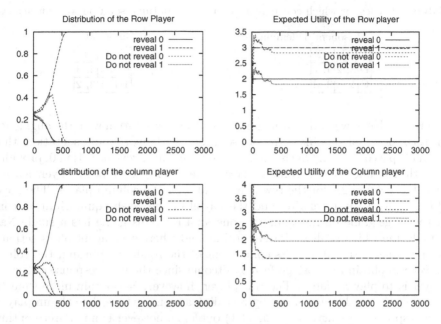

Fig. 2. Learning to play game 27 - not augmented

its action 1, the column player learns not to reveal, which was not possible with earlier expression of the expected utility. These observations confirm that the augmentation can improve the performance of both players.

Comparing protocol outcome with Nash Equilibrium. 51 of the 57 games in the testbed have a unique Nash equilibrium (9 of these games have a mixed strategy equilibrium and 42 have pure strategy equilibrium), the remaining 6 have multiple equilibria (two pure Nash equilibria and and a mixed strategy Nash equilibrium). Of the 42 games that have a unique pure strategy Nash equilibrium, 4 games have a Nash equilibrium that is not Pareto-optimal: the prisoners' dilemma, game #27, #28 and #48 have a unique Nash equilibrium which is dominated.

The Pareto optimal outcome is reached games #27, #28 and #48 with the augmented algorithm. The non-augmented protocol converges to the Pareto equilibrium for game #28, but it failed to do so for games #27 and #48. We noticed that in some games, namely games #41, #42, #44, the players learn not to reveal. Revealing does not help improve utility in these games. Incidentally, these games also have a single mixed strategy Nash equilibrium.

We found that the augmented mechanism fails to produce a Pareto optimal solution in only two games: the Prisoner's dilemma game (Table 4(a)) and game #50 (Table 4(b)) fails to converge because of the opportunity to reveal.

The Prisoner's dilemma game has a single Nash equilibrium where each player plays D. If a player reveals that it is going to cooperate (i.e. play C), the opponent's myopic best response is to play defect (i.e. to play D). With the revelation mechanism, the players learn to play D (by revealing or not). Hence, the players do not benefit from the revelation protocol in the Prisoner's dilemma game.

Table 4. Games for which convergence to a Pareto optimal solution was not achieved

(a) Prisoners' Dilemma

	D	C
D	2, 2	4, 1
C	1, 4	3, 3

(b) Game 50

	0	1
0	2, 4	4, 3
1	1, 1	3, 2

From Table 3, we find that in game #50, the new solution with the augmented protocol does not dominate the old solution. Without the augmentation, there are multiple equilibria. One is when the column player reveals action 0, providing 2 for the row and 4 to the column player. The other is when both players learn to reveal, providing 2.5 for the row player and 3 for the column player. The payoff obtained with the revelation and the payoff of the Nash equilibrium outcome of the stage game do not dominate one another. This game has a single Nash equilibrium which is also a Pareto optima and where each agent plays action 0. By revealing action 0, i.e., its component of the Nash equilibrium, the column player can obtain its most preferred outcome since the best response of the row player is to play action 0. The row player, however, can obtain more than the payoff of the Nash equilibrium by revealing action 1 where the column player's best response is its action 1. The (1,1) outcome, however is not Pareto optimal since it is dominated by the (0,1) outcome. The dynamics of the learning process in this game is shown in Figure 3. Both the players learn to reveal and hence each reveals about 50% of the time, and in each case the other agent plays its best response, i.e., the outcome switches between (0,0) and (1,1). The interesting observation is that the average payoff of the column player is 3, which would

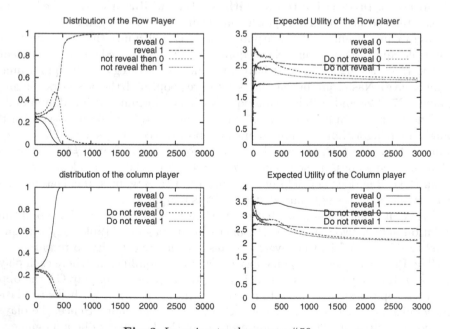

Fig. 3. Learning to play game #50

be its payoff if the column player played 1 instead of a myopic choice of 0 to row player's revealing action 0. Hence, revealing an action does not improve the outcome of this game because of a myopic best response by the opponent.

4.2   Results on Randomly Generated Matrices

As shown in the restricted testbed of 2x2 conflicting games with a total preference over the outcomes, the structure of some games can be exploited by the augmented protocol to improve the payoffs of both players. We have not seen cases where both agents would be better off by playing the Nash equilibrium (i.e. we have not encountered cases where revelation worsens the outcome). To evaluate the effectiveness of the protocol on a more general set of matrices, we ran experiments on randomly generated matrices as in [7].

We generated 1000 matrices of size 3x3, 5x5 and 7x7. Each matrix entry is sampled from a uniform distribution in $[0, 1]$. We computed the Nash equilibrium of the stage game of all these games using Gambit [13]. We compare the payoff of the Nash equilibrium with the average payoff over 10 runs of the game played with the revelation protocol. We are interested in two main questions:

 - In what proportion of the games does the revelation protocol dominate all the Nash equilibria of the stage game?
 - Are there some games where a Nash equilibrium dominates the outcome of the game played with the revelation protocol?

Results from the randomly generated matrices with both the augmented and non-augmented variations are presented in Figure 4. The top curve on each figure represents the percentage of games where all the Nash equilibria (NE) are dominated by the outcome of the revelation protocol. We find that the augmented protocol is able to significantly improve the percentage of Nash dominating outcomes and improves the outcome over Nash equilibria outcomes on 20–30% of the games. The percentage of such games where a Nash Equilibrium is better than the outcome reached by the revelation protocol is represented in the lower curve. We observe that this percentage decreases significantly with the

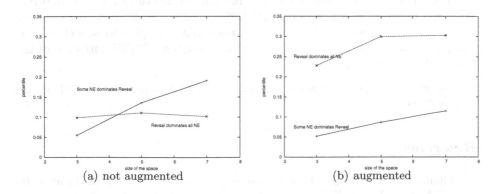

(a) not augmented   (b) augmented

Fig. 4. Results over random generated matrices

augmentation and is now at the 5–10% range. Although these results show that the proposed augmentation is a clear improvement over the previous protocol, there is still scope for improvement as the current protocol does not guarantee PONE outcomes.

5   Conclusion and Future Work

In this paper, we augmented a previous algorithm from [7] with the goal of producing PONE outcomes in repeated single-stage games. We experiment with two-player two-action general-sum conflict games where both agents have the opportunity to commit to an action and allow the other agent to respond to it. Though the revealing one's action can be seen as making a concession to the opponent, it can also be seen as an effective means to force the exploration a subset of the possible outcomes and as a means to promoting trusted behavior that can lead to higher payoffs than defensive, preemptive behavior that eliminates mutually preferred outcomes in an effort to avoid worst-case scenarios. The outcome of a Nash equilibrium of the single shot, stage games can be seen as outcomes reached by myopic players. We empirically show that our augmented protocol can improve agent payoffs compared to Nash equilibrium outcomes of the stage game in a variety of games: the search of a mutually beneficial outcome of the game pays off in many games. The use of the testbed of all structurally distinct 2x2 conflict games [8] also highlights the shortcomings of the current protocol. Agents fails to produce Pareto optimal outcomes in the prisoners' dilemma game and game #50 . The primary reason for this is that a player answers a revelation with a myopic best response.

To find a non-myopic equilibrium, an agent should not be too greedy! We are working on relaxing the requirement of playing a best response when the opponent reveals. We plan to allow an agent to estimate the effects of its various responses to a revelation on subsequent play by the opponent. This task is challenging since the space of strategies, using the play history, used by the opponent to react to one's play is infinite.

Another avenue of future research is to characterize the kind of equilibrium we reach and the conditions under which the algorithm converges to a outcome that dominates all Nash equilibria of the stage game. We plan to actively pursue modifications to the protocol with the goal of reaching PONE outcomes of the repeated game in all or most situations.

Acknowledgments. This work has been supported in part by an NSF award IIS-0209208.

References

1. Littman, M.L., Stone, P.: Leading best-response strategies in repeated games. In: IJCAI Workshop on Economic Agents, Models and Mechanisms. (2001)
2. Watkins, C.J.C.H., Dayan, P.D.: Q-learning. Machine Learning **3** (1992) 279 – 292

3. Fudenberg, D., Levine, K.: The Theory of Learning in Games. MIT Press, Cambridge, MA (1998)
4. Littman, M.L., Stone, P.: A polynomial-time nash equilibrium algorithm for repeated games. Decision Support Systems **39** (2005) 55–66
5. Conitzer, V., Sandholm, T.: Awesome: A general multiagent learning algorithm that converges in self-play and learns a best response against stationary opponents. In: Proceedings ont the 20th International Conference on Machine Learning. (2003)
6. Bowling, M., Veloso, M.: Multiagent learning using a variable learning rate. Artificial Intelligence **136** (2002) 215–250
7. Sen, S., Airiau, S., Mukherjee, R.: Towards a pareto-optimal solution in general-sum games. In: Proceedings of the Second International Joint Conference On Autonomous Agents and Multiagent Systems. (2003)
8. Brams, S.J.: Theory of Moves. Cambridge University Press, Cambridge: UK (1994)
9. Claus, C., Boutilier, C.: The dynamics of reinforcement learning in cooperative multiagent systems. In: Proceedings of the Fifteenth National Conference on Artificial Intelligence, Menlo Park, CA, AAAI Press/MIT Press (1998) 746–752
10. Littman, M.L.: Friend-or-foe q-learning in general-sum games. In: Proceedings of the Eighteenth International Conference on Machine Learning, Morgan Kaufmann (2001) 322–328
11. Greenwald, A., Hall, K.: Correlated-q learning. In: Proceedings of the Twentieth International Conference on Machine Learning. (2003) 242–249
12. Aumann, R.: Subjectivity and correlation in randomized strategies. Journal of Mathematical Economics **1** (1974) 67–96
13. McKelvey, R.D., McLennan, A.M., Turocy, T.L.: Gambit: Software tools for game theory version 0.97.0.7. http://econweb.tamu.edu/gambit (2004)

Unifying Convergence and No-Regret
in Multiagent Learning

Bikramjit Banerjee and Jing Peng

Department of Electrical Engineering & Computer Science,
Tulane University, New Orleans, LA 70118
{banerjee, jp}@eecs.tulane.edu
http://www.eecs.tulane.edu/Banerjee

Abstract. We present a new multiagent learning algorithm, $RV_{\sigma(t)}$, that builds on an earlier version, ReDVaLeR . ReDVaLeR could guarantee (a) convergence to best response against stationary opponents and *either* (b) constant bounded regret against arbitrary opponents, *or* (c) convergence to Nash equilibrium policies in self-play. But it makes two strong assumptions: (1) that it can distinguish between self-play and otherwise non-stationary agents and (2) that all agents know their portions of the *same* equilibrium in self-play. We show that the adaptive learnng rate of $RV_{\sigma(t)}$ that is explicitly dependent on time can overcome both of these assumptions. Consequently, $RV_{\sigma(t)}$ theoretically achieves (a') convergence to near-best response against *eventually* stationary opponents, (b') no-regret payoff against arbitrary opponents *and* (c') convergence to some Nash equilibrium policy in some classes of games, in self-play. Each agent now needs to know its portion of *any* equilibrium, and does not need to distinguish among non-stationary opponent types. This is also the first successful attempt (to our knowledge) at convergence of a no-regret algorithm in the Shapley game.

1 Introduction

Multiagent learning (MAL) in a reinforcement learning setting has been an active field of study recently. The problem is simply of multiple controllers trying to learn individually "optimal" control policies in a shared Markov Decision Process (MDP), often called a *stochastic game* or a *Markov game*. The difficulty arises from the fact that all agents are learning simultaneously, which means the MDP faced by each agent is essentially *non-stationary*. Hence, the concept of "optimal" policy becomes ill-defined, and depends on the collective behavior of the other agents. Previous research has attempted to tackle this problem by considering various *opponent classes* such that there is a well-defined "optimal policy" for the learner *for each class of opponents*. Typically the research contributions in this aspect has been to design learning algorithms that learn the appropriate behaviors for the corresponding class of opponents, *without any access to the class information*.

The present paper follows this line of research and makes several fundamental contributions. In particular, we point out that the class taxonomy of the opponents suggested so far is incomplete. We then fill the void and present the first algorithm that can tackle all opponent classes. More specifically, we present a new multiagent learning algorithm

K. Tuyls et al. (Eds.): LAMAS 2005, LNAI 3898, pp. 100–114, 2006.
© Springer-Verlag Berlin Heidelberg 2006

for repeated games, with the general philosophy of policy convergence against some classes of opponents but otherwise ensuring high payoffs. We build on our previous algorithm, ReDVaLeR [1], that we proved to guarantee (a) convergence to best response against stationary opponents and either (b) constant bounded regret against arbitrary opponents or (c) convergence to Nash equilibrium policies in self-play. It was shown to achieve both (b) and (c) empirically but needed to assume that all agents must know their portions of the *same* equilibrium. In this paper we present a new technique extending ReDVaLeR , called $RV_{\sigma(t)}$, that theoretically achieves (a') convergence to near-best response against *eventually* stationary opponents, (b') no-regret payoff against arbitrary opponents and (c') convergence to Nash equilibrium policies in some classes of games, in self-play. Each agent now needs to know only its portion of *any* equilibrium, besides the other assumptions made in ReDVaLeR . Additionally, since $RV_{\sigma(t)}$can achieve both (b') and (c') simultaneously, it does not need to distinguish between a self-play agent and an otherwise non-stationary agent.

No-regret has been an attractive property for a learner facing unknown opponents - the case that precludes any meaningful definition of a "desirable behavior" even for the agent designer. In such cases, no-regret stipulates a specific behavior sequence that achieves "safe" play in terms of payoffs, but otherwise does not attempt convergence to any specific behavior. However, depending on the opponents, we may want a no-regret learner to indeed converge to some policy, e.g., we would want it to converge to Nash equilibrium policy in self-play. Previous research [2] has empirically shown that in some games (such as the Shapley game in Table 1), no-regret learners are unable to converge in self-play. A major consequence of our theoretical results is that $RV_{\sigma(t)}$is *both no-regret and convergent* in self-play in some classes of games that includes the Shapley game. The rest of the paper is organized as follows: sections 2 and 3 present the background and the related work respectively. In section 4 we present the $RV_{\sigma(t)}$technique and in section 5, its analysis. We present our conclusions in section 6.

2   Multiagent Reinforcement Learning

A Multiagent Reinforcement Learning task is usually modeled as a Stochastic Game (SG, also called *Markov Game*), which is a Markov Decision Process with multiple controllers. We focus on stochastic games with a single state, also called repeated games. This refers to a scenario where a matrix game (defined below) is played repeatedly by multiple agents. We shall represent the action space of the ith agent as A_i.

Definition 1. *A matrix game with n players is given by an n-tuple of matrices,* $\langle \mathbf{R}_1, \mathbf{R}_2, \ldots, \mathbf{R}_n \rangle$ *where $\mathbf{R}_i$ is a matrix of dimension $|A_1| \times |A_2| \ldots \times |A_n|$, such that the payoff of the ith agent for the joint action $(a_1, a_2, \ldots, a_n)$ is given by the entry* $R_i(a_1, a_2, \ldots, a_n), \forall i.$

As is usual, we assume that payoffs are bounded, $R_i(a_1, a_2, \ldots, a_n) \in [\underline{r}_i, \bar{r}_i]$, for real $\underline{r}_i, \bar{r}_i$. Table 1 shows an example game of 2 players with 3 actions per player, called the Shapley game.

A *mixed policy*, vector $\pi_i \in \Delta(A_i)$ for agent i, is a probability distribution over A_i. If the entire probability mass is concentrated on a single action (some actions), it

Table 1. The Shapley Game

$$R_1 = \begin{pmatrix} 1 & 0 & 0 \\ 0 & 1 & 0 \\ 0 & 0 & 1 \end{pmatrix}, \qquad R_2 = \begin{pmatrix} 0 & 1 & 0 \\ 0 & 0 & 1 \\ 1 & 0 & 0 \end{pmatrix}$$

is also called a *pure policy* (*partially mixed policy*). The joint policies of the opponents of the ith agent will be given by the vector π_{-i}. We shall usually refer to the ith agent as the learner and the rest of the agents as the opponents. The expected payoff of the learner at any stage in which the policy tuple $\langle \pi_1, \pi_2, \ldots, \pi_n \rangle$ is followed is given by $V_i(\pi_i, \pi_{-i}) = \sum_{(a_1, \ldots, a_n) \in \prod_k A_k} \pi_1(a_1) \ldots \pi_n(a_n) R_i(a_1, \ldots, a_n)$.

Definition 2. *For an n-player matrix game, an ϵ-best response ($BR^i_{\epsilon, \pi_{-i}}$) of the ith agent to its opponents' joint policy (π_{-i}), for some $\epsilon \geq 0$, is given by*

$$BR^i_{\epsilon, \pi_{-i}} = \{\pi_i | V_i(\pi_i, \pi_{-i}) \geq V_i(\pi'_i, \pi_{-i}) - \epsilon, \ \forall \pi'_i \in \Delta(A_i)\}$$

Definition 3. *A mixed-policy Nash Equilibrium (NE) for a matrix game $\langle \mathbf{R}_1, \mathbf{R}_2, \ldots, \mathbf{R}_n \rangle$ is a tuple of probability vectors $\langle \pi^*_1, \pi^*_2, \ldots, \pi^*_n \rangle$ (policy profile) such that each is a best response to the rest, i.e., $\pi^*_i \in BR^i_{\pi^*_{-i}} \ \forall i$. In terms of payoffs, these conditions can be restated as*

$$V_i(\pi^*_i, \pi^*_{-i}) \geq V_i(\pi_i, \pi^*_{-i}) \ \forall \pi_i \in \Delta(A_i), \forall i$$

No player in this game has any incentive for unilateral deviation from the Nash equilibrium policy, given the others' policy. There always exists at least one such equilibrium profile for an arbitrary finite matrix game [3]. As an example, the only NE of the 2 player Shapley game in Table 1 is $\langle [\frac{1}{3}, \frac{1}{3}, \frac{1}{3}], [\frac{1}{3}, \frac{1}{3}, \frac{1}{3}] \rangle$.

Definition 4. *For a given time range $t = 0 \ldots T$, the regret of a learner (agent i), Rg^T_i is given by $Rg^T_i = \max_{\pi_i} \sum_{t=1}^{t=T} V_i(\pi_i, \pi^t_{-i}) - \sum_{t=1}^{t=T} V_i(\pi^t_i, \pi^t_{-i})$.*

This compares the total payoff of the actual sequence of policies of the learner with the best response to the empirical distribution of the opponent.

3 Related Work

Multiagent Reinforcement Learning has produced primarily two types of algorithms. One type learns some fixed point of the game e.g., NE (Minimax-Q [4, 5], Nash-Q [6], FFQ [7]) or correlated equilibrium (CE-Q [8]). These algorithms can guarantee a certain minimal expected payoff asymptotically, but it may be possible to guarantee higher payoff in certain situations if the learner is adaptive to the opponents' play, instead of learning the game solution alone. This brings us to the other type of learners that learn a best response to the opponents' actual play e.g., IGA [9], WoLF-IGA [10, 11], AWE-SOME [12]. Since mutual best response is an equilibrium, two similar best responding players (such situations referred to as *self-play*) should be able to converge to an equilibrium. WoLF-IGA achieves this in 2×2 games (assuming it knows its portion of any equilibrium) and AWESOME achieves it for arbitrary sized games. But an AWESOME agent needs to know an entire equilibirum profile, meaning that it not only knows the others' equilibrium policy, but also that all agents agree on which equilibrium they know in games with multiple equilibria.

Performance guarantees *during* the learning process are provided by *regret matching* learners. These are algorithms that achieve $\lim_{T \to \infty} \frac{Rg_i^T}{T} \leq 0$ (called *no-regret* algorithms) but their convergence properties in policies are unknown [13, 14, 15, 16] or at best limited [2]. A generalized version of IGA, called GIGA, was shown to be no-regret [17] but its convergence property is unknown. Clearly, there was a need for a MAL algorithm that could address (eventually) stationary opponents and self-play *as well as other types of opponents*. Our previous work on ReDVaLeR [1] filled this void and allowed a learner to be no-regret against this large class of opponents, in addition to satisfying the base cases agaitt stationary and self-play opponents. Subsequently, the WoLF version of GIGA [18] was shown to be also no-regret but convergent to NE only in 2×2 games against GIGA. Our previous algorithm, ReDVaLeR [1] also had limitations. It was shown to achieve both convergence and no-regret in arbitrary sized games, but for conflicting settings of a parameter σ. Each ReDVaLeR agent was also assumed to know its portion of *some* equilibrium, i.e., there was agreement on equilibrium selection. Our present work builds on ReDVaLeR and uses a single time dependent σ that achieves both convergence and no-regret properties simultaneously. More importantly, we relax the assumption that agents agree on which equilibrium they know their portions of. Another recent work proposed a similar set of properties for a MAL algorithm, with a greater focus on payoff [19]. This algorithm achieves near best response against stationary players (in contrast we guarantee near best response against the larger set of eventually stationary opponents), at least non-Pareto dominated (by another equilibrium) equilibrium payoff in self-play (in contrast we provide convergence to some equilibrium policy), and at least the minimax payoff against all other players (in contrast, we guarantee the stronger property of no-regret payoff that could be greater than the minimax payoff depending on the opponents) in polynomial time. However, this algorithm needs to know the game matrix of *all* agents which is stronger than our 2 assumptions combined that the learner knows only its own game matrix and its portion of any equilibrium policy.

4   Our Approach: ReDVaLeR with Variable σ

We make the following assumptions for the current work,

1. that the learner knows its own bounded game payoffs (like AWESOME)
2. that the agents can observe each other's instantaneous policies [1] and can use vanishing step sizes for policy improvement (similar to IGA and WoLF-IGA).

---

[1] This assumption is only used in Theorem 10 but it is dispensable. It is possible to collapse this and the previous assumption into a single assumption that the learner can *only* observe its payoff vector at every round, as in [18]. We shall show the details in a consolidated version.

3. that the agents are given at the start, their portions of *any* equilibrium policy profile (like WoLF-IGA). They might see their portions of different equilibria in games with multiple equilibria.

We write the probability of the jth action of the ith agent at time t as $\pi_i^t(j)$ and the expected payoff of this action against the opponent's current policy as $V_i(j, \pi_{-i}^t)$ and note that $\sum_j \pi_i^t(j)V_i(j, \pi_{-i}^t) = V_i(\pi_i^t, \pi_{-i}^t)$.

We use the ReDVaLeR algorithm (see [1] for details) with a time-varying schedule for σ in place of a constant. The discrete form of the algorithm (slightly different from [1]) is

$$\pi_i^{t+1}(j) = \frac{\pi_i^t(j) + \eta\pi_i^t(j)l_i^t(j)V_i(j, \pi_{-i}^t)}{1 + \eta\sum_j l_i^t(j)\pi_i^t(j)V_i(j, \pi_{-i}^t)} \tag{1}$$

for η being a small step size and initial condition: $\pi_i^0(j) = \frac{1}{|A_i|}$. Note that the probability values generated above are automatically bounded in the range $[0, 1]$ if $\underline{r}_i \geq 0$. Also the distribution is indeed a probability distribution (i.e., sum 1) without the need of a projection operation unlike GIGA or GIGA-WoLF.

In continuous time, i.e., as $\eta \to 0$, the above equation yields the same differential equation as ReDVaLeR for the dynamics of the n-player system

$$\frac{d}{dt}(\pi_i^t(j)) = \pi_i^t(j) \times [l_i^t(j)V_i(j, \pi_{-i}^t) - \sum_j l_i^t(j)\pi_i^t(j)V_i(j, \pi_{-i}^t)] \tag{2}$$

$j = 1\ldots|A_i|$, $i = 1\ldots n$. In contrast with [1], the learning rates ($l_i^t(j)$) for this algorithm, $RV_{\sigma(t)}$, are defined as

$$l_i^t(j) = \begin{cases} 1 + \sigma(t) \text{ if } \pi_i^t(j) < \pi_i^*(j) \\ 1 - \sigma(t) \text{ if } \pi_i^t(j) \geq \pi_i^*(j) \end{cases} \tag{3}$$

for a suitable σ-schedule as defined below.

Definition 5 (σ-Schedule). *A time decaying schedule for $\sigma(t)$ is defined by the 3 conditions:*

1. $\sigma(t)$ *is continuous and* $1 \geq \sigma(t) \geq 0, \forall t$,
2. $\sigma(t) \geq \sigma(t'), \forall t' \geq t$,
3. $\sigma(t) \to 0$ *as* $t \to \infty$.

5   Analysis of $RV_{\sigma(t)}$

In the following analysis, we shall use the symbol $\|\mathbf{x}\|$ to mean the $\mathcal{L}_\infty$ norm of a vector, i.e., $\|\mathbf{x}\| = \max_i |x_i|$ and the symbol $\mathbf{1}$ to mean a vector of all 1's. We also assume that the game payoffs are all positive (i.e., $\underline{r}_i \geq 0$), which is merely a technical assumption, since if the agent knows its game payoffs it can easily make an affine transformation to satisfy this assumption. The new game is strategically unchanged and the no-regret property also holds in the original game.

For the sake of brevity, we write $V_i(j, \pi^t_{-i})$ simply as V^j_i. Let $D_i(\tilde{\pi}_i, \pi^t_i)$ be the Kullback Leibler divergence between the ith agent's policy at time t and an *arbitrary* distribution $\tilde{\pi}_i$, given by

$$D_i(\tilde{\pi}_i, \pi^t_i) = \sum_j \tilde{\pi}_i(j) \log \left(\frac{\tilde{\pi}_i(j)}{\pi^t_i(j)} \right) \tag{4}$$

With a slight abuse of notation, we will refer to $\dot{D}_i$ or $\frac{dD_i}{dt}$ as the projection of the gradient of the function D_i (equation 4) along the solution trajectory of (2) for a given initial policy profile. When the trajectory follows the unmodified Replicator Dynamics, we write the same as $\frac{dD^{RD}_i}{dt}$. The following result is crucial to all subsequent analyses.

Lemma 1. [1] *For any fixed policy $\tilde{\pi}_i$,*

$$\frac{d}{dt}(D_i(\tilde{\pi}_i, \pi^t_i)) = \sum_j l^t_i(j)\pi^t_i(j)V^j_i - \sum_j l^t_i(j)\tilde{\pi}_i(j)V^j_i$$

$$\frac{d}{dt}(D^{RD}_i(\tilde{\pi}_i, \pi^t_i)) = V_i(\pi^t_i, \pi^t_{-i}) - V_i(\tilde{\pi}_i, \pi^t_{-i})$$

5.1 Convergence Against Eventually Stationary Opponents

Here we establish that $RV_{\sigma(t)}$ with σ-schedule of definition 5 converges to the set of ϵ-best responses against stationary opponents from which follow the convergence against eventually stationary opponents. The following lemma is used and is straightforward to prove.

Lemma 2 (Payoff-continuity). *If π_{i1} and π_{i2} are two policy vectors of agent i against the stationary joint policy of the opponents π_{-i} and if $\|\pi_{i1} - \pi_{i2}\| \leq \alpha$ for some $\alpha > 0$, then*

$$|V_i(\pi_{i1}, \pi_{-i}) - V_i(\pi_{i2}, \pi_{-i})| \leq \alpha |A_i| \bar{r}_i$$

In other words, if two policies are close then so are their payoffs against a given joint policy of the opponents.

The following Theorem establishes that $RV_{\sigma(t)}$ with a non-stationary σ (Definition 5) converges to the set of ϵ-best responses against stationary opponents.

Theorem 3. *For a given $\epsilon > 0$, there exists a time τ, such that after τ a $RV_{\sigma(t)}$ agent i using σ-schedule in Definition 5 against $n - 1$ stationary agents, is guaranteed to converge to the set of ϵ-best response policies, $BR^i_{\epsilon, \pi_{-i}}$.*

Proof: Suppose the opponents' joint stationary policy is given by π_{-i}, and let us consider some $\bar{\pi}_i \in BR^i_{0, \pi_{-i}}$. Clearly the payoff of all policies in $BR^i_{0, \pi_{-i}}$ have the same value and let this value be $\bar{V}_i$. At any given time t we consider the following two cases:

Case 1: $\pi^t_i \notin BR^i_{\epsilon, \pi_{-i}}$
    This means

$$V(\pi^t_i, \pi_{-i}) < \bar{V}_i - \epsilon \tag{5}$$

Now substituting $\bar{\pi}_i$ in place of the arbitrary policy in Lemma 1, we get

$$\frac{d}{dt}(D_i(\bar{\pi}_i, \pi_i^t)) = \sum_j l_i^t(j)\pi_i^t(j)V_i^j - \sum_j l_i^t(j)\bar{\pi}_i(j)V_i^j$$

$$\leq (1 + \sigma(t))V_i(\pi_i^t, \pi_{-i}) - (1 - \sigma(t))V_i(\bar{\pi}_i, \pi_{-i})$$
$$= V_i(\pi_i^t, \pi_{-i}) - V_i(\bar{\pi}_i, \pi_{-i}) + \sigma(t)[V_i(\pi_i^t, \pi_{-i}) + V_i(\bar{\pi}_i, \pi_{-i})]$$
$$< -\epsilon + \sigma(t)[V_i(\pi_i^t, \pi_{-i}) + V_i(\bar{\pi}_i, \pi_{-i})] \text{ , by (5)}$$
$$\leq -\epsilon + 2\sigma(t)\bar{V}_i$$

Now according to Definition 5 there exists a time (τ) such that for all $t' > \tau$, $\sigma(t') < \frac{\epsilon}{2\bar{V}_i}$. Thus at all such times $\frac{d}{dt}(D_i(\bar{\pi}_i, \pi_i^{t'})) < 0$ whenever $\pi_i^{t'} \notin BR_{\epsilon, \pi_{-i}}^i$. This means, the policy approaches a best response at such times. By Lemma 2, the policy cannot approach a best response without its payoff approaching $\bar{V}_i$. Thus at some point t', the value of the policy will exceed $\bar{V}_i - \epsilon$ and so, $\pi_i^{t'} \in BR_{\epsilon, \pi_{-i}}^i$. This brings us to the 2nd case.

Case 2: $\pi_i^t \in BR_{\epsilon, \pi_{-i}}^i$. Also $t \geq \tau$

If $\pi_i^{t'} \in BR_{\epsilon, \pi_{-i}}^i$, $\forall t' > t$ then we are done. Otherwise, there exists a time $t' > t$ such that $\pi_i^{t'-\eta} \in BR_{\epsilon, \pi_{-i}}^i$ and $\pi_i^{t'} \notin BR_{\epsilon, \pi_{-i}}^i$, where η is the time step size used in Equation 1. So $V_i(\pi_i^{t'-\eta}, \pi_{-i}) \geq V_i(\pi_i^{t'}, \pi_{-i})$. Also

$$\|\pi_i^{t'-\eta} - \pi_i^{t'}\| \leq \eta(1 + \sigma(t' - \eta))\bar{r}_i$$
$$\leq 2\eta\bar{r}_i$$

Then by Lemma 2,

$$V_i(\pi_i^{t'-\eta}, \pi_{-i}) - V_i(\pi_i^{t'}, \pi_{-i}) \leq 2\eta|A_i|\bar{r}_i^2$$

that is

$$V_i(\pi_i^{t'}, \pi_{-i}) \geq \bar{V}_i - (\epsilon + 2\eta|A_i|\bar{r}_i^2)$$

So even though $\pi_i^{t'}$ is not an ϵ-best response, it is an $(\epsilon + 2\eta|A_i|\bar{r}_i^2)$-best response. Also from time t' case 1 applies and both of the policy and the payoff approach that of a strict best response. Thus after τ, the payoff never falls below $\bar{V}_i - (\epsilon + 2\eta|A_i|\bar{r}_i^2) = \bar{V}_i - \epsilon$, since $\eta \to 0$. Lastly, π_i^t may not converge to any specific policy in $BR_{\epsilon, \pi_{-i}}^i$, only stay in this set asymptotically. $\square$

An immediate corollary of Theorem 3 is that $RV_{\sigma(t)}$ will converge to an ϵ-best response even if the opponents do not always play stationary policies, as long as they *settle down to a stationary profile at some finite time*, τ_1. This is justified by replacing τ in the proof of Theorem 3 by $\max\{\tau, \tau_1\}$. We state this result as the following corollary.

Corollary 4. *If there exists a time τ_1 such that all other agents play stationary policies at all times $t > \tau_1$, then for a given $\epsilon > 0$, there exists a time τ, such that after $\max\{\tau_1, \tau\}$ an $RV_{\sigma(t)}$ agent i using σ-schedule in definition 5, is guaranteed to converge to the set of ϵ-best response policies, $BR_{\epsilon, \pi_{-i}}^i$.*

Note that this does not require all of the opponents to start playing a stationary profile simultaneously, only that the last opponent to settle down should do so at some finite time point τ_1. Also note that this notion of eventually stationary opponent profile is a stronger condition than the non-stationary opponent policies *with a limit* considered in [20]. In the latter the opponents may never actually settle down but continue with an ever decreasing distance from a limiting profile.

5.2 No-Regret Property

Here we prove the no-regret property of $RV_{\sigma(t)}$. Compared to ReDVaLeR , now the regret is no longer constant bounded but can grow with time. However, with the help of the following lemma (stated without proof) we can show that the average regret goes to 0.

Lemma 5 (Vanishing average). *Given definition 5 for* $\sigma(t)$, *we have* $\lim_{T\to\infty} \frac{\int_0^T \sigma(t)dt}{T} = 0.$

Theorem 6. *If a* $RV_{\sigma(t)}$ *agent i uses the decaying* σ-*schedule of definition 5, then*

$$\lim_{T\to\infty} \frac{Rg_i^T}{T} \leq 0$$

i.e., the algorithm is asymptotically no-regret.

Proof: As in Theorem 2 in [1], we have

$$-D_0 \leq \int_0^T \left(\sum_j l_i^t(j)\pi_i^t(j)V_i^j - \sum_j l_i^t(j)\tilde{\pi}_i(j)V_i^j \right) dt$$

$$\leq \int_0^T (1+\sigma(t))V_i(\pi_i^t, \pi_{-i}^t)dt - \int_0^T (1-\sigma(t))V_i(\tilde{\pi}_i, \pi_{-i}^t)dt$$

$$= \int_0^T V_i(\pi_i^t, \pi_{-i}^t)dt - \int_0^T V_i(\tilde{\pi}_i, \pi_{-i}^t)dt$$

$$+ \int_0^T \sigma(t)\left[V_i(\pi_i^t, \pi_{-i}^t) + V_i(\tilde{\pi}_i, \pi_{-i}^t)\right] dt$$

Rearranging and again noting that $D_0 \leq \log|A_i|$ and that $\tilde{\pi}_i$ was chosen arbitrarily, we have

$$\int_0^T V_i(\pi_i^t, \pi_{-i}^t)dt \geq \max_{\tilde{\pi}_i} \int_0^T V_i(\tilde{\pi}_i, \pi_{-i}^t)dt - \log|A_i|$$

$$- \int_0^T \sigma(t)\left[V_i(\pi_i^t, \pi_{-i}^t) + V_i(\tilde{\pi}_i, \pi_{-i}^t)\right] dt$$

$$\geq \max_{\tilde{\pi}_i} \int_0^T V_i(\tilde{\pi}_i, \pi_{-i}^t)dt - 2\bar{r}_i \int_0^T \sigma(t)dt - \log|A_i|$$

Thus the regret of the ith agent is bounded by

$$Rg_i^T \leq 2\bar{r}_i \int_0^T \sigma(t)dt + \log|A_i|$$

The result now follows from Lemma 5.   □

We postpone the choice of actual form of $\sigma(t)$ till the end of section 5.3 in order to satisfy both convergence and no-regret, whereby we also compare the emerging expression of regret with those from GIGA, GIGA-WoLF.

5.3   Convergence in Self-play

Since we do not assume any coordination in the choice of the equilibrium, for games with multiple equilibria, the agents may be given their portions of different equilibria. Although this is not difficult to handle in 2×2 games [11], in larger games this becomes a daunting task. In this paper we show that the variable learning rate is useful for this purpose, in games *of any size* but with a unique mixed equilibrium. Even though coordination in equilibrium selection is by default in such games, it has proven to be a hard case for convergence in self-play beyond 2×2 games. $RV_{\sigma(t)}$ is the first algorithm that extends this property to such games of arbitrary size, and this is also experimentally validated in two such games, viz., the Shapley game (Table 1) and the game in Table 2 with a unique partially mixed equilibrium. This is addition to $RV_{\sigma(t)}$ being convergent in *all* 2×2 games with possibly multiple equilibria, which we show next.

2×2 games. In all 2×2 games, the $RV_{\sigma(t)}$ algorithm can be shown to be equivalent to WoLF-IGA. In cases where IGA converges (in policy) in self-play, only the direction of the gradient matters and this remains same for $RV_{\sigma(t)}$. In the special case where WoLF-IGA (but not IGA) converges in policy, the learning rate change in $RV_{\sigma(t)}$ turns out to be the same as WoLF-IGA thus guaranteeing convergence like WoLF-IGA. Hence $RV_{\sigma(t)}$ always converges to an equilibrium policy in all 2×2 games, when given its portion of *any* equilibrium, similar to WoLF-IGA.

Games with unique mixed equilibrium. Here we prove that a σ-schedule can be designed satisfying definition 5 such that convergence to equilibrium can be achieved in these games. We make another technical assumption, that the minimum game payoff of i is strictly positive, $\underline{r}_i > 0$, for all i. Again this is easy to satisfy in self-play without changing the game strategically. The following lemmas will be used in the proof of the final Theorem for convergence of $RV_{\sigma(t)}$ in self-play.

As a first step we show that the requirement on the value of σ (i.e., $\sigma = 1$; Theorem 3 in [1]) from the perspective of any learner i can be relaxed in two ways. The first is a direct but minor relaxation given by the lemma below.

Lemma 7. *If the policy of i is not ϵ_i-close to its equilibrium, i.e., $\min_j |\pi_i^t(j) - \pi_i^*(j)| > \epsilon_i$, for some $\epsilon_i > 0$, then $\frac{d}{dt} D_i(\pi_i^*, \pi_i^t) < -\alpha$ for some $0 < \alpha < \epsilon_i \underline{r}_i$, if i uses*

$$\sigma > \frac{1}{1 + \frac{\epsilon_i \underline{r}_i - \alpha}{\bar{r}_i + \alpha}}.$$

Proof: The proof closely follows Theorem 3 in [1]. In case 1 of that proof, σ only needs to be positive. It is really case 2 that needs to be relaxed. It is easily seen that the proof of case 2 in that theorem can be stated for individual agents as well. Consequently when $\frac{dD_i^{RD}}{dt} > 0$, we have

$$\frac{dD_i^{RD}}{dt} - \frac{dD_i}{dt} = \sigma \sum_j |\pi_i^t(j) - \pi_i^*(j)| V_i^j \tag{6}$$

Now since $\min_j |\pi_i^t(j) - \pi_i^*(j)| > \epsilon_i$, there is at least one action, say k, such that $\pi_i^t(k) < \pi_i^*(k)$. Therefore, $|\pi_i^t(k) - \pi_i^*(k)|V_i^k \geq \epsilon_i \underline{r}_i$. So,

$$\frac{dD_i^{RD}}{dt} = \sum_{j \neq k}(\pi_i^t(j) - \pi_i^*(j))V_i^j + (\pi_i^t(k) - \pi_i^*(k))V_i^k$$

$$= \sum_{j \neq k}(\pi_i^t(j) - \pi_i^*(j))V_i^j - |\pi_i^t(k) - \pi_i^*(k)|V_i^k$$

$$\leq \sum_{j \neq k}(\pi_i^t(j) - \pi_i^*(j))V_i^j - \epsilon_i \underline{r}_i$$

Hence,

$$\sum_{j \neq k}(\pi_i^t(j) - \pi_i^*(j))V_i^j \geq \frac{dD_i^{RD}}{dt} + \epsilon_i \underline{r}_i \tag{7}$$

Equation 6 gives us $\frac{dD_i^{RD}}{dt} - \frac{dD_i}{dt} \geq \sigma \sum_{j \neq k}(\pi_i^t(j) - \pi_i^*(j))V_i^j$. Substituting from Equation 7, we have $\frac{dD_i^{RD}}{dt} - \frac{dD_i}{dt} \geq \sigma(\frac{dD_i^{RD}}{dt} + \epsilon_i \underline{r}_i)$. The result follows noting that $\frac{dD_i^{RD}}{dt} \leq \bar{r}_i$. $\square$

To illustrate the nature of this relaxation, if $\epsilon_i = 2 \times 10^{-3}$, $\bar{r}_i = 2$, $\underline{r}_i = 1$, and $\alpha = 10^{-3}$, then we have $\sigma > 0.9995$. The main Theorem on convergence of $RV_{\sigma(t)}$ in self-play, however, depends on this to be maintained for only a finite time ($O(\frac{1}{\alpha})$).

The following lemma allows σ to approach 0 in self-play, but applies only when the others are *sufficiently close* to their portions of the equilibrium. First we define "sufficiently close". Let us write the vector of ith agents payoff, V_i^j over index j ($j \in A_i$), as $\mathbf{V}_i$. Also from Game Theory [21] we know that for a non-negative game with a unique completely mixed equilibrium there is a constant $V_i^* > 0$ for each i such that, $V_i(j, \pi_{-i}^*) = V_i^*$, $\forall j$. Clearly when the opponents' policies are close to their respective equilibria, $V_i^j = V_i(j, \pi_{-i}^t)$ is also close to $V_i(j, \pi_{-i}^*) = V_i^*$, since payoffs are bounded.

Definition 6. *The opponents of agent i are said to be* sufficiently close *to their equilibria if* $\|\mathbf{V}_i - V_i^* \mathbf{1}\| < V_i^*$, *and this distance does not exceed* V_i^* *at any future time.*

Now the following Lemma relaxes the the value of σ from 1 when the opponents are *sufficiently close* to their equilibria.

Lemma 8. *In self-play in non-negative games with a unique completely mixed equilirium, when the opponents of agent i are sufficiently close to their equilibria, the value of σ used by i need only satisfy $\sigma(t) > \frac{\|\mathbf{V}_i - V_i^*\mathbf{1}\|}{V_i^*}$ to ensure convergence of π_i^t to π_i^*.*

Proof: Let us call $c = \|\mathbf{V}_i - V_i^*\mathbf{1}\|$. Note that under the given conditions, $V_i^* - c \leq V_i^j \leq V_i^* + c, \forall j$. Then the rate of variation in $D_i(\pi_i^*, \pi_i^t)$ can be given as before by,

$$\frac{dD_i}{dt} = \sum_j (\pi_i^t(j) - \pi_i^*(j))l_i^t(j)V_i^j$$

$$= \sum_{j:\pi_i^t(j)\geq\pi_i^*(j)} (\pi_i^t(j) - \pi_i^*(j))(1 - \sigma(t))V_i^j + \sum_{j:\pi_i^t(j)<\pi_i^*(j)} (\pi_i^t(j) - \pi_i^*(j))(1 + \sigma(t))V_i^j$$

$$\leq \sum_{j:\pi_i^t(j)\geq\pi_i^*(j)} (\pi_i^t(j) - \pi_i^*(j))(1 - \sigma(t))(V_i^* + c)$$

$$+ \sum_{j:\pi_i^t(j)<\pi_i^*(j)} (\pi_i^t(j) - \pi_i^*(j))(1 + \sigma(t))(V_i^* - c)$$

$$= (1 - \sigma(t))(V_i^* + c) \sum_{j:\pi_i^t(j)\geq\pi_i^*(j)} (\pi_i^t(j) - \pi_i^*(j))$$

$$+ (1 + \sigma(t))(V_i^* - c) \sum_{j:\pi_i^t(j)<\pi_i^*(j)} (\pi_i^t(j) - \pi_i^*(j))$$

$$= (1 - \sigma(t))(V_i^* + c) \sum_{j:\pi_i^t(j)\geq\pi_i^*(j)} (\pi_i^t(j) - \pi_i^*(j))$$

$$- (1 + \sigma(t))(V_i^* - c) \sum_{j:\pi_i^t(j)\geq\pi_i^*(j)} (\pi_i^t(j) - \pi_i^*(j))$$

$$= \left[\sum_{j:\pi_i^t(j)\geq\pi_i^*(j)} (\pi_i^t(j) - \pi_i^*(j)) \right] [(1 - \sigma(t))(V_i^* + c) - (1 + \sigma(t))(V_i^* - c)]$$

The equality of the last but one step follows from the fact that $\sum_{j:\pi_i^t(j)\geq\pi_i^*(j)}(\pi_i^t(j) - \pi_i^*(j)) + \sum_{j:\pi_i^t(j)<\pi_i^*(j)}(\pi_i^t(j) - \pi_i^*(j)) = 0$. Since the factor in the first square braces in the last step is strictly positive, the only situation when this is strictly negative is when $\sigma(t) > \frac{c}{V_i^*}$. This makes D_i Lyapunov implying convergence to π_i^*. $\square$

Interestingly, if all agents are *sufficiently close* to their equilibria and all use the σ as in Lemma 8, then all of them will converge to their respective equilibria. This means for each i, $\|\mathbf{V}_i - V_i^*\mathbf{1}\|$ will decrease and that agent will be able to further decrease its σ with time while satisfying Lemma 8. The key is to get them *sufficiently close* to their equilibria. We show how in the next Theorem but before that we state one last necessary Lemma.

Lemma 9 (KLD-$\mathcal{L}_\infty$ correspondence). *For any two probability distributions, $\mathbf{x}, \mathbf{y}$, we have $\|\mathbf{x} - \mathbf{y}\| \leq \epsilon$ for some $1 > \epsilon > 0$ if $D(\mathbf{x}, \mathbf{y}) \leq \frac{2\epsilon^2}{\log 2}$.*

The following Theorem establishes the convergence of $RV_{\sigma(t)}$ to Nash equilibrium in self-play under appropriate assumptions.

Theorem 10. *There exists a σ-schedule satisfying definition 5, which when followed by n $RV_{\sigma(t)}$ agents guarantees the convergence of their policies to the unique completely mixed equilibrium profile of the strictly positive game, provided each agent knows*

1. *the maximum game payoff of any agent, $R_{\max} = \max_i \bar{r}_i$,*
2. *the maximum size of action space among all agents, $\max_i |A_i|$,*
3. *the minimum equilibrium payoff among all agents, $\min_i V_i^*$*
4. *the total number of agents, n.*

Proof: The proof is stated in two steps. In step 1, we establish how agents can get *sufficiently close* to their equilibria. In step 2, we show how they can continue to approach their equilibria in self-play satisfying condition 3 of Definition 5.

Step 1: For each i, we need the opponents $(-i)$ to be *sufficiently close* to their equilibria. Now any agent p can make $\|\pi_p^t - \pi_p^*\| \le \delta_p$ for some δ_p by using $\sigma_p > \frac{1}{1+\frac{\epsilon_p \tau_p - \alpha_p}{\bar{\pi}_p + \alpha_p}}$ (Lemma 7) for sufficiently long (say τ) to bring $D_p(\pi_p^*, \pi_p^t)$ down from initial value $D_p(\pi_p^*, \pi_p^0) = \log|A_p| + \sum_j \pi_p^*(j) \log \pi_p^*(j)$ to $D_p(\pi_p^*, \pi_p^\tau) \le \frac{2\delta_p^2}{\log 2}$ (Lemma 9) at the rate of α_p (Lemma 7). Therefore,

$$\tau \ge \frac{D_p(\pi_p^*, \pi_p^0) - D_p(\pi_p^*, \pi_p^\tau)}{\alpha_p}$$

and this can be easily computed. Note that agent p can also compute appropriate ϵ_p and α_p since it has the knowledge of the necessary policies, π_p^t and π_p^*.

Now if $\|\pi_p^t - \pi_p^*\| \le \delta_p$ $\forall p \in \{-i\}$, then $\|\pi_{-i}^t - \pi_{-i}^*\| \le \sum_p \delta_p$ approximately (ignoring the terms in second and higher powers of δ). As a consequence, i's opponents will be *sufficiently close* to their equilibria if

$$\|\mathbf{V}_i - V_i^* \mathbf{1}\| \le \max_j |V_i^j - V_i^*|$$
$$\le |A_i||\bar{r}_i| \|\pi_{-i}^t - \pi_{-i}^*\|$$
$$\le |A_i||\bar{r}_i| \sum_p \delta_p$$

is less than V_i^*. This can be ensured for all agents p, by forcing

$$\delta_p \le \frac{\min_i V_i^*}{n R_{\max} \max_i |A_i|}$$

Hence the conditions in the Theorem statement. Thus all agents can be brought *sufficiently close* to their equilibria by some σ-schedule following Definition 5.

Step 2: After τ, each agent i must always satisfy Lemma 8. Since the starting value $(\sigma(\tau))$ has been specified in **Step 1**, i only needs to know an appropriate $\frac{d\sigma}{dt}$ to keep changing its σ satisfying Lemma 8. It is easy to see that a suitable $\frac{d\sigma}{dt}$ is

$$0 > \frac{d\sigma}{dt} > \left(\frac{-1}{V_i^*}\right) \max_j \left| \sum_{a_{-i}} R_i(j, a_{-i}) \frac{d}{dt}\left(\pi^t_{-i}(a_{-i})\right) \right| \tag{8}$$

where a_{-i} is a joint action played by i's opponents. The appropriate rate in (8) can be computed from i's observation of its opponents' policies at all times. Also since (8) requires $\frac{d\sigma}{dt}$ be always negative after τ, Definition 5 is satisfied. This completes the proof. $\qquad\qquad\square$

Note that while in self-play (8) will lead $\frac{d\sigma}{dt}$ to approach 0 from below as $t \to \infty$, if the opponents are not self-play $\frac{d\sigma}{dt}$ may not approach 0. But since $\frac{d\sigma}{dt}$ is negative, the no-regret property (Theorem 6) will be preserved if we make $\left|\frac{d\sigma}{dt}\right|$ explicitly decay with time. A sample schedule that does this and satisfies (8) is (for $t \geq 1$)

$$\frac{d\sigma}{dt} = \left(\frac{-1}{V_i^*\sqrt{t}}\right) \max_j \left| \sum_{a_{-i}} R_i(j, a_{-i}) \frac{d}{dt}\left(\pi^t_{-i}(a_{-i})\right) \right| \tag{9}$$

Table 2. A 3 actions game with lone mixed equilibrium

$$R_1 = \begin{pmatrix} 1 & 3 & 1 \\ 1 & 10 & 1 \\ 5 & 1 & 2 \end{pmatrix}, \qquad R_2 = \begin{pmatrix} 7 & 1 & 1 \\ 1 & 0 & 1 \\ 10 & 15 & 1 \end{pmatrix}$$

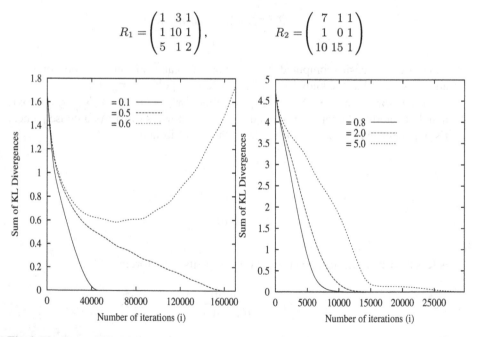

Fig. 1. The Sum of KL Divergences in the Shapley game (left) and in the game in Table 2 (right), with $\sigma = \frac{1}{1+\beta\sqrt{t}}$

Thus a $RV_{\sigma(t)}$ agent can use the above σ-schedule for convergence to equilibrium in self-play while being oblivious of the nature of the others. In case the others are not self-play agents, the same schedule will guarantee the results of Theorem 3, Corollary 4 and Theorem 6.

Theorem 10 basically says that if σ decays slow enough, then monotonic convergence of the sum of KL divergences can be achieved in self-play. For the following experiments we use a σ-schedule $\sigma(t) = \frac{1}{1+\beta\sqrt{t}}$ (of the form of (9)) and show the results for various values of β in Figure 1 corresponding to the Shapley game (Table 1) and the game in Table 2 respectively. We used $\eta = 2 \times 10^{-4}$ and the starting policies were selected close to the edges of the probability simplex since these are the policies that make convergence most difficult in RD. Note that the game in Table 1 is not strictly positive, and that in Table 2 is not strictly positive for the column agent. Also note that σ does not really need to be close to 1 as long as step 1 of Theorem 10 requires. In both experiments, in just 2000 iterations σ climbs down to less than 75% for the middle values of β as shown in Figure 1.

6   Conclusion

We have presented a modification of ReDVaLeR that could guarantee (a) convergence to best response against stationary opponents and *either* (b) constant bounded regret against arbitrary opponents, *or* (c) convergence to Nash equilibrium policies in self-play. The original ReDVaLeR algorithm was shown to achieve both (b) and (c) empirically but assumed that all agents must know their portions of the *same* equilibrium. The new algorithm, $RV_{\sigma(t)}$, theoretically achieves (a') convergence to near-best response against *eventually* stationary opponents, (b') no-regret payoff against arbitrary opponents *and* (c') convergence to some Nash equilibrium policy in some classes of games, in self-play. Each agent now needs to know only its portion of *any* equilibrium. Although we have shown property c' in games with unique mixed equilibrium only, we have also found it to hold in some other classes of games, like coordination games (omitted here). Future work include further generalization and discrete analysis. We also intend to experiment further with learning rate schedules identical to GIGA to directly compare their regret growth rates.

References

1. Banerjee, B., Peng, J.: Performance bounded reinforcement learning in strategic intercations. In: Proceedings of the 19th National Conference on Artificial Intelligence (AAAI-04), San Jose, CA, AAAI Press (2004) 2 – 7
2. Jafari, A., Greenwald, A., Gondek, D., Ercal, G.: On no-regret learning, fictitious play, and Nash equilibrium. In: Proceedings of the 18th International Conference on Machine Learning. (2001) 216 – 223
3. Nash, J.F.: Non-cooperative games. Annals of Mathematics **54** (1951) 286 – 295
4. Littman, M.L.: Markov games as a framework for multi-agent reinforcement learning. In: Proc. of the 11th Int. Conf. on Machine Learning, San Mateo, CA, Morgan Kaufmann (1994) 157–163

5. Littman, M., Szepesvári, C.: A generalized reinforcement learning model: Convergence and applications. In: Proceedings of the 13th International Conference on Machine Learning. (1996) 310 – 318
6. Hu, J., Wellman, M.P.: Nash Q-learning for general-sum stochastic games. Journal of Machine Learning Research **4** (2003) 1039 – 1069
7. Littman, M.L.: Friend-or-foe Q-learning in general-sum games. In: Proceedings of the Eighteenth International Conference on Machine Learnig, Williams College, MA, USA (2001)
8. Greenwald, A., Hall, K.: Correlated Q-learning. In: Proceedings of AAAI Symposium on Collaborative Learning Agents. (2002)
9. Singh, S., Kearns, M., Mansour, Y.: Nash convergence of gradient dynamics in general-sum games. In: Proceedings of the Sixteenth Conference on Uncertainty in Artificial Intelligence. (2000) 541–548
10. Bowling, M., Veloso, M.: Rational and convergent learning in stochastic games. In: Proceedings of the 17th International Joint Conference on Artificial Intelligence, Seattle, WA (2001) 1021 – 1026
11. Bowling, M., Veloso, M.: Multiagent learning using a variable learning rate. Artificial Intelligence **136** (2002) 215 – 250
12. Conitzer, V., Sandholm, T.: AWESOME: A general multiagent learning algorithm that converges in self-play and learns a best response against stationary opponents. In: Proceedings of the 20th International Conference on Machine Learning. (2003)
13. Auer, P., Cesa-Bianchi, N., Freund, Y., Schapire, R.E.: Gambling in a rigged casino: The adversarial multi-arm bandit problem. In: Proceedings of the 36th Annual Symposium on Foundations of Compter Science, Milwaukee, WI, IEEE Computer Society Press (1995) 322 – 331
14. Fudenberg, D., Levine, D.K.: Consistency and cautious fictitious play. Journal of Economic Dynamics and Control **19** (1995) 1065 – 1089
15. Freund, Y., Schapire, R.E.: Adaptive game playing using multiplicative weights. Games and Economic Behavior **29** (1999) 79 – 103
16. Littlestone, N., Warmuth, M.: The weighted majority algorithm. Information and Computation **108** (1994) 212 – 261
17. Zinkevich, M.: Online convex programming and generalized infinitesimal gradient ascent. In: Proceedings of the 20th International Conference on Machine Learning, Washington DC (2003)
18. Bowling, M.: Convergence and no-regret in multiagent learning. In: Proceedings of NIPS 2004/5. (2005)
19. Powers, R., Shoham, Y.: New criteria and a new algorithm for learning in multi-agent systems. In: Proceedings of NIPS 2004/5. (2005)
20. Weinberg, M., Rosenschein, J.S.: Best-response multiagent learning in non-stationary environments. In: Proceedings of the 3rd International Joint Conference on Autonomous Agents and Multiagent Systems (AAMAS). Volume 2., New York, NY, ACM (2004) 506 – 513
21. Owen, G.: Game Theory. Academic Press, UK (1995)

Implicit Coordination in a Network of Social Drivers: The Role of Information in a Commuting Scenario

Ana L.C. Bazzan*, Manuel Fehler, and Franziska Klügl

[1] Instituto de Informática, UFRGS, Caixa Postal 15064,
Porto Alegre 91.501-970, RS, Brazil
bazzan@inf.ufrgs.br
[2] Dep. of Artificial Intelligence, University of Würzburg,
Am Hubland, Würzburg 97074, Germany
{fehler, kluegl}@informatik.uni-wuerzburg.de

Abstract. One of the major research directions in multi-agent systems is dedicated to learning how to coordinate and whether individual agents´ decisions can lead to globally optimal or at least acceptable solutions. Our long term goal is to study the effect of several types of information to guide the decision process of the individual agents. This present paper addresses simulation of agents' decision-making regarding route choice, and the role of an information component. This information can be provided by group colleagues, by acquaintances from other groups (small-world), or by route guidance. Besides, we study the role of agents lying about their choices. We compare these scenarios, concluding that information (from some kind of source) is beneficial in general: lying helps only to a certain extent, and route guidance is the best type of information.

1 Introduction

In multi-agent systems it is almost impossible to oversee the issue of learning how to coordinate. In particular, we focus here on a route choice scenario, in which social drivers have to select a route based on information sharing. The behavior of these agents is influenced by information, be it route recommendation, be it driving experiences exchanged within a group. Thus, we address not only the individual agent behavior, but also how information sharing and recommendations could influence this behavior so that a coordinated situation emerges.

A route choice scenario is normally characterized by an agent facing repeated action selection. In a previous paper [7], we concluded that the more reliable the information that an agent gets about the current and future state of the environment is, the more his actions depend on his beliefs about the decisions of the other agents.

The rest of this paper is organized as follows. The next section briefly reviews some background ideas on decision-making regarding binary choice and organization of agents in groups, with and without information sharing. In Section 3 we present the scenarios used to simulate route choice under several conditions, whereas the results of the corresponding simulations are presented in Section 4. The last section summarizes the conclusions and outlines the possible extensions.

---

* Author partially supported by CNPq.

K. Tuyls et al. (Eds.): LAMAS 2005, LNAI 3898, pp. 115–128, 2006.

2   Background

2.1   Coordination Games and Route Choice

The *El Farol* Bar Problem (EFBP) [1], and, more generally, the Minority Game (MG) [5] are particular instances of coordination models. Basically, these deal with the situation in which N players or agents have the choice between two alternatives (e.g. buy/sell stocks, go to a bar, use route A or B). Variants of these games have been proposed in economics, computer science, and physics. Two relate to multi-agent systems and traffic problems. In [2], personalities are introduced in the MG and populations of agents with these personalities interact in a commuting scenario.

In the second one [6] under the focus of dynamic adaptation, in a commuting scenario, in which drivers have to daily select a route to drive from home to office and back. One route, namely M (main), provides more capacity. The other alternative is a secondary one (thus S). At the end of the trip, every agent gets a reward that is computed based on the number of agents who selected the same alternative. This mimics the actual travel time experienced by the driver himself. The agents know nothing about the reward function or about other agents, but their decisions do influence the reward each receives. Rewards for each agent i were computed based on the the number of agents selecting each route; the less agents select one alternative, the more reward each of them receive for their choice. The overall goal is to reach the best distribution of agents. This is the case when the system reaches the user equilibrium and no agent can change to another alternative at a strictly lower cost. Also, especially for traffic scenarios, the Wardrop Second Principle (optimum) states that the average travel time is minimal [9]. This corresponds to the best social optimum in economic terms.

To investigate this, a simple model for adaptive choice was initially developed [6]. Each agent decides which route to select based on the probability according to which it selects the main route. In the adaptive scenario the agent updates this heuristic with a certain periodicity according to the rewards he has obtained selecting that alternative up to that point. An important factor is how often and in which intervals the heuristic is updated. Changes in this and other parameters are detailed in [6]. Without any information from outside, this yields a configuration where, on average, the agents learn the optimal heuristic.

2.2   Social Attachments and Networks

Also related to the present paper, we discuss some previous works on simulating the Iterated Prisoner's Dilemma (IPD) under different conditions, with agents having various kinds of social attachment.

Watts and Strogatz [10] studied networks of coupled elements through an analogy with the *small-world phenomenon*. The small-world concept is based on the fact that, in large societies, there is normally a shortcut between any two persons via a path of acquaintances [8].

In [3], the performance of a society composed of agents playing the IPD in the presence of agents with attachment to others was analyzed. These agents may have an altruistic behavior towards its acquaintances. These so-called altruistic agents are interested in the good performance of their group as a whole, as well as on their own, since the social group provides also a base for support in case the agent itself is not performing well.

This contributes to the further understanding of how coordination mechanisms can be developed. It is not enough to consider pure rationality when agents are autonomous but also interact in a social group.

3   Description of the Information Sharing Scenarios

The main motivation is to check whether egoistic agents who seek only to maximize a utility function or are overconcerned with self-interest can miss good opportunities for themselves. We use a scenario similar to the one described in Section 2.1 adding the issue of people interacting in groups, using the iterated route choice and the two options (main and secondary routes). The goal remains to have agents distributed between the two routes so that no agent is better off by deviating from its selection. The learning scheme is based on information sharing among the group and, in some scenarios, among people in a network of acquaintances, bringing in the idea of small world explained in Section 2.2. The reward functions are slightly changed here, as explained next.

The N agents acting in these scenarios have to select one of the two available routes as explained in Section 2.1. After all agents have made their decisions and have driven, they receive their rewards, which are inversely proportional to their travel times. Since we use an abstract model here, the travel time is actually computed as in Eq. 1.

$$R_i = \begin{cases} \frac{4}{3} - \frac{M}{N} & \text{if } M \text{ selected} \\ \\ 1 - \frac{S}{N} & \text{if } S \text{ selected} \end{cases} \tag{1}$$

where:

- R_i is the reward for driver i
- M and S are the number of drivers driving main and secondary routes respectively
- N is the total number of drivers ($M + S$)

These formulas arise from the fact that we assume that topological constraints of both routes allow twice more vehicles at the main route than at the secondary one (this is a more didactic example than just allowing 50-50% distribution). Thus, at the equilibrium, $\frac{2}{3}$ of the vehicles should drive on main. The reward on main would then be, for each driver i, $R_i = \frac{2}{3} - \frac{M}{N}$. Similarly, the reward on the secondary route would be $R_i = \frac{1}{3} - \frac{S}{N}$. However, these formulas would yield negative rewards (e.g. in case all drivers go to side, the reward would be $-\frac{2}{3}$), which is not desirable. Therefore, we normalize the rewards adding $\frac{2}{3}$ in all cases, what puts the distribution of rewards between 0 and $\frac{4}{3}$. Table 1 shows rewards for some particular distributions of drivers.

When agents meet their colleagues, they can share information about which route was the best in the group. As said before, from time to time these agents can meet acquaintances from other groups, sharing information about routes as well.

This set of simulations is based on groups composed by either "social" people (in the sense that they share their information within their group and with acquaintances

Table 1. Rewards for particular distribution of drivers between main and secondary routes, for N=150

#nb. main	#nb. sec.	rew. main	rew. sec.
149	1	$\approx 1/3$	≈ 1
1	149	$\approx 4/3$	≈ 0
100	**50**	**2/3**	**2/3**
50	100	1	1/3
75	75	5/6	1/2

about which route is good), "nasty" people (always lie giving the opposite information), and "noisy" drivers (do not belong to any group since they do not commute
frequently).

We can see these groups as being formed by colleagues (e.g. people working together). Agents in the group can ask for rewards of colleagues (or, more directly, which
route was good) and eventually (if the reward is higher) do what other(s) have done.
This is important because even if agent i has a good driving history (e.g. it is always on
time because it has a good strategy for selecting routes), it does not bring much to be the
only one on time in the office. Ideally, assuming that they work together or meet every
morning for important decisions, it is desirable that *every one* in the group is on time!
(thus the motivation for route information sharing).

Some of these agents also know people belonging to other groups (e.g. partners in
leisure activities, etc.) in a small-world-like configuration, so that they have opportunity
to ask for route tips from time to time. Finally, there are agents who like to experiment
a different route with a given probability.

Noisy drivers select routes randomly and do not ask for information. However, they
might meet other non-noisy agents (e.g. at the gas station) and give information.

Nasty agents have an operational behavior similar to the social drivers except that
they do not care about the group or acquaintances; they just want to drive in the route
with as few drivers as possible. Thus, in a quite "naïve" way, they give the opposite
information (e.g. if one used the main route and got a good reward, it advises others to
use the secondary one, if asked). In fact, in some scenarios, given that the information
propagates, this can be a good strategy, as it will be shown. At this stage, we do not
have groups of mixed people because we want to compare performance at the group
level.

Finally, in some scenarios, we introduced a private message system (PMS) which
recommends drives what to do. The aim of the PMS is to direct people to an equilibrium
situation, based on the optimal distribution of drivers. Again, we assume that noisy
drivers do not get this kind of message.

Several scenarios were simulated, changing the composition of groups, the characteristics of agents, and the presence or not of PMS. These scenarios are summarized in
Table 2.

All scenarios of type 1 are without PMS, and without noisy and nasty drivers. In
scenario **1A**, infos are exchanged among group colleagues only; everyone select the
route of the best colleague in the group. Scenario **1B** is pretty much the same, except
that agents have a probability p_1 **of trying a different route**. **1C** is also similar to 1A,
except that agents have a probability p_2 **of asking for infos outside their groups**.

Table 2. Description of scenarios (∗ means that the parameter assumed different   values, as described in the experiment's specific section)

scenario	PMS	nb. of nasty	nb. of noisy	p_1	p_2	p_3
1A	no	0	0	0	0	0
1B	no	0	0	∗	0	0
1C	no	0	0	0	∗	0
2A	no	0	∗	0	0	0
2B	no	0	∗	0.01	0	0
2C	no	0	∗	0	0.2	0
3A	no	∗	0	0	0	0
3B	no	∗	0	0.01	0	0
3C	no	∗	0	0	0.2	0
4A	yes	0	0	0	0	0
4B	yes	0	0	0.01	0	∗
4C	yes	0	0	0	0.2	∗
5A	yes	∗	0	0	0	0
5B	yes	∗	0	0.01	0	0
5C	yes	∗	0	0	0.2	0
5D	yes	∗	0	0	0	∗
6A	yes	0	∗	0	0	0
6B	yes	0	50	0	0	∗
6C	yes	0	50	0	0.2	0

Scenarios of type 2 are similar to type 1 but include noisy drivers. In **2A** we changed only their number. In **2B** we also have a non zero probability p_1. **2C** is similar to 2B but p_2 is used instead of p_1.

Scenarios of type 3 are similar to type 2 but include nasty instead of noisy drivers. Their number was changed in scenario **3A** while **3B** and **3C** are similar to 2B and 2C respectively.

Scenarios of type 4, 5, and 6 all have agents receiving recommendations from the PMS. In type 4 there are no noisy or nasty drivers. In **4A** all agents do follow the recommendation. In **4B** they **deviate from the recommendation with probability** p_3 (this means doing the opposite as recommended), plus they try different routes with probability p_1. **4C** is similar to 4B but we use p_2 instead of p_1.

In type 5, there are nasty drivers. In **5A** we change only the number of them. In **5B** and **5C** p_1 and p_2 are non zero respectively. In **5D** we also vary p_3.

Type 6 is similar to type 5 but includes noisy instead of nasty drivers. In **6A** we vary the number of noisy drivers. The other drivers all follow the recommendations. In **6B** the number of noisy drivers is constant and we vary the probability to deviate from the recommendation (p_3), and in **6C** we vary the probability p_2.

Simulations take 500 time steps (in the graphics we show up to 1000 *simulation steps* because each time step takes two simulation steps due to the nature of the simulation: decide and drive). The parameters used in the simulations are: $N = 150$ drivers, and these are divided in 15 groups. Since agents are created with a probability of belonging to a group, groups may not have exactly $N/15$ members. Depending on the scenario, two of those groups are fixed: one group with only noisy and one group with only nasty drivers.

4 Results

We now present and discuss the main results regarding the scenarios just described. In the graphics we depict only the number M of drivers on main (the secondary is given by $N - M$). In fact, we measure both the actual number at each time step and a discounted average (by a factor δ) as follow: $\overline{M_\delta} = \delta \times \overline{M}_{old} + (1 - \delta) \times M_{current}$. In the simulations presented here $\delta = 0.9$ so that we put much less weight on the current time step. In most graphics we plot only the discounted average which is more smooth than the actual number M (see for instance how it looks when both are plotted at Fig. 2). Remember that the optimal situation is when two-thirds of the drivers (100) are on main and one-third (50) on the secondary route.

4.1 Scenarios Without Recommendation

In Fig. 1 we depict all simulations of type 1: case 1A is the topmost curve in the upper box. Here we see that after a short time the N agents select the main route! This happens because they share the information and all copy the best strategy in the group. Since there is no probability of trying something new, they are all stuck in a very poor situation in terms of performance (see Table 1). Similar performance is noticed for case 1C. This happens because, although agents do ask acquaintances in other groups, since they all behave the same regarding copying strategies and there are no noisy

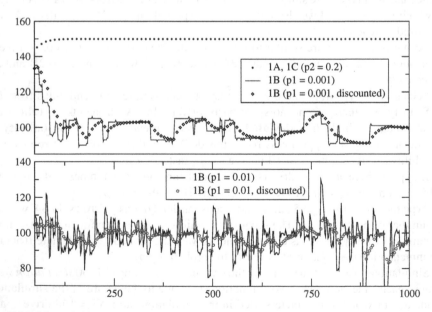

Fig. 1. Number of drivers on main for scenarios 1A, 1B, and 1C, with $p_1 = 0.001$ (upper box) and $p_1 = 0.01$ (lower box)

drivers, this behavior brings nothing. Thus, the result is that again all N drivers end up selecting main.

Of course these are determinisitic and thus very unrealistic situations. In case 1B we used probability p_1 of people trying different routes. This is depicted in Fig. 1 as well. The curves in the upper box are for $p_1 = 0.001$ and the curves in the lower box are for $p_1 = 0.01$. We can see that in both cases the average number of drivers on main fluctuates around 100 drivers, with a much higher deviation in the latter case, which is explained by the fact that the experimentation happens more frequently.

Fig. 2 shows the simulations for scenario 2A for various numbers of noisy drivers, with $p_1 = p_2 = 0$. From top to bottom, their numbers are 10, 50, 100, and 150. When there are only 10, on average 5 go to main and 5 to secondary, what puts the number of people at main to 145 on average (remember that the non-noisy just copy the best route and thus go to main as in 1A). Similar situation happen with 50 (125 on main), 100 (100 on main), and when all are noisy (of course 75 go to each route on average). Notice that the deviation from the expected average increases with increasing number of noisy drivers.

In the simulations depicted on Fig. 3 (scenario 2B), a probability $p_1 = 0.01$ of trying another route was used, and the number of noisy drivers varied: 10, 30, and 50. From now on, in most of the figures, we show only the discounted average in order to plot several curves in a single graphic. The overall average is below 100 due to the noisy drivers who select randomly thus bringing the average as close to 75 the higher their number is.

In scenario 2C, the probability p_2 was set to 0.2 (keeping $p_1 = 0$), changing the number of noisy drivers (10, 30, and 50). Fig. 4 show the results: the more noisy drivers,

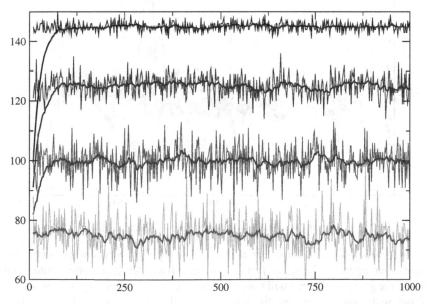

Fig. 2. Number of drivers on main for scenario 2A, for 10, 50, 100, and 150 (from top to bottom) noisy drivers

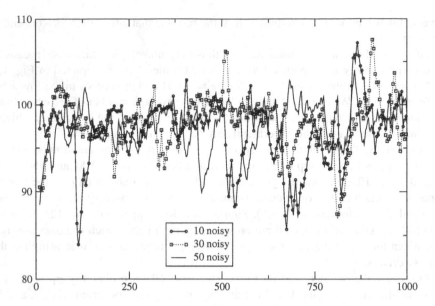

Fig. 3. Number of drivers on main for scenario 2B

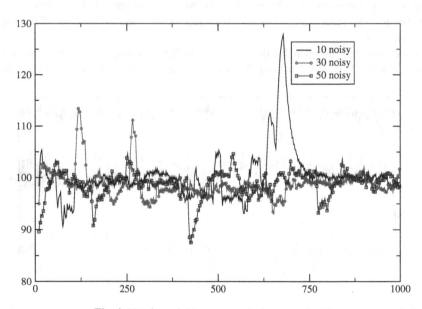

Fig. 4. Number of drivers on main for scenario 2C

the more the small-world metaphor is effective. The high/low peaks in the curves appear because when agent i asks agent j in another group and learns a better route, then all agents of the group of agent i will copy and change, if agent i got a good reward.

Cases with nasty drivers are discussed next. In 3A, p_1 and p_2 are zero and we vary only the number of nasty drivers: 10, 30, 50, 75, 100, and 140. With 10 nasty drivers, those who select the side route at the beginning (5 on average) perform very well because

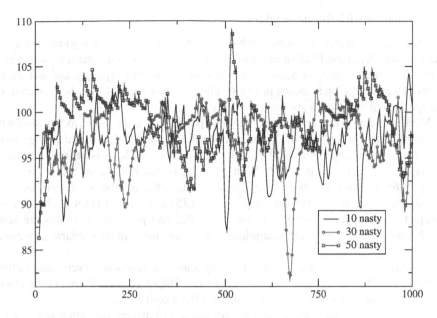

Fig. 5. Number of drivers on main for scenario 3B

all social drivers go to main (again, because they copy the best route in their groups). The remaining nasty drivers get wrong information from the others in the group and go to main as well. Thus, a few nasties are better off driving the secondary route. Similar situations happen for 30 and 50. However, with 75, 100, and 140 nasty drivers their performance decreases (in this order) because around 50% of them go to each route and they are simply too many in each. Compared to situations 1A and 1C (no nasty drivers), here, with the presence of false information, at least some of the nasty drivers have a good performance (especially when they are few).

To escape from this unrealistic situation, simulations were performed in which both social and nasty drives have a probability p_1 (here equal to 0.01) to try another route. Results are depicted in Fig. 5. There is not so much difference comparing cases 3B and 1B: nasty drivers do not cause more fluctuation because every driver can find a better route.

The scenario with nasties was also combined with the small world (3C) using $p_2 = 0.2$. Only 10 nasty drivers are not enough to influence the other 140 (in a situation similar to 1C – see Fig. 1, topmost box), so that all social drivers get stuck selecting main, while the nasty drivers go to both and those on the side route have a much better reward. However, when we increase the number of nasty drivers, the wrong information they give to people outside their group plays the role of diversity and makes other agents select a different route, avoiding everyone being stuck. Because nasty drivers also get information from outside their group, they find out the best route (from someone who does not lie) and eventually all go to either main (2/3) or side (1/3).

An interesting conclusion here is that nasty drivers, although not intensionally, provide the diversity necessary for the whole society to converge to the equilibrium, which is not in the best interest of those nasty drivers who give the false information (since this was actually intended to free their own routes!).

4.2 Scenarios with Recommendation

Now we discuss similar scenarios in which all drivers (except for noisy) receive a recommendation from the PMS in order to direct $2/3$ of them to the main route. In case of 4A, there are no nasty or noisy drivers and all probabilities (p_1, p_2, and p_3) are set to zero. One simulation is shown in Fig. 6. The top most curve shows the expected: on average, $2/3$ of the drivers use the main route.

More interesting are the cases where those probabilities are non-zero. We start with variations in the probability of deviating from the recommendation and change route (4B), i.e. p_3 assuming values of 0.01, 0.1, 0.5, and 1.0, while p_1 is set to 0.01. These results are also depicted in Fig. 6. With $p_3 = 0.01$, the number of drivers on main is not different from the above case. For $p_3 = 0.1$, the number of drivers on main goes down to around 95. Similar for $p_3 = 0.5$ (75) and $p_3 = 1.0$ (50). The case 4C is depicted in the same figure, only for $p_2 = 0.2$ and $p_3 = 0.01$ (others are similar). Asking people from other groups introduces more noise in the scenario (compared to 4A).

Summarizing case 4, the best situation happens of course when everybody follows the recommendation; however this is not realistic. The more noise there is (introduced by the probabilities p_3), the less drivers deviate from equilibrium.

However, case 4 does not account for noisy or nasty drivers. The latter is studied in case 5. We have simulated case 5A with different number of nasty drivers, keeping p_1, p_2, and p_3 at zero. Nasty drivers also get recommendations but, when asked, give the wrong selection. In all cases the average fluctuates around 100 drivers on main because nasty drivers have low influence due to the recommendation. This is pretty much the case also regarding cases 5B and 5C. Neither probability p_1 nor probability p_2 affects the distribution which is in equilibrium.

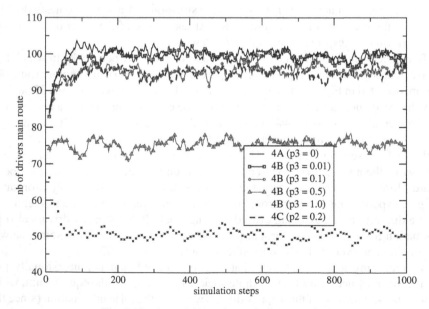

Fig. 6. Number of drivers on main for scenario 4

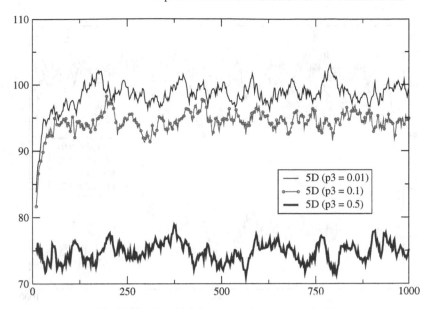

Fig. 7. Number of drivers on main for scenario 5D

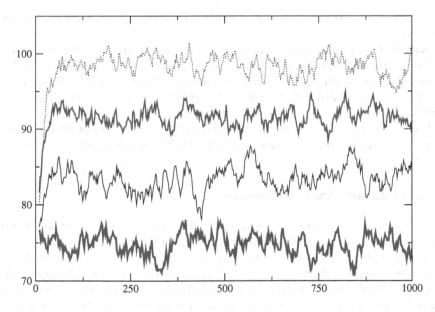

Fig. 8. Number of drivers on main for scenario 6A, for 10, 50, 100, and 150 (top to bottom) noisy drivers

However, this changes when we introduce the probability p_3 of drivers deviating from the recommendation. Fig. 7 shows this situation for different values of p_3 (0.01, 0.1, and 0.5), while keeping p_1 and p_2 at zero. As expected, the number of drivers on main decreases and this happens the more drivers deviate from the recommendation.

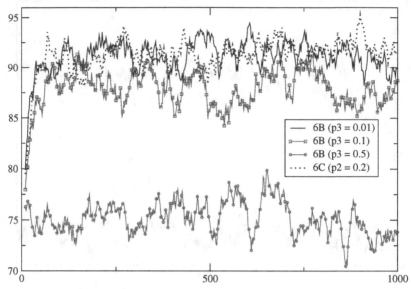

Fig. 9. Number of drivers on main for scenarios 6B and 6C

With $p_3 = 0.5$, the overall behavior is similar to random selection, even if no noisy driver is present.

Scenario 6A includes noisy drivers, and p_1, p_2, and p_3 are zero. Fig. 8 shows the results of the simulations for number of noisy drivers equal to 10, 50, 100, and 150 (from top to down). As expected, in each case we have 2/3 of the social drivers who follow the recommendations and half of the noisy drivers in the main route, which destroys the equilibrium.

Now, when we add non-zero probability for p_3 (6B), the number of drivers on main decreases further because some drivers deviate (Fig. 9). In this figure we also plot for $p_2 = 0.2$ (6C).

4.3   Final Remarks About All Scenarios

Regarding the *performances of groups*, we discuss only cases which are far from the equilibrium because these situations indicate the performance of a given group.

Regarding the analysis of the simulations *without recommendation*, generally, the performance of *noisy drivers* is just boring: they tend to perform around the equilibrium when they are too many (see last entry on Table 1 whose average reward for main and side is $\frac{5}{6} * \frac{1}{2} + \frac{1}{2} * \frac{1}{2} = 2/3$) or when they are too few (they have little influence). In other cases, they tend to destroy the equilibrium pattern, pushing the number of drivers on main below 100.

In the case of *nasty drivers*, their best performance happens for 3A with 10 nasty drivers since only half of these few go to S because of the false information they give inside their group. With the increasing number of nasty drivers, their performance as a group drops. In fact, their worst performance is in case 3A with 140 nasty drivers, followed by 3A with 100 nasty.

In the case of *social drivers*, their best performance is case 3A when there are 140 nasty drivers (which, not surprisingly is the worst performance for these). All of the nasty drivers go to secondary route most of the time, leaving the main route for the few social ones.

The worst performance for social people are 1A and 1C because they all copy the best route in the group and select the same route. In 2A, the performance of social drivers is bad only when there are few noisy drivers; when there are many, these select randomly leaving less people on main, thus increasing the reward of the social drivers. 3A is also bad for social drivers because the few nasty drivers do very well as explained above.

Regarding the performance for the situations *with recommendation*, the observations above do not apply (except for noisy drivers). Regarding nasty drivers, in no case they do very good or very bad. There are high fluctuations over the average for case 5D when p_3 is 0.5 because drivers deviate from the recommendation frequently. Social drivers do well in case 6A, when there is a high number of noisy drivers (again, these select randomly leaving less people on main). They have a low performance in case 4B when p_3 is 1.0 because they all deviate from the recommendation, thus ending up in a situation opposed to the equilibrium.

5   Conclusions and Future Work

This paper discusses the effect of information sharing in a scenario of adaptation regarding which route to take in a route choice scenario. The simulations of the situations described in Section 3 show that it is interesting to have a system giving recommendations to the drivers. However, the performance of the groups decreases when too many drivers deviate from the recommendation, which seems to be a current practice regarding driving because people not always trust the recommendation given bad past experiences or they just want to experiment new routes.

Also, when there is no social attachment and the behavior is myopic towards maximization of short time utility, the performance is bad for nasty drivers (at least), except when they are few. Being a nasty driver pays off up to a certain level only. Another point that can be stressed is that in scenario 3C nasty drivers help the social ones, even if this is not intended.

Regarding the noisy drivers, these tend to destroy good patterns of equilibrium (and hence performance). However they also help social drivers when these are stuck in a bad choice in situations, especially when the probability of meeting acquaintances is non-zero. Therefore, the recommendation system must consider the ratio of noisy drivers. When the number of noisy drivers is unknown or too high, the recommendation may fail.

Finally, this work is based on a series of assumptions that may not be bearable in every real world application. For instance, we assume a global control component that is able to compute the exact utility of the agent decisions for producing the recommendation. In [4], we investigate a scenario in which the control system has imperfect information.

In the future, we plan to also investigate the influence of group size. Also, we will add an adaptation component to the social and nasty drivers, as well as to the PMS so that they can adapt to the changing conditions, with an eventual recognition of nasty drivers in order to mark them as untrustable as information source.

Acknowledgments

The first author is partially supported by CNPq. We also thank the anonymous reviewers for their valuable suggestions.

References

1. B. Arthur. Inductive reasoning, bounded rationality and the bar problem. Technical Report 94–03–014, Santa Fe Institute, 1994.
2. A. L. C. Bazzan, R. H. Bordini, G. Andriotti, R. Viccari, and J. Wahle. Wayward agents in a commuting scenario (personalities in the minotity game). In *Proc. of the Int. Conf. on Multi-Agent Systems (ICMAS)*. IEEE Computer Science, July 2000.
3. A. L. C. Bazzan and A. P. Cavalheiro. Influence of social attachment in a small-world network of agents playing the iterated prisoners dilemma. In S. Parsons and P. Gmytrasiewicz, editors, *5th Workshop of Game Theoretic and Decision Theoretic Agents*, pages 17–24, July 2003. held together with AAMAS 2003.
4. A. L. C. Bazzan and R. Junges. Congestion tolls as utility alignment between agent and system optimum. In *Proceedings of the Fifth Int. Joint Conference on Autonomous Agents and Multiagent Systems*, 2006. submitted to AAMAS 2006.
5. D. Challet and Y. C. Zhang. Emergence of cooperation and organization in an evolutionary game. *Physica A*, 246:407–418, 1997.
6. F. Klügl and A. L. C. Bazzan. Route decision behaviour in a commuting scenario. *Journal of Artificial Societies and Social Simulation*, 7(1), 2004.
7. F. Klügl, A. L. C. Bazzan, and J. Wahle. Selection of information types based on personal utility - a testbed for traffic information markets. In *Proceedings of the Second International Joint Conference on Autonomous Agents and Multi-Agent Systems (AAMAS)*, pages 377–384, Melbourne, Australia, July 2003. ACM Press.
8. S. Milgram. The small world problem. *Psychol. Today*, 2, 1967.
9. J. G. Wardrop. Some theoretical aspects of road traffic research. In *Proceedings of the Institute of Civil Engineers*, volume 2, pages 325–378, 1952.
10. D. J. Watts and S. H. Strogatz. Collective dynamics of 'small-world' networks. *Nature*, 393(6684):397–498, June 1998.

Multiagent Traffic Management:
Opportunities for Multiagent Learning

Kurt Dresner and Peter Stone

Department of Computer Sciences, University of Texas at Austin,
Austin, TX 78712, USA
{kdresner, pstone}@cs.utexas.edu

Abstract. Traffic congestion is one of the leading causes of lost productivity and decreased standard of living in urban settings. In previous work published at AAMAS, we have proposed a novel reservation-based mechanism for increasing throughput and decreasing delays at intersections [3]. In more recent work, we have provided a detailed protocol by which two different classes of agents (intersection managers and driver agents) can use this system [4]. We believe that the domain created by this mechanism and protocol presents many opportunities for multiagent learning on the parts of both classes of agents. In this paper, we identify several of these opportunities and offer a first-cut approach to each.

1 Introduction

Traffic congestion is one of the leading causes of lost productivity and decreased standard of living in urban settings. According to a recent study of 85 U.S. cities [18], annual time spent waiting in traffic has increased from 16 hours per capita to 46 hours per capita since 1982. In the same period, the annual financial cost of traffic congestion has swollen from $14 billion to more than $63 billion (in 2002 US dollars). Each year, Americans burn approximately 5.6 billion gallons of fuel while idling in heavy traffic. Recent advances in artificial intelligence suggest that autonomous vehicle navigation will be possible in the near future. Individual cars can now be equipped with features of autonomy such as cruise control, GPS-based route planning [14,16], and autonomous steering [10,12]. It is inevitable that before long many of the cars on the road will have such capabilities, thus opening up the possibility of autonomous interactions among multiple vehicles.

Multiagent Systems (MAS) is the subfield of AI that aims to provide both principles for construction of complex systems involving multiple agents and mechanisms for coordination of independent agents' behaviors [17]. In earlier work published at AAMAS, we have proposed a MAS-based approach to alleviating traffic congestion, specifically at intersections [4].

Current methods for enabling traffic to flow through intersections include building overpasses and installing traffic lights. However, the former is very expensive and forbids turning, while the latter can be quite inefficient, often requiring cars to remain stopped even when no cars are present on the intersecting road.

At this time, it is possible to create a small-scale system in which all cars are piloted by a central computer. Consider, for example, the task of controlling ten vehicles on an

K. Tuyls et al. (Eds.): LAMAS 2005, LNAI 3898, pp. 129–138, 2006.

open factory floor. However, scaling such a system to handle an intersection in which a city's worth of cars might turn up would involve prohibitively expensive and inefficient communication and control infrastructure. Our goal is to maximize the efficiency of moving cars through intersections with minimal centralized infrastructure. We assume that intersections can be outfitted with a simple wireless communication system and a protocol (which we introduced in a previous paper[2]) for communicating with oncoming traffic and giving permission for cars to pass. In the system we developed, vehicles must traverse intersections according to a set of parameters agreed upon by the vehicle and the intersection manager (as they do today by obeying red and green lights), but otherwise are free to decide for themselves how to drive. Each car is an autonomous agent, and in particular need not surrender control to any centralized decision maker.

We have demonstrated that our novel reservation system dramatically outperforms systems used in common practice, including traffic lights and stop signs. We began with a model in which cars could only go straight and move at constant velocity through the intersection [3]. In our latest results, we have extended the system to allow for turns and acceleration in the intersection [4].

In all of this prior work, the behaviors of both the driver agents and the intersection control agent were all identical and fixed throughout the simulation. However, a main feature of our research has been the definition of an agent-indepedent protocol for car-intersection interaction. In particular, we expect that in general, intersections will have different traffic control algorithms (perhaps depending on the topology of the intersection and/or expected traffic flows), and that indeed each vehicle manufacturer will create proprietary vehicle control algorithms. As long as they adhere to our pre-defined protocol, there is no reason to prevent such diversity.

Once we open the possibility of varying behaviors on the part of the agents, the intersection scenario becomes, in a sense, a multiagent game, admitting for the possibility of strategic behavior on the part of the agents, and ultimately multiagent learning-based approaches.

In this paper, we identify several possible directions for extending our current model that will require such multiagent learning. For each direction, we discuss the strategic issues and propose a first approach towards multiagent learning.

The remainder of this paper is organized as follows. In Section 2, we present a list of properties we believe a multiagent intersection control mechanism should have. In Section 3 we describe the reservation-based system that we have created (in simulation) which we believe has these properties. In Sections 5 and 6 we present several opportunities for using machine learning in the intersection manager and driver agents, respectively. In Section 7, we mention other work that has been done in this area. We conclude in Section 8.

2   Desired Properties

In the process of developing our system we outlined several properties we believed should hold in order for the system to be realistic and practical.

1. The agents should only communicate information which is necessary for the system to function properly.

2. The agents should only have access to information that can be reliably obtained with current technology.
3. Communication failure (dropped messages) should not violate the system's safety properties.
4. The vehicles should be treated as individual agents, and no centralized controller should have any more control over them than necessary.
5. The system should incorporate a simple communication protocol that allows agents to know only a minimal amount about each other. As long as agents obey and understand the protocol, no extra information exchange or other interaction should be required.
6. Every vehicle should eventually make it through the intersection (i.e. no deadlocks or starvation).

Many of these properties also ensure that the system will be amenable to machine learning techniques. Specifically, the simple, reliable protocol ensures that agents are more or less self-contained — the intersection manager isn't extensively involved in the driver agent's decision making process (and vice versa). Furthermore, the requirement that every vehicle makes it through the intersection means that a machine learning algorithm in its early stages will not bring the system to a halt as a result of risky exploration.

3 The Reservation System

In our previous work, we proposed a novel reservation-based multi-agent approach to alleviating traffic, specifically at intersections. This system consisted of two types of agents: *intersection managers* and *driver agents*. Each system consists of an intersection manager for each intersection and a driver agent for each vehicle. Intersection managers are responsible for directing the vehicles through the intersection, while the driver agents are responsible for controlling the vehicles to which they are assigned. To improve the throughput and efficiency of the system, the driver agents "call ahead" to the intersection manager and request space-time in the intersection. The intersection manager then determines whether or not these requests can be met. Depending on the decision the intersection manager makes, the driver agent either records the parameters of the request (the *reservation*) and attempts to meet them, or it makes another request at a later time. We have described our implementation of a driver agent in previous papers [4,2]. Note that our implementations of the reservation system and the driver agent are just two possibilities. As long as the agents adhere to the protocol, the system will still work. In practice, each agent could run a different algorithm or use a different heuristic to improve performance.

To determine whether or not a request can be met, the reservation manager simulates the journey of the vehicle across the intersection, which it divides into a grid of $n \times n$ tiles. The parameter n is called the *granularity* of the reservation manager. At each time step of the simulation, it determines which tiles the vehicle occupies. If throughout this simulation, no required tile is occupied by another vehicle (from a previous reservation), the manager reserves the tiles for this vehicle.

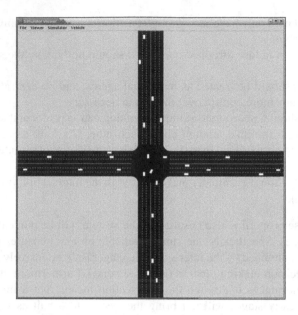

Fig. 1. A screenshot of our simulator in action

In order to evaluate the performance of the reservation system, we created a custom simulator. A screenshot of the simulator in action can be seen in Figure 1. We tested the reservation system against two other *intersection control policies* - the overpass and the traffic light. An intersection control policy is a method the intersection managers use to determine when specific vehicles are allowed in the intersection. Using the simulator, we showed that using the reservation-based policy, vehicles crossing an intersection experience much lower *delay* (increase in travel time from the optimal) versus the traffic light. Furthermore, we showed that the reservation-based policy also drastically increases the throughput of the intersection. For any realistic intersection control policy, there exists an amount of traffic above which vehicles arrive at the intersection more frequently than they can go through the intersection. At this point, the average delay experienced by vehicles travelling through the intersection grows without bound. Compared to the traffic light, this amount of traffic is much higher for the reservation system. Videos of our most recent developments can be found at http://www.cs.utexas.edu/users/kdresner/papers/2005aamas/.

4   Communication Protocol

In our latest work, we added the protocol by which the agents can communicate the bare minimum of information necessary to function appropriately. The protocol consists of several message types for each kind of agent, as well as some rules governing when the messages should be sent and what sorts of guarantees accompany them. A detailed specification of the protocol including full syntax and semantics is available in our technical report [2]. We believe that this protocol will help facilitate the application of machine learning techniques to the intersection domain. Here we give a brief overview of the types of messages available to the agents using this protocol.

4.1 Vehicle → Intersection

There are four types of messages that can be sent from vehicles to the intersection.

1. REQUEST — This is the message a vehicle sends when it does not have a reservation and wishes to make one. It contains the properties of the vehicle (ID number, performance, size, etc.) as well as some properties of the proposed reservation (arrival time, arrival velocity, type of turn, arrival lane, etc.).
2. CHANGE-REQUEST — This is the message a vehicle sends when it has a reservation, but would like to switch to a different set of parameters.
3. CANCEL — This is the message a vehicle sends when it no longer desires its current reservation.
4. RESERVATION-COMPLETED — This message is used when the vehicle has completed its traversal of the intersection. This message can be used to collect statistics for each vehicle, which can be recorded in order to analyze and improve the performace of the intersection manager.

4.2 Intersection → Vehicle

There are three types of messages that can be sent from the intersection to the individual vehicles.

1. CONFIRMATION — This message is a response to a vehicle's REQUEST (or CHANGE-REQUEST) message. It can contain a counter-offer by the intersection. The reservation parameters in this message are implicitly accepted by the vehicle, and must be explicitly cancelled if the driver agent of the vehicle does not approve. Note that this is safe to faulty communication — the worst that can happen is that the intersection reserves space that does not get used.
2. REJECTION — By sending this message, an intersection can inform a vehicle that the parameters sent in the latest REQUEST (or CHANGE-REQUEST) were not acceptable, and that the intersection either could not or did not want to make a counter-offer. This message also contains a field indicating whether or not the rejection was because the reservation manager requires the vehicle to stop at the intersection before entering. This lets the driver agent know that it should not attempt any more reservations until it reaches the intersection.
3. ACKNOWLEDGMENT — This message acknowledges the receipt of a CANCEL or RESERVATION-COMPLETED message.

5 Learning Opportunities for the Intersection Manager

At this point in the paper we have described the current state of our implementation, describing mainly the aspects required to motivate the multiagent learning opportunities we see in the future. We now turn our attention to those opportunities. Our goal at the outset of this project was to improve the efficiency of intersections. It seems natural, then, to start with the agent controlling which vehicles have access to the intersection: the intersection manager.

5.1   Delayed Response

Incorporating any nontrivial learning into the intersection manager may require a few conceptual changes to the intersection manager. As it stands, all intersection managers in the system respond immediately to requests made by vehicles. Given this constraint, the current reservation system performs as well as it can — it can't tell what is going to happen in the future. However, if we relax this constraint and allow the reservation manager to respond to requests at a later time, the intersection manager would have time to get a feel for the competing requests and can make a more well-informed decision.

This modification suggests a straightforward method for determining whether or not to grant reservations. When the intersection manager receives a request, it can calculate the last possible point at which it can respond without forcing the sending vehicle to slow down for lack of having a reservation. The intersection manager holds on to the reservation request until that time. In the meantime, it considers other vehicles' requests and can then grant reservations more efficiently.

Allowing this delayed response offers an immediate improvement over the current system. Consider the following example in which three vehicles, A, B, and C all send reservation requests to the intersection manager a short time after one another. Now suppose that vehicle A's request conflicts with both B's and C's (that is, they require the same reservation tile at a specific time), but that B's request does not conflict with C's. With our current system, the reservation manager would approve A's request, but reject both B and C. With the new system, only A would be rejected.

In addition to improving the efficiency of the system, adding a delayed response creates some opportunites to apply machine learning. In particular, as the number of outstanding reservation requests increases, the number of possible responses scales exponentially. Since timeliness is an important constraint, the intersection manager will need to intelligently search through set of possible responses in order to optimize the overall performance. Learned search control knowledge based on off-line optimization trials could play an important role in this regard.

Furthermore, projected incoming traffic can also play an important role. Once a reservation is accepted, it can't be cancelled. However, the parameters of reservations made in the near future are going to be related to the parameters of the reservations made now. For example, in heavy traffic, it may be best to reject a reservation request even when it doesn't conflict with many other requests in the same time frame — granting that reservation may cause the system to perform much more poorly at a slightly later time. In this sense, a learned model of incoming traffic as a function of time of day, day of week, and/or recent history could improve performance by serving as an input to the forward simulations of the impact of any given decision.

5.2   Vehicles with Priorities

In our current simulation, all vehicles are treated as equally important with regards to the performance metric. However in practice, the intersection should be able to give preferential treatment to a subset of vehicles, such as emergency vehicles. For example, a normal commuter would have a low priority, a police car would have a high priority, and an ambulance or fire truck en route to a fire would have yet a higher priority.

The first-cut solution to this problem is straightforward: whenever the reservation manager receives a request that conflicts with a request which it is currently holding, it rejects the lower priority request. This does enforce the constraint that higher priority vehicles are given preference, but is not optimal by any stretch of the imagination. Consider again three vehicles: a daily commuter, a police car, and an ambulance racing a heart-attack victim to the hospital. If the commuter is in front of the ambulance and it is forced to yield to the police car, it will hold up the ambulance as well. If the intersection manager instead just allowed the commuter through, the ambulance may have been able to pass unhindered. The actual relationship between the times of a particular vehicle's reservation, that vehicle's priority, the characteristics of other approaching vehicles, and how much it is worth to the intersection to accept the reservation is very complicated. However, a reinforcement learning algorithm may be able to capture this relationship. When vehicles complete a trip across the intersection, the intersection manager could be given a reward signal inversely proportional to the delay the vehicle experienced. The manager could eventually learn to grant reservations based on the vehicles' priorities and the current traffic patterns so as to maximize the system's overall future reward.

5.3   The Intersection as a Market

Another consideration is that vehicles might have to pay to use the intersection. With states in the U.S. such as Oregon and California already considering taxing motorists by the mile, this is not far-fetched. Along with reservation requests, vehicles would transmit a bid. The reservation manager's goal would be to collect the most revenue. A first-cut solution would be analagous to the example with vehicle priorities: when a reservation comes in, reject any currently pending reservations that conflict with it and have a lower bid. This is obviously not optimal — consider any set of n vehicles such that for all $0 < i < n$, vehicle i and $i+1$ conflict. As long as the bid for vehicle $i+1$ is greater than that of vehicle i, the reservation manager will wind up only letting through vehicle n. Instead, it might have been able to allow through vehicles $1, 3, \ldots$. This is approximately $\frac{n}{2}$ vehicles and would generate a lot more revenue.

In this context, the intersection can be framed as a continually clearing combinatorial auction. The decision for any given grid cell must occur whenever the first car that needs it is about to enter the intersection. There is a tradeoff between letting a car through and retaining flexibility for later that the intersection manager must maintain. That is, letting an individual car through is good for the intersection manager. However, not letting that car through may lead to more positive benifits later on. Since even a single combinatorial auction can be computationally costly to solve, continually clearing, interacting combinatorial auctions are likely to be intractable. However, based on off-line simulation, the intersection manager could learn expected marginal values for granting a request to a given driver and therefore more effectively balance the above tradeoff.

6   Learning Opportunities for the Driver Agent

While there are many opportunities for the intersection manager to improve, they are mostly of the form of a single agent learning how to interact with multiple fixed agents (the drivers). The true *multiagent* learning opportunities lie in the vehicles.

6.1   Bidding in the Market System

In Section 5, we showed how a market could play an important role in the intersection management problem. In the example we gave, it wasn't clear how the agents should determine what bid to place with their reservation requests. An agent could start with a low bid and then continue raising it until one gets accepted, but this process takes time and it could wind up severely delayed just because it wasn't willing to commit to the higher bid up front. This is a very challenging problem — to solve it effectively would require a more detailed response from the intersection manager: the amount of the bid that caused the request to be rejected, the average bid amount for this particular intersection at this time of day, and so forth. Even with this type of information, though, it is unclear how to proceed. Learning the relationship between time of day, day of week, recent traffic reports, and a reasonable price for a reservation is a task well-suited to a neural network or other supervised learning algorithm. In off-line simulation, many vehicles could be run through the intersection, and when one gets a reservation, it could use the cost it eventually had to pay as a target value, weighted perhaps by how quickly it got the reservation.

6.2   Lane Changing

One of the features of our reservation system is the complete autonomy of driver agents while they are outside the intersection. Thus, when considering how to incorporate some sort of lane changing behavior, ideally we'd like to avoid having the intersection manager tell the vehicles which lane they should be in. However, as in the previous example, having the reservation manager (or some other source) provide the vehicle with relevant information could be extremely useful. For example, if an intersection manager realizes that one lane has a lot of cancelled reservations (e.g. from a stalled vehicle in that lane preventing other vehicles from fulfilling their reservations), this information might let vehicles know that they should switch to another lane instead of trying to make it through in the lane with the stalled car. It would then be interesting to explore how much and what kind of information the intersection manager is required to give the vehicles such that they can best choose which lane to use. If the driver agents were able to learn a better policy for lane choice, we could examine which information is useful for making that decision without having to first determine precisely how they are using it.

6.3   Making Better Reservations

In the current implementation, driver agents must find a way to make reservations that they can keep. To do this, they must be able to accurately predict when they will reach the intersection, accounting for delays from other vehicles and road hazards. In a real-life implementation, statistics and data the intersection manager has collected may be useful and thus made available to the driver agent. For example, as in both the bidding and lane-changing examples, the intersection manager may be able to provide vehicles with statistics on recent reservations. Once again, how to use these data is not immediately obvious and certainly depends on the algorithms (learning or otherwise) used by the other drivers. While the sensors in our simulated vehicles do not do it currently, they might be able to track the speed of the vehicle in front over the 10 seconds before making a reservation, or determine that the vehicle in front is a public bus and therefore might stop before the intersection for a long period of time. Given these new inputs, the driver agent could learn to better predict when and how it will arrive at the intersection.

7 Related Work

Rasche and Naumann have worked extensively on decentralized solutions to intersection collision avoidance problems [9,11]. Many approaches focus on improving current technology (systems of traffic lights). For example, Roozemond allows intersections to act autonomously, sharing the data they gather [15]. The intersections then use this information to make both short- and long-term predictions about the traffic and adjust accordingly. This approach still assumes human-controlled vehicles. Bazzan has used an approach using both MAS and evolutionary game theory which involves multiple intersection managers (agents) that must focus not only on local goals, but also on global goals [1].

Work is also being done with regard to the control of the individual vehicles. Hallé and Chaib-draa have taken a MAS approach to collaborative driving by allowing vehicles to form *platoons*, groups of varying degrees of autonomy, that then coordinate using a hierarchical driving agent architecture [5]. While not focusing on intersections, Moriarty and Langley have shown that reinforcement learning can train efficient driver agents for lane, speed, and route selection during freeway driving [8].

On real autonomous vehicles, Kolodko and Vlacic have created a primitive system for intersection control which is very similar to the granularity-1 reservation system [7].

Actual systems in practice (not MAS) for traffic light optimization include TRANSYT [13], which is an off-line system requiring extensive data gathering and analysis, and SCOOT [6], which is an advancement over TRANSYT, responding to changes in traffic loads on-line. However, almost all of the methods in practice or discussed above still rely on traditional signalling systems.

8 Conclusion

The intersection management problem presents a challenging yet promising domain for multi-agent learning research. The intersection control mechanism we developed is a vast improvement over current methods, but with a few extensions poses some challenging problems. We have provided several examples of such problems where machine learning could be used to improve the performance of both intersection managers and driver agents. These examples are at this point speculative. In ongoing research we are investigating how to bring them and other learning opportunities into practice.

References

1. A. L. C. Bazzan. A distributed approach for coordination of traffic signal agents. *Autonomous Agents and Multi-Agent Systems*, 10(2):131–164, March 2005.
2. K. Dresner and P. Stone. Multiagent traffic management: A protocol for defining intersection control policies. Technical Report UT-AI-TR-04-315, The University of Texas at Austin, Department of Computer Sciences, AI Laboratory, December 2004.

3. K. Dresner and P. Stone. Multiagent traffic management: A reservation-based intersection control mechanism. In *The Third International Joint Conference on Autonomous Agents and Multiagent Systems*, July 2004.

4. K. Dresner and P. Stone. Multiagent traffic management: An improved intersection control mechanism. In *The Fourth International Joint Conference on Autonomous Agents and Multiagent Systems*, pages 471–477, July 2005.

5. S. Hallé and B. Chaib-draa. A collaborative driving system based on multiagent modelling and simulations. *Journal of Transportation Research Part C (TRC-C): Emergent Technologies*, 2005. To appear.

6. P. B. Hunt, D. I. Robertson, R. D. Bretherton, and R. I. Winton. SCOOT - a traffic responsive method of co-ordinating signals. Technical Report 1014, TRL Laboratory, 1981.

7. J. Kolodko and L. Vlacic. Cooperative autonomous driving at the intelligent control systems laboratory. *IEEE Intelligent Systems*, 18(4):8–11, July/August 2003.

8. D. Moriarty and P. Langley. Learning cooperative lane selection strategies for highways. In *Proceedings of the Fifteenth National Conference on Artificial Intelligence*, pages 684–691, Madison, WI, 1998. AAAI Press.

9. R. Naumann and R. Rasche. Intersection collision avoidance by means of decentralized security and communication management of autonomous vehicles. In *Proceedings of the 30th ISATA - ATT/IST Conference*, 1997.

10. D. A. Pormerleau. *Neural Network Perception for Mobile Robot Guidance*. Kluwer Academic Publishers, 1993.

11. R. Rasche, R. Naumann, J. Tacken, and C. Tahedl. Validation and simulation of decentralized intersection collision avoidance algorithm. In *Proceedings of IEEE Conference on Intelligent Transportation Systems (ITSC 97)*, 1997.

12. C. W. Reynolds. Steering behaviors for autonomous characters. In *Proceedings of the Game Developers Conference*, pages 763–782, 1999.

13. D. I. Robertson. TRANSYT — a traffic network study tool. Technical Report TRRL-LR-253, Transport and Road Research Laboratory, Crowthorne, 1969.

14. S. Rogers, C.-N. Flechter, and P. Langley. An adaptive interactive agent for route advice. In O. Etzioni, J. P. Müller, and J. M. Bradshaw, editors, *Proceedings of the Third International Conference on Autonomous Agents (Agents'99)*, pages 198–205, Seattle, WA, USA, 1999. ACM Press.

15. D. A. Roozemond. Using intelligent agents for urban traffic control control systems. In *Proceedings of the International Conference on Artificial Intelligence in Transportation Systems and Science*, pages 69–79, 1999.

16. T. Schonberg, M. Ojala, J. Suomela, A. Torpo, and A. Halme. Positioning an autonomous off-road vehicle by using fused DGPS and inertial navigation. In *2nd IFAC Conference on Intelligent Autonomous Vehicles*, pages 226–231, 1995.

17. P. Stone and M. Veloso. Multiagent systems: A survey from a machine learning perspective. *Autonomous Robots*, 8(3):345–383, July 2000.

18. Texas Transportation Institute. 2004 urban mobility report, September 2004. Accessed at http://mobility.tamu.edu/ums in December 2004.

Dealing with Errors in a Cooperative Multi-agent Learning System

Constança Oliveira e Sousa and Luis Custódio

Institute for Systems and Robotics, Instituto Superior Técnico,
Av. Rovisco Pais 1049-001 Lisboa, Portugal
c.osousa@sapo.pt, lmmc@isr.ist.utl.pt

Abstract. This paper presents some methods of dealing with the problem of cooperative learning in a multi-agent system, in error prone environments. A system is developed that learns by reinforcement and is robust to errors that can come from the agents sensors, from another agent that shares wrong information or even from the communication channel.

1 Introduction

In robotics, learning a specific task in an efficient manner is usually considered individually for one robot. However, when the application involves a set of robots with common objectives, it can be an advantage if the robots work as a team, and share knowledge to accelerate the learning process. Unfortunately, in real environments there are often errors that interfere in the agents perception and delay learning.

In this paper three sources of errors are considered:

- Perception errors: an agent can have errors in perceiving the environment due to, e.g., its sensors malfunctioning, causing an inaccurate representation of the world.
- Communication errors: in a multi-agent system with communication between agents, the information shared can contain errors. In this case, it is important to have a robust system that prevents errors propagating from agent to agent.
- Position errors: with real robots it is common to have errors that mislead the robot about its location in the world, e.g., odometry errors. This source of errors is not predictable and its negative effects are not easy to handle.

In this work we build robust agents by developing methods that handle these errors, so that they do not interfere in the worlds learning process.

To increase the applicability of the methods developed, the learning process was made independent of the world to explore: the agents start learning with no knowledge of the world, and stop their learning process autonomously. A limitation of this method is that the world to be explored must be bounded by walls. We have also introduced a method of self-orientation so that the agents

K. Tuyls et al. (Eds.): LAMAS 2005, LNAI 3898, pp. 139–154, 2006.

can relate their frames of reference, because communication between agents is possible only if they are oriented.

In this paper we also propose some innovative methods to accelerate the worlds learning rate. We have introduced (i) a method that varies the initial position of the agents at the beginning of each episode, in order to improve the learning process and to make it independent of the environment, (ii) a change in the learning algorithm so that an agent learns faster, and (iii) a criteria so that the agents know what and when to communicate. This criteria is based on how important a Q-value is. If it is very important, it shall be communicated. If not, it shall not be communicated. Note that if there is too much sharing of information, the communication system can be full and, therefor, work improperly. However, the maximum communication quantity is ignored in this work, although it can be specified.

The price to pay for the improvements obtained is an increase in the memory that an agent must have available.

2   Reinforcement Learning

One of the computational approaches to learning by interaction that is often used is Reinforcement Learning (RL), by which an agent learns based on the information that it receives from the world: rewards are received if the action executed by the agent provides a positive contribution to reaching the goal, and penalties otherwise [1].

2.1   Reinforcement Learning Elements

The RL problem involves an *agent* that decides and learns, and an *environment* (or *world*), composed of everything external to the agent.

Let us assume an experiment takes place during a discrete time $t=0,1,2,....$ At each instant t, the agent receives a representation of the environment state, $s_t \in S$, where S is the set of possible states, based on which it chooses an action $a_t \in A(s_t)$, where $A(s_t)$ is the set of possible actions in state s_t. As a response to the action taken, the agent receives a numerical reinforcement, $r_t \in R$, where R is the set of possible reinforcements, and moves to a new state, s_{t+1}.

At each time instant, the agent maps the state space to a probability space that weights each possible action in that instant. This mapping is called a policy π_t, where $\pi_t(s,a)$ is the probability of choosing the action a in state s at instant t ($s_t = s$ and $a_t = a$). The agent's objective is to find a policy that maximizes the reinforcements, i.e., to find a sequence of actions that leads to the goal state with the minimum possible costs [1].

2.2   Decision Making in a Stochastic World

In classical Artificial Intelligence, the *objective* for a certain task is a desired state of the world, and *planning* is finding an optimal path to the goal state. When the world is deterministic, planning can be reduced to a graph search problem,for which a wide variety of solution methods exist [2]. In a stochastic world, planning is not a graph search problem because transitions between states are non-deterministic [1].

In a stochastic world with a transition model $P(s_{t+1}|s_t, a_t)$, an agent currently in state s_t will choose the optimal action a_t^* that maximizes the expected utility [3].

2.3   Markov Decision Process

An agent's sequential decision making in an observable stochastic world with a Markovian[1] transition model is called a Markov Decision Process (MDP). In an MDP it is assumed that an agent receives an immediate reinforcement $r_t \in R$ from the environment, in each state s_t. The agent's task is to maximize its total *discounted future reward*

$$R_t = r_t + \gamma r_{t+1} + \gamma^2 r_{t+2} + \ldots = \sum_{k=0}^{T} \gamma^k r_{t+k} \tag{1}$$

where, assuming an episodic environment, T is the terminal time instant and $\gamma \in [0, 1]$ is a discount rate that ensures that even with infinite sequences the sum is finite.

The state-action pair value function for a certain policy, also known as *Q-value*, defines the future discounted expected reward by choosing, at each time instant t, an action a_t for state s_t, following an optimal policy, and can be described by the *Bellman optimality equation* for Q-values,

$$Q^*(s_t, a_t) = r_t + \gamma \sum_{s_{t+1} \in S} P(s_{t+1}|s_t, a_t) \max_{a \in A} Q^*(s_{t+1}, a) . \tag{2}$$

Note that rule (2) corresponds to updating the policy, in a state s_t, for a given action that maximizes the Q-value of the next state s_{t+1} [1].

An optimal policy is any policy that allows an optimal sequence of actions to be found

$$a^*(s) = \arg\max_{a \in A} Q^*(s, a) . \tag{3}$$

Equation (3) is simple to calculate because it is not necessary to know the worlds transition model [3].

2.4   Q-Learning

The *Q-Learning* method qualifies state-action pairs: at each time instant t, an agent in state s_t will choose an available action a_t using an exploring strategy, execute that action a_t which takes it to the next state s_{t+1} and register the reinforcement r_t that the world provides. The agent then updates the state-action pair value correspondent to action a_t in state s_t, based on the following update rule:

---

[1] A world is said to be Markovian if the information that each state gives in a certain instant t summarizes all of the information of the past that is relevant to fulfil a given task [3]. For a more accurate definition see [1, section 3.5].

$$Q(s,a) \leftarrow Q(s,a) + \alpha[r + \gamma \max_{a'} Q(s',a') - Q(s,a)] \tag{4}$$

where α is the step size, and $0 < \alpha < 1$ can change from iteration to iteration and

$$\sum_t \alpha_t = +\infty \text{ and } \sum_t \alpha_t^2 = const . \tag{5}$$

All that is needed to guarantee the convergence of the method is the continuous updating of the pairs, using well studied exploration strategies such as ε-greedy and *Softmax*. If this condition is verified and if conditions in (5) hold, Q converges to the optimal value Q^* with probability one [1].

3   Proposed Approach

The basic generic principles of RL were presented in the previous section. In the following section an environment is specified, as well as the agents structure used to develop the proposed methods. Then, the agent's performance will be evaluated. Assuming there is a team of agents, we want every agent to find the optimal policy in an environment with errors.

3.1   The Environment

A discrete, stochastic, episodic and bounded world is used in this work, represented by a grid map in Fig.1. There are three types of states, distinguished by the value of the reinforcement with which they respond to an agents action:

- *walls* undesirable states; these states constitute the worlds boundaries; represented in Fig.1 by crosses; respond to an agents action with a penalty of -10;
- *goal* state terminal state; responds to the agents action with a reward of +1; identified in Fig.1 by a star;
- *passing* states all other states; respond to an agents action with reinforcement -1/33.

There is only one *goal* state, and the initial state cannot be a wall. The world must have two *pillars*, for agents to orientate themselves and communicate with each other. A pillar can be any state of the world which not only responds with the corresponding reinforcement, but also identifies itself as a fixed mark, a reference to all agents, allowing them to be oriented in relation to this mark.

3.2   The Agent

All agents used in this work are identical and very simple, in order to facilitate the analysis of the results and the causes of the observed behaviors. An agents task is to learn the shortest path, minimizing the Manhattan distance, from any state of the world to the goal state. This means that each agent must find the optimal policy of the world, from any state to the goal state, as shown in Fig.1.

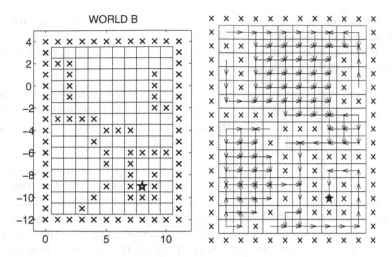

Fig. 1. World B, used to test the developed ideas. The arrows in the figure on the right show the set of optimal policies that can be found in World B.

Movement. The actions an agent can take are to move North, South, East or West and changing direction therefore implies a rotation and a translation. When there are multiple agents, it is assumed that they move sequentially, one at a time, and thus a communication order known by all the agents is imposed [3].

A priori knowledge. What an agent knows when it starts:

★ its learning parameters (in this work it was used $\alpha = 0.4$ and $\gamma = 0.9$);
★ the actions it can take;
★ its own identification number;
★ its sensors uncertainty as well as some other parameters used for error detection.

An agent does not know the other agents characteristics nor the worlds (neither its size nor its own position in the worlds frame).

Memory. As an agent moves, it holds the following information in its memory:

★ a *World Model* with the knowledge acquired, which is a grid map representing the states visited, for each possible action. This is only updated by the individual agent;
★ a *Shared World*, another model of the world, where the values of the state-action pairs are updated with information provided by all agents. This Shared World will have an important role in accelerating learning and will help the agents to be more robust to incorrect information coming from other agents;
★ the number of visits to each state;
★ the reinforcements received and the information shared;
★ transformation matrices between agents internal frames;
★ a mail box to keep the other agents responses to the questions that the agent itself posed.

The growth in memory is the price to pay for the robustness of the agents, as the amount of memory needed to save all information is minimized by $(6 + n) * N$, where n is the number of agents learning the world, and N is the number of state-action pairs the world has.

State Machine. An agent can operate in two modes: a *Learning* mode where it chooses an action and learns the world following the method mentioned above, and a *Directional* mode in which the agent executes a sequence of previously planned actions that lead it to a certain state of the world.

Orientation. Consider a fixed world frame, identified by two pillars, in which the agents are moving. While exploring, each agent will eventually find the pillars and, when it does, it will transmit the pillars location in its internal frame to the other agents. When the other agents receive these coordinates, they can relate them with the pillars coordinates in their own internal frame and then determine the transformation matrix that relates both agents frames. Note that an agent does not know, and does not need to know, its location in the world frame: it just has to know its relation to the other agents internal frame, in order to understand what they communicate.

This orientation method is very simple because it does not require a large amount of memory nor a large data analysis, and it is easy to implement: recognizing a pillar can be as easy as identifying a color, and the only requirement is that both pillars must be in different states of the world and distinguishable from each other.

Shared Worlds and Trust Factor. A formal way to describe communication is to consider each communicative act as an action that updates the agents knowledge about a certain state.

Ideally, it would be desirable that each agent share all its knowledge. In practice, sharing all information is not reasonable because, even if communication between agents were reliable, there would be a large amount of information traveling between agents requiring extensive and complex data analysis and consequent processing time.

Each agent has its independent world model and policies map. When an agent finds a result that it considers relevant to share, it transmits the obtained Q-value and the correspondent state-action pair. An agent that receives the shared information updates its world by adding that information to its knowledge, updating the correspondent state-action pair following the rule

$$Q_R(s,a) = \frac{g_R Q_R(s,a) + g_T Q_T(s,a)}{g_R + g_t} \tag{6}$$

where index R refers to the agent that receives the shared state-action pair, $Q(s,a)$, sent by the transmitter agent represented by index T. $g_T \in [0,1]$ is a certain trust factor that quantifies how much agent R trusts agent T, and $g_R \in [0,1]$ is the trust that agent R has in itself.

The trust factor defines how much an agent believes in the information received which, in turn, depends on how much it trusts the transmitting agent:

* $g_T = 0 \rightarrow$ the agent R does not believe in the information sent by agent T, and does not update its own state with this new information. This may be useful if agent T sends incorrect information as a result of, e.g., a malfunction of its sensors.
* $g_T = 1 \rightarrow$ agent R fully believes in the information sent, and absorbs it totally.
* $g_R = 0 \rightarrow$ agent R does not believe in itself and refuses its own knowledge. This can occur if the information of the agent itself is incorrect because, e.g., of a malfunction of its own sensors. Here an agent continues its learning "seeing through other agent's eyes".
* $g_R = 0$ and $g_T = 0 \rightarrow$ the state action pair is not updated. If this happens it means that the agent does not trust anyone, not even itself.
* g has another value $\rightarrow$ updates the world by weighing the received information by value g.

When trust factors are zero, the presence of the respective agents does not contribute to increase worlds knowledge nor to accelerate the joint learning. However, an agent that does not believe in itself (because it is not working correctly) can be guided by the others and will not be lost, which is a form of cooperation.

The trust factor can change. Whenever an error, coming from the agent itself or from another agent, is detected, the correspondent trust factor decreases following $g_{k+1} = \frac{g_k}{\tau}$, where k is the instant where the errors occur and $\tau > 1$ is a variation rate previously defined.[2] If an error is detected more than a certain number of successive times, the correspondent trust factor becomes null. This predefined limit is introduced before the learning process begins.

In the same way, if the errors are no longer detected, the trust factor for the source increases following $g_{k+1} = g_k \cdot \tau$. If the error is no longer detected for a certain number of consecutive times, the trust factor is fixed at its maximum value. This predefined limit from which the agent considers that the information source is correct, is the same as the one referred above.

If, for any reason, an agent receives incorrect information during its learning process, it will no longer believe in the values shared by that agent from that point onwards. However, values sent earlier could also be incorrect, resulting in a deficient update of both worlds. To avoid these cases of misleading the learning process from its objective, each agent has two world models: one that is only updated with its own knowledge, and other that is also updated with the information received by the other agents, the *Shared World*. An agent generally decides using its Shared World values, however every time it notices that the information received could have been incorrect, it appeals to its own World Model, which should still be free of errors.

As this Shared World is updated with information that comes from all agents, the policies found are different from the ones found using the World Model updated by each agent individually, and converge faster to an optimal policy.

---

[2] In this work $\tau = 10$ was used for the simulations.

3.3   The Learning Algorithm

Initially the algorithm used in this work was Q-Learning, but later a small change was made to this method in order to speed up learning convergence. For instance, consider the state (10,0) in world B in Fig.1. If the agent chooses to go South, which takes it to state (10,-1), the Q-Learning updating rule considers the best state-action pair of this last state, which corresponds, in this specific case, to go North, which takes the agent back to state (10,0), because the other directions would lead it to walls. In this case, and in all other cases in which the best action of the next state is the one that brings the agent back to its actual position, it would be preferable, when updating the Q-value, only to consider the best action that is not the reverse action. This method can be reduced to Q-learning with the following update rule

$$Q(s,a) \leftarrow Q(s,a) + \alpha[r + \gamma \max_{a'} Q(s',a') - Q(s,a)] \qquad (7)$$

$$\text{with } a' \neq reverse\_action(a)$$

where $reverse\_action(a)$ is the action that leads the agent from state s back to state s. Note that this rule does not limit the actions that the agent can take. It only removes the reverse action from the set of possible actions that can be taken in the next state, from which the state-action pair with maximum value will be elected.

This method increases learning performance in worlds with many walls or mazes, such as world B, where about 9,1% of the steps are speared. In a world with no inner walls, changing the Q-Learning algorithm as mentioned above does not bring any advantage; on the contrary, it introduces a relay of 25% of steps because it is ignoring one of each possible actions, which are 4, thereby ignoring 1/4 of the information.

In this work, we developed criteria so that the agent could decide autonomously when to stop the learning process. Focusing on the various states Q-values, as time increases, it is expected that the Q-values get closer to the respective optimal values, which implies that the variation between successive actualizations of each Q-value decreases. When this variation is inferior to a small threshold, called *Stop Limit*, the optimal value can be considered achieved and the correspondent state-action pair learnt.

An agent can know when it has found an optimal value, but does not know which states are worth learning to fulfil its task, so it keeps learning until it knows the entire world. We assume that the world is learnt when all states reach that Stop Limit.

For this work the Stop Limit was fixed at 0.04% of the maximum Q-value attained.[3] The higher this percentage, the fewer steps an agent will give to reach the end of the learning process but, at the same time, it is important to find a percentage small enough to ensure that all states are correctly learnt. The highest value that verifies this last condition for world B is 0.04%.

---

[3] The maximum Q-value attained is 10 given the learning parameters ($\alpha = 0.4$ and $\gamma = 0.9$) and the reinforcements used.

3.4   Cooperative Learning in Environments with Errors

In this section we will analyze how we can protect learning from errors. Given the different types of possible consequences of the errors, let us separate the errors into three distinct sets *Perception Errors, Communication Errors* and *Position Errors*.

Results presented here were obtained using agents that:

→ use *initial state variation*: in order to allow an agent to return autonomously to an initial position, it was endowed with a state machine, as mentioned in section 3.2, allowing it to return directly (Directional mode) to a new starting position after it finishes an episode. An agent saves the number of visits to every state, and which are already learnt (i.e., which crossed the Stop Limit). Therefore, at the end of each episode, it can find out which area is less visited and not learned yet, and return to a state of that area by a path found using a breadth-first search. When it reaches its new starting position (which varies from episode to episode), it restarts the learning process (Learning mode). This automatically provides a more uniform distribution of the agents over the physical space of the world thereby improving the learning process and making it independent of the environment to explore.

→ share only information that they are sure is correct, which is walls[4] and all states that have already passed the Stop Limit. Crossing the Stop Limit is the criteria used to know which states are already learnt and also what information is relevant to share. Results considering self-interested agents exploring the world in the presence of other exploring agents can be found in [4]. It addresses the issues of communication and cooperation, and how one influences the other, as well as a comparison with non-cooperative scenarios.

Perception errors. Perception errors include all errors that limit the worlds perception, generally caused by sensors faulty operation or perceptual aliasing.[5] They will not allow an agent to identify correctly in which type of state they are. If there was no communication, these errors would no be propagated between agents, and they would only interfere in the learning process of the agent in which they occurred. The presence of these errors can be detected if a certain state-action pair receives a different reinforcement from what it usually receives when that action is taken in that state. In order to have a robust multi-agent learning system, each agent keeps a register with the reinforcements received, and compares them at all instants with the ones it received earlier. Each time

---

[4] When an agent finds a wall it assumes that the state-action pair that led it to that wall is already learnt.

[5] Perceptual aliasing is an inherent property of an environment that reflects the incapacity of the robots sensors to perceive complete information about the state of the world, which can mislead the robot when identifying the environment. In other words, two states may look the same to an agent, although they are distinct from each other.

an agent receives an unexpected reinforcement, it decreases the trust factor for itself and, after detecting a certain number of consecutive errors, informs the other agents that it has Perception errors. When the other agents receive this information, they decrease the trust factor in this agent.

If these errors are not permanent, the agent increases the trust factor in itself every time it receives the expected reinforcements. If it receives a certain number of consecutive expected reinforcements, the agent informs the other agents that there are no more problems in its sensors and that it has became a credible source of information again.

If these errors are permanent (such as when the sensors are badly damaged), the agent informs the others about its limitation and stops sending information. At this point, this agents presence can no longer increase learning knowledge and so it returns to a pre-defined position (e.g., the initial state) and stays still. This agent will not learn the world.

For simulation effects, errors are applied to the reinforcement $r(s, a)$ with which the world responds to the action a taken by the agent in state s. The reinforcement $\hat{r}(s, a)$ received is described by a probability distribution

$$\hat{r}(s, a) = \begin{cases} r(s, a) & \text{with probability} \quad (1 - p) \\ r(s, a) + \delta & \text{with probability} \quad p \end{cases} \tag{8}$$

where p is the probability of an error δ. The sensors' uncertainty $\Delta > 0$, usually specified by the devices' vendor, is also considered and introduced a priori in the agents' parameter set. In this way, error detection by the agent can be described as

$$\begin{aligned} &\text{if} \quad \hat{r}(s, a) \in [r(s, a) - \Delta, r(s, a) + \Delta], \text{there is no error;} \\ &\text{if} \quad \hat{r}(s, a) \notin [r(s, a) - \Delta, r(s, a) + \Delta], \text{there is error.} \end{aligned} \tag{9}$$

The reinforcements $r(s, a)$ used as reference are the ones received the first time that the agent visits the correspondent state-action pair. This assumes that an agent does not have errors initially. Note that this type of error does not include those coming from the agents movement, like odometry errors, which are handled as Position errors. Assuming that the errors are only provided by sensors malfunction and perceptual aliasing and that the robot has been revised before starting to learn, it is natural to assume that robot sensors should start by working well apart from normal uncertainties, which are handled in rule 9.

The described error prevention measures revealed to be efficient (see Table 1) where the agent with errors is agent 1:

- when errors are not permanent, the other agents' learning process was not delayed, and agent 1 is the only one affected, but only with a small delay. The values presented here were simulated for the worst case, i.e., forcing $p = 1$ and $|\delta| > |\Delta|$ during a limited time period after the agent visited at least once each state-action pair, so that reinforcements $r(s, a)$ used as reference have no errors.
- errors are permanent, agent 1 returns to the initial position and stops, and other agents continue learning. Agent 1's policy map is wrong, but the other

agents are able to find optimal policies. The values presented in Table 1 were also simulated for the worst case, i.e., forcing $p = 1$ and $|\delta| > |\Delta|$ for an unlimited time period after agent 1 visited at least once each state-action pair.

Communication Errors. This type of errors was divided in two groups:

* ⋆ *Receptors Communication Errors*, which include all errors that can occur in the agents reception device;
* ⋆ *Transmitters Communication Errors*, which include all errors that can occur in the communication channel or in the agents transmitter device.

The influence of the distance between agents and the presence of walls were not considered in the communication errors.

Once again, the agent detects that the received information is wrong using the reinforcements. If the reinforcement received for a certain state-action pair is different from the one received earlier from the same agent, there could be communication errors, arising from the receptor or the transmitter. The agent that detected this irregularity, after decreasing the trust factor of the transmitter agent, asks all the other agents if any of them detected that same error. If no more agents have detected the problem, the agent concludes that it has problems in its reception device. If these errors persist, the agent ignores all information shared by other agents.

On the other hand, if the other agents, other than the transmitter, also detect this irregularity, it is a communication problem with the transmitter agent or in the communication channel. If the error persists, the transmitter is informed that transmitting is useless, and it stops transmitting; however, it still receives what other agents share.

To allow this conversation, it is essential to have at least three agents, and it is this interchange of questions and answers that allows an agent to find the errors source.

Note that communication is only used to accelerate the world learning rate, but it is not essential for each agent to learn the world. So, loss of communication can never damage each individual learning process. In the worst case, which happens when all communications are lost, the agents will learn the world individually.

Tests performed to deal with this type of errors revealed the efficiency of the method adopted (Table 1). Once again it is agent 1 who has errors, but, given there is no significant variation of other agents number of steps, we can conclude that the negative effect was not propagated.

To simulate this, an error δ was applied to the Q-values and to the reinforcements sent, if they were transmitter's errors, or received, if they were receptor's errors. The reinforcement $\hat{r}(s, a)$, received or sent, is described as a probability distribution following (5) and its detection can be described by (5) , where Δ is the sensors' uncertainty of the agent that sent the information.

The reinforcements $r(s, a)$ used as reference are the ones received for the first time that the agent receives a sharing for the correspondent state-action pair.

Table 1. Errors influence in learning World B: Perception Errors (PeE), Receptor's Communication Errors (RCE), Transmitter's Communication Errors (TCE), Position Errors (PoE). Results are presented in number of steps needed to learn the world, in the form: (mean) ± (standard deviation).

	Agent # 1	Agent # 2	Agent#3
Without errors	30 928.88±2 393.45	30 010.90±1 850.21	30 105.18±1 441.19
PeE - limited period	33 190.80±2 686.36	31 821.30±1 417.90	30 661.70±1 495.04
PeE - permanent	5 043.50± 7.30	29 926.50± 910.60	30 400.00±1 880.40
RCE - limited period	32 382.50±2 597.30	29 668.70±1 425.70	30 764.10±1 520.10
RCE - permanent	33 066.90±2 260.30	30 600.60±2 224.12	30 679.30±2 594.90
TCE - limited period	30 240.50±1 637.30	30 842.80±1 460.60	30 104.30±1 944.36
TCE - permanent	30 306.20±2 131.80	30 693.00±1 604.40	30 876.20±1 748.60
PoE	36 320.33±8 738.22	30 883.44±2 668.05	30 146.49±1 577.26

This assumes that communication errors only happen after agents share at least once each state-action pair.

Values in Table 1 were simulated for the worst case, where all reinforcements arrive with errors bigger than the considered uncertainty, forcing $p = 1$ and $|\delta| > |\Delta|$ for an unlimited or a limited time interval, depending on whether their errors are or not permanent.

Position Errors. Position errors can happen frequently if robots actuators are not well calibrated, or simply caused by odometry errors, and they can have a more drastic effect than the errors mentioned above because they are usually detected too late. Detection of errors is based on unexpected reinforcements, however, there are similar reinforcements for different states, so an agent with position errors[6] can only detect its error if it finds a wall or a goal state in an unexpected position, and even in this case it will think that the errors are due to its sensors bad operation.

The only way an agent can really detect position errors is if it finds a pillar in an unexpected position. In this case, the agent decreases the trust factor in itself and warns all other agents that it has position errors. As it cannot know for how long it has these errors, all agents erase the information they have in their Shared Worlds and continue learning using their own World Models information. This way, learning is delayed but not all information is lost.

There is no way to correct an agent with position errors, unless it finds the pillars. In this case the other agents cannot help because they do not know where the lost agent is. The agent with position errors keeps moving randomly through the world: physically the agent does not leave the worlds limits, however, in its internal World Model, it might. This map can grow significantly and bring memory problems. The other agents are robust to these errors (Table 1), but the agent who has them cannot correct itself.

If the World Model of the agent with position errors grows too much before it notices it, the agent shares states out of the worlds limits, allowing the other

---

[6] If it is in a position $(\widehat{x}, \widehat{y}) \neq (x, y)_{real}$.

agents to detect this irregularity and to protect themselves from these errors as mentioned above.

Another negative consequence of the position errors is the probable communication saturation because, while an agent doesn't realize that it is lost, it thinks that the errors it detects are due to sensors problems, and is constantly warning the others about it.

To simulate these errors, a deviation error was applied to the actions taken by the agent.

Again, the reference values to decide if there are errors are based on the first time step, which, in this type of error, is unrealistic. It is also very probable that an agents position error increases as the robot moves. To avoid this, an agent should keep updating its localization using some more complex and efficient technique.

4   Related Work

The field of multi-agent RL in which many agents are simultaneously learning by interacting with the environment and with each other is not yet mature. The number of parameters to learn in a cooperative system increases dramatically with the increase in the number of agents. One way to deal with this problem is to use Hierarchical RL, e.g. the MAXQ method [5], which allows the agent to learn simultaneously more than one task and limits the exponential growth of the required memory. Based on this idea, many other works, such as [6] [7], used hierarchies to avoid the growth of the state space and to speed up learning. However, these methods build a world map for each task to be learned, which is not efficient in the way that the knowledge acquired to execute one task is not used to update the policy maps of other tasks. This is equivalent to learning the world as many times as the number of goals to reach and, at the same time, the required computer memory increases with the number of tasks to execute.

When improving methods focused on reduction of complexity, caused by the high number of agents and goals, some cooperative potentialities are ignored, and this subject has been studied in order to develop new approaches to the RL problem [8][9][10][11][12], such as the Profit-Sharing method, latter used by [13]. This method also deals with the problem of non-stationarity, which is essential because, when there are multiple agents executing actions at the same time, the environment becomes non-stationary, and frequently non Markovian, and some of the convergence conditions that guarantee the correct function of the developed methods for individual RL fail. Profit-Sharing is a robust multi-agent learning method to use in dynamic domains with uncertainties.

Other authors explored communication in multi-agent systems, and varied the type and the amount of the shared information. In [15] three forms of communicating are identified. In the first one, agents can instantaneously communicate information, such as actions, reinforcements and state-action pairs. This is equivalent to sharing all information from all agents, which can be unbearable to communicate. In the second form of communicating, agents share episodes, which are sequences of triples (action, Q(s,a), reinforcement) that the agents experienced. This approximation has the inconvenient of sharing information only at the end of each episode, which can already be obsolete. There is also a big amount of information to be communicated. In the third form of communicating, agents share the policies learned.

In this paper we introduced new criteria to establish communication, similar to the approach presented in [14] since it shares instantaneous information, but we create a filter to avoid sharing irrelevant information. The problem of this filter is that it evaluates what is important based on a rule (crossing the Stop Limit) which is reached very late in the learning process. So, when agents share information, other agents already know much of it. It may be more useful to assign each agent to a specific part of the world, however, this will have to remain for future work.

Learning to communicate has also been studied in [14], but in a hierarchical approach. A communication level was added to the hierarchical decomposition of the problem, allowing agents to learn to balance the amount of communication needed for proper coordination, and communication cost.

Recently, experiments have been made that apply game theory to multi-agent RL [16], combining matrix games with MDPs. This has opened up new ways of studying cases where agents are limited, and where it is not possible to guarantee convergence and full observation of the environment, two properties usually considered separately, allowing agents to make decisions based on principles like the WoLF (Win or Learn Fast) [17].

5   Conclusions and Future Work

This paper presents methods for dealing with perception, communication and positioning errors in cooperative reinforcement learning frameworks. In order to have a learning process independent of the environment:

- each agent starts learning without knowing anything about the worlds characteristics;
- agents can communicate with each other and orientate themselves using a self-orientation method based on pillars fixed in certain states of the world;
- agents return to an initial position at the end of each episode in an autonomous way, and this initial position can change according to a rule that finds regions which are less explored;
- agents stop learning autonomously when they find the optimal Q-values of the world, which is detected based on a Stop Limit.

To avoid error propagation among agents, each agent constructs a World Model and updates it only with information obtained by itself, while, at the same time, constructs another model of the world, the Shared World, that is updated with information shared by all the other agents.

A trust factor is attributed to each agent, allowing the increase or decrease of the influence of the shared Q-values accordingly to the sources credibility. In this manner, an agent is protected against negative effects of errors and has the possibility to ignore all knowledge acquired jointly with other agents, given it has its own individual World Model.

Methods were developed to protect agents against errors from sensors (including perceptual aliasing), from communication between agents and position errors. This last case is sometimes unsolvable, but error propagation between agents was avoided.

The price paid for these improvements is the increase of memory an agent must have available.

Based on the work developed, the following possibilities of future work have been identified: (i) to make the multi-agent system robust to errors by using a probabilistic model where shared Q-values are the model's samples and errors are dealt as outliers; (ii) to study these methods in dynamic worlds; (iii) to develop a way to learn multiple goals.

References

1. Sutton, R. S. and Barto, A. G., Reinforcement Learning, An Introduction, The MIT Press, UK (1998).
2. Russel, S. J. and Norvig, P., Artificial Intelligence, A Modern Approach, Prentice Hall, New Jersey, USA (2003).
3. Vlassis, N., Multiagent Systems and Distributed AI, Intelligent Autonomous Systems, Informatics Institute, University of Amsterdam (2003).
4. Sousa, C. and Custdio, L., Cooperative Reinforcement Learning: exploring Communication and Cooperation Problems. In: Proceedings of the 6th IEEE International Symposium on Computational Intelligence in Robotics and Automation (2005).
5. Dietterich, T. G., The MAXQ Method for Hierarquical Reinforcement Learning. In: International Conference on Machine Learning (1998).
6. Parr, R. and Russel, S., Reinforcement Learning with Hierarchies of Machines, Computer Science Division, UC Berkeley, CA (1998).
7. Makar, R., Mahadevan, S. and Ghavamzadeh, M., Hierarquical Multi-Agent RL, Department of Computer Science, Michigan State University (2001).
8. Arai, S. and Sycara, K., Credit Assignment Method for Learning Effective Stochastic Policies in Uncertain Domains. In: Proceedings of Genetic and Evolutionary Computation Conference (2001).
9. Arai, S., Sycara, K. and Payne, T., Experience-based RL to Acquire Effective Behaviour in a Multi-agent Domain. In: Proc. of the 6th Pacific Rim Int. Conference on Artificial Intelligence, Lecture Notes in AI 1886, Springer-Verlag (2000), pp.125-135.
10. Arai, S. and Sycara, K., Effective Learning Approach for Planning and Scheduling in Multi-agent Domain. In: Proceedings oh the 6th ISAB - From animals to animats 6 (2000), pp. 507-516.
11. Arai, S. and Sycara, K., Multi-agent RL for Planning and Conflict Resolution in a Dynamic Domain, Carnegie Mellon University (2000).
12. Arai, S., Sycara, K. and Payne, T., Multi-agent Reinforcement Learning for Planning and Scheduling Multiple Goals. In: Proceedings of Fourth International Conference on Multi-Agent Systems (2000).
13. Wahab, M., Reinforcement Learning in Multi-Agent Systems, McGill Univ. School of Computer Science.

14. Ghavamzadeh, M. and Mahadevan, S, Learning to Communicate and Act in Co-operative Multiagent Systems using Hierarchical Reinforcement Learning. Third International Joint Conference on Autonomous Agents and Multiagent Systems - Volume 3 (AAMAS'04), (2004), pp. 1114-1121.
15. Tan, M., Multi-Agent RL: Independent vs. Cooperative Agents. In: Proceedings of the Tenth International Conference on Machine Learning (1993), pp.330-337.
16. Bowling, M. and Veloso, M., An Analysis of Stochastic Game Theory for Multiagent Reinforcement Learning, CMU-CS-00-165 (2000).
17. Bowling, M., Multiagent Learning in the Presence of Agents with Limitations, PhD. Thesis (2003), Carnegie Mellon University, Pittsburg.

The Success and Failure of Tag-Mediated Evolution of Cooperation

Austin McDonald and Sandip Sen

University of Tulsa, Mathematics and Computer Science Department,
600 S College, Tulsa 74104, OK
{austin, sandip}@utulsa.edu

Abstract. Use of tags to limit partner selection for playing has been shown to produce stable cooperation in agent populations playing the Prisoner's Dilemma game. There is, however, a lack of understanding of how and why tags facilitate such cooperation. We start with an empirical investigation that identifies the key dynamics that result in sustainable cooperation in PD. Sufficiently long tags are needed to achieve this effect. A theoretical analysis shows that multiple simulation parameters including tag length, mutation rate and population size will have significant effect on sustaining cooperation. Experiments partially validate these observations. Additionally, we claim that tags only promote mimicking and not coordinated behavior in general, i.e., tags can promote cooperation only if cooperation requires identical actions from all group members. We illustrate the failure of the tag model to sustain cooperation by experimenting with domains where agents need to take complementary actions to maximize payoff.

1   Introduction

Learning and reasoning in single or multistage games have been an active area of research in multiagent systems [1,2,3,4,5,6,7]. Most of this research has concentrated on simultaneous move games with solution concepts like Nash equilibria [8,9]. Nash Equilibrium, however, does not guarantee that agents will obtain the best possible payoffs, i.e., Nash Equilibrium does not ensure Pareto-optimal solutions. Some non-Nash Equilibrium action combinations may yield better payoffs for both agents, which may be reached if the agents look ahead to future iterations of the game while selecting actions [10].

That Nash Equilibria may not be the preferred outcome is particularly evident in the widely-studied Prisoner's Dilemma (PD) game (see Figure 1). In this game, the only Nash Equilibria is the strategy profile (D,D) which is also the only non-Pareto-optimal outcome! The (D,D) strategy profile is dominated by the (C,C) strategy profile. Unfortunately, in a single-shot PD game, rational play will produce the Nash Equilibrium strategy profile. In repeated or iterated play, however, learning approaches can produce higher payoff by choosing the (C,C) strategy profile. Numerous researchers in game theory and in multiagent systems have attempted various mechanisms to induce cooperation in iterated PDs [11,12,7,13,14,15].

We are particularly interested in recent work using tags in a population of interacting players (agents) [16,17]. Tags have been proposed by John Holland as a primitive means

K. Tuyls et al. (Eds.): LAMAS 2005, LNAI 3898, pp. 155–164, 2006.
ⓒ © Springer-Verlag Berlin Heidelberg 2006

	C	D
C	R, R	S, T
D	T, S	P, P

Fig. 1. Utilities to players in a two-player Prisoner's Dilemma game. Constraints on the utility values are T>R>P>S and 2R>T+S>2P.

of communication that can aid in the evolution of a group [18]. Tags have also been used by other researchers to promote cooperation in variations of PDs [19,20]. Whereas these papers provided a reasonable high-level explanation of how the use of tags promotes cooperation, a detailed analysis that clearly explains the fundamental subtleties of the interactions in the population was missing. As a result, design of tag systems was based on trial and error and did not explain why certain parameter choices for such systems succeeded in inducing cooperation whereas others did not.

Another key observation was that all the domains to which tags have been applied so far contained a narrow characterization of cooperation as imitation of behavior. In multiagent domains in general, cooperation requires a richer, divergent collection of behaviors. It was unclear from the current state of knowledge whether tags can support cooperation in a broad spectrum of multiagent problems.

In this paper, we plan to carefully characterize the detailed interactions of agents using tags. The goal is to identify domains where tags would be useful for promoting cooperation and to develop a methodology for choosing parameter values in the tag framework that will actually facilitate the evolution of cooperation in such domains.

2   Related Work

The usage of tags to bias interactions on iterated Prisoner's Dilemma has been suggested by [21,22,18]. Riolo performed the pioneering experiments in [19]. Riolo's agents were modeled as a stochastic strategy, based on Tit-For-Tat, combined with a real-valued tag and a real-valued bias, both on the interval [0, 1]. Agents then attempt to pair up, where the difference between the agents' tags is less than each agents' bias. If no suitable pairing can be found within a small number of tries, the agent simply chooses a partner at random. When each agent has an identical, fixed bias, Riolo's model results in increased performance for the society. However, when each agent's bias is allowed to evolve, behavior varies drastically according to initial conditions and the results are less clear.

Hales and Edmonds [17] used a different model where the population consists of a collection of agents represented as a binary string of $l + 1$ bits. The first bit represents a pure strategy (always cooperate or always defect), while the remaining l bits are the tag. In each population generation, every agent plays a PD game against one other agent with an identical tag. If an agent has a unique tag in the population, it plays against a randomly selected opponent. The next generation is formed via fitness proportionate reproduction where the fitness of an agent is the payoff received in this round of play. Mutation is then applied to each bit. This process is described in Algorithm 1.

Algorithm 1. Hales and Edmond's model of population evolution with tags

---

for some number of generations **do**
    for each agent a in the population **do**
        Select a game partner agent b with the same tag (if possible)
        Agent a and b invoke their strategies and a gets corresponding payoff.
    end for
    Reproduce agents in proportion to their average payoff (with some low level of mutation)
end for

---

3   Tag-Based Model for Population Evolution

Our model is characterized as follows: Each agent in a population of size N is represented by two numbers: an integer s representing its strategy $0 \leq s \leq$ (number of valid strategies), and a real number t representing its tag $0 \leq t \leq 1$. The real number representation of the tag provides for an infinite tag space. Additionally, we divide the interval $[0, 1]$ into subintervals of length δ called *tag groups*.

The population is evolved over a number of generations. Each generation, every agent chooses another agent in the same tag group and plays a round of the game with the other agent. If an agent is the only member of a tag group, it randomly chooses another agent from the population. The first agent receives the payoff from that round. This process is repeated for all agents. Thus, an agent may interact with many agents per generation, but receives only one payoff per generation. This prevents singleton agents from interfering with other groups, while still giving them a chance to play, and hence survive.

The next generation is selected by a payoff proportionate reproduction scheme. For each selected agent the mutation operator, which replaces the current value of a parameter with a new number randomly chosen from the range for that parameter, is applied to the strategy with probability μ_S and to the tag with probability μ_T. The new generation is then evolved as described above.

The goal of this framework is to enable consistent evaluation of the performance of agent societies on a variety of games. Our proposed setup can be used to approximate a variety of existing tag models. It is similar to Riolo's model using a global fixed bias, with two exceptions: we use a pure strategy, and being in the same tag group is transitive in our model (but such is not necessarily the case in Riolo's). To compare to Hales' and Edmonds' model, we observe that there are 2^l distinct tag groups possible when using a tag with l bits. So we use $\frac{1}{\delta} = 2^l$, which lets us choose a corresponding δ for any given l. Additionally, in Hales' and Edmonds' original model[1], the mutation rate of the tag was a function of tag length, which is not the case here.

4   Tags in Prisoner's Dilemma and Related Games

We recount Hales' [17] explanation of how tags help promote cooperation in the PD game. A homogeneous group of cooperators will prosper and grow. When such a group is

---

[1] This was changed in a later paper [23].

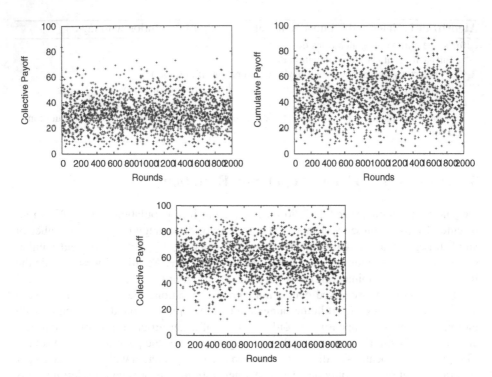

Fig. 2. Average payoffs for $l = 0$ (left), 4 (right), and 32 (bottom) for the Prisoner's Dilemma game

invaded, via mutation of the strategy or tag, by a defector, the defector will prosper, resulting in imitators in the next generations. Over time, the group will fill with defectors, resulting in worsening performance and eventual extinction. Thus defectors, even if formed by chance, will not live long, and hence a majority of the population will be cooperators.

Our additional observation is that individuals with unique tags, i.e., singletons, can prosper if the randomly chosen individual they interact with is cooperative in nature. If the singleton is cooperative, then it will perform well, leading to perhaps more agents copying its tag bits and strategy and thus the group expands as a group of cooperators. If the singleton is a defector, when others copy its strategy and tag, all agents in this group will be defectors, they will perform poorly in the following generation and the group will die out.

We were puzzled, however, by the observation by Hales that sufficiently long tags were required to sustain cooperation in the PD game. For example, Hales observed that while 32 bit tags were able to sustain cooperation, 8 bit tags were not for a population of 100 agents! Note that this translates into the requirement of huge tag spaces, e.g., 32-bit tags produce a tag space of 2^{32}! The explanation of how tags facilitate cooperation has no apparent requirement for such massive tag spaces. We also did not find any theoretical justification in Hales's work on characterizing the effect of tag length on promoting cooperation. This led us to believe that the current understanding of the working of the tag mechanism is incomplete and we need to improve on it in order to design working tag-based systems for arbitrary populations playing the iterated PD game and for other applications.

We are interested in investigating whether longer tags are required solely for the associated increase in mutation rate, or whether there were other beneficial effects. Additionally, we sought to validate the claim that tags are useful only in cases where mimicry is a desirable strategy.

To investigate tag length, we chose a game that tags were known to perform well on: the Prisoner's Dilemma (Figure 1). We chose T=1.9, R=1.0, P=.002, and S=.001 in order to accentuate the differences in the outcomes. Using closer values yields results that are similar to those presented here. Unless otherwise stated, all experiments use $\mu_s = \mu_t = .1$. Since we are primarily interested in comparisons to Hales' and Edmonds' work, we will specify δ in terms of bits of tag length, l. The average payoffs per agent over time in a set of typical Prisoner's Dilemma runs are presented in Figure 2. The left plot is equivalent to not using tags, and is presented to demonstrate that tags do produce improvement. We see that for shorter tags, the payoffs are clustered around a lower average than for progressively higher tag lengths.

The population characteristic that we found most distinguished runs with long versus short tags was the number of populated groups. We present the corresponding plot for the number of groups over a run in Figure 3. The left plot uses $l = 8, \mu_T = .001$ and the right plot uses $l = 32, \mu_T = .1$. The figures clearly denote significant differences in the population features with larger number of groups and smaller average group sizes in the case of longer tags and higher mutation rates.

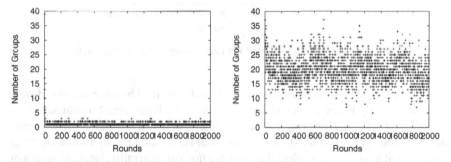

Fig. 3. Number of populated groups in Prisoner's Dilemma for $l = 8, \mu_T=.001$ (left) and $l = 32, \mu_T = .1$ (right)

This observation is key to the following conjecture: *Cooperation is sustained in a population of tag-based players playing PD and evolved based on fitness if sufficient number of cooperative groups are created via mutation.* The conjecture is supported by the following reasoning. If there are too few cooperative groups, invasion by defectors will destroy them. If there are sufficiently many cooperative groups, destroying a few will still leave the possibility of other groups spawning more new cooperative groups via mutation. The basic argument is that there has to be enough groups such that the rate of destruction via invasion by defectors is less than the formation of new groups by mutation.

To further investigate this conjecture, we now attempt a partial theoretical characterization of this phenomena. We first calculated the expected number of new groups formed each generation, M.

$$M = N(1 - \delta g)\mu_T$$

where g is the current number of populated groups and N is the population. This is only an approximation; after a new group is formed, the value of g changes. However, when $N \ll \frac{1}{\delta}$, this approximation is valid. From this equation, consider $P = M/N$, the fraction of agents in the population that formed new groups. Higher values for P can be thought of as having two complementary effects: the likelihood of an agent forming a new group is increased, and the likelihood of an agent joining an existing group is decreased. This directly increases the rate of formation of new cooperative groups (proportional to the aggregate payoffs of cooperative agents) while decreasing the rate that groups are invaded by defectors from outside. However, P cannot be allowed to become too high; this would result in too many agents forming new groups and not staying behind to achieve the cooperative payoff.

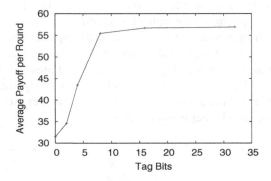

Fig. 4. Average payoffs per round with decreasing δ (increasing tag length)

So by varying P, we should enhance the payoffs obtained by a population. However, we cannot directly lower g, even if doing so were to be beneficial. So instead we focus on δ and μ_T. By simply lowering δ to zero, we can ensure that any mutation will result in a new tag group being formed (note that this would correspond to an infinite tag length). Then, we will have $P = \mu_T$. Note that we have not lost generality, since all values of P we could achieve with any given δ are still achievable with μ_T. We present the effect of progressively lowering δ in Figure 4.

The above characterization explains how smaller δ (or equivalently, longer tags) can increase the performance of a population on Iterated Prisoner's Dilemma (up to a certain bound) despite a fixed mutation rate. According to our theory, then, when $\delta = 0$ there should be a μ_T with which we can achieve the best performance possible from the system. When $\delta = 0$, the only way agents can be in the same group is if they have identical real-valued tags. Since the chances of an agent randomly mutating to an existing tag are infinitely small, agents with identical tags must have been reproduced from the same parent.[2] So, it is likely that they will share common strategy bits. This behavior leads us to speculate that tag systems are merely promoting mimicry, rather than cooperation.

---

[2] This is only theoretically true. In practice, machines have a finite precision for representing real numbers. However, this precision is typically large enough that we can consider it to be infinite.

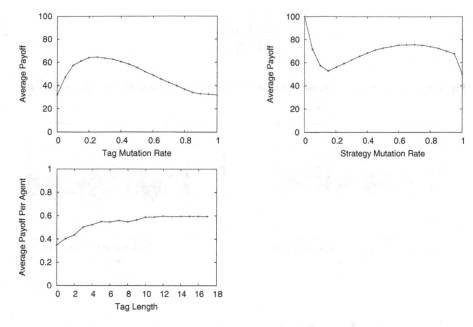

Fig. 5. Average payoffs as we increase μ_T (left) μ_S (center) and N (right)

Having decided on a fixed $\delta = 0$, we now investigate the effects of altering μ_T and μ_S. (Figure 5). From the figure, we see that there exists an optimal value for μ_T near $\mu_T = .2$. Higher values result in groups not remaining together long enough for cooperation to occur; lower values result in fewer new groups being formed, and thus a higher proportion being lost due to defection. With regards to μ_S, we conjecture that higher values are causing agents to switch strategies too quickly to be able to cooperate, while lower values aren't producing enough cooperators.

5 Effect of Tags Where Cooperation $\neq$ Mimicry

Several authors have suggested other applications of tags [24,16,20]. However, we observed that in all of the applications mentioned mimicry is an effective strategy for increasing performance. Though mimicking behavior can produce cooperation in PD and other domains, for a large gamut of multiagent interactions complementary, rather than identical behavior is required for cooperation. For tags to be used as an effective facilitator for promoting cooperation in general, it is imperative that we better understand their role in aiding cooperation through complementary behavior. Our own experiments (see above) suggest that tags may only be helpful in games where cooperative actions are identical.

To investigate the performance of tag systems on a game where complementary actions are required to maximize payoff, we look at the performance of a tagged system on a game where mimicry is useless: the Anti-Coordination game. In this game, cooperation occurs when players choose ιcomplementary actions; note that this game is not a dilemma

	0	1
0	L, L	H, H
1	H, H	L, L

Fig. 6. Utilities to players in Anti-Coordination. Constraints on the utility values are $H > L$.

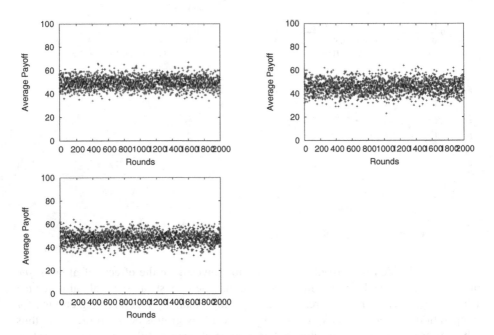

Fig. 7. Average payoffs for $l = 0$ (left), 8 (middle), and 32 (right) for the Anti-Coordination game

(ie, one player cannot succeed at the other player's expense). We expect that tags can improve the performance of a society on this game by increasing the likelihood of pairing a 1 with a 0 from the expected equilibrium strategy without tags, which is an even spread across the strategies (half 1's, half 0's). Next we present similar results for the anti-coordination game (Figure 6).

Figure 7 shows the average payoffs of a society over time with varying tag lengths. We see that changing l has no noticeable effect on the population. We show the effects of changing l over time in Figure 8, where each point is an average of 5 runs. We also present the average performance of the population as we alter the strategy mutation rate μ_S while holding fixed $\delta = 0$. The tagging mechanism has no effect on the society playing this game.

To explain why tags fail to increase performance on this game, assume we begin with an equally distributed population of 0's and 1's. Without tags, this is the optimal distribution. Any increase in 0's or 1's will be detrimental to the society. For example, say the number of 0's increases. Then the average 0 will receive a lower payoff than the average 1, and so the number of 0's will decrease and the number of 1's will increase, pushing the system back to equilibrium.

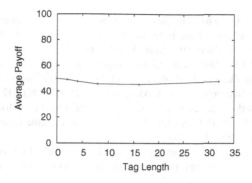

Fig. 8. Average payoffs as tag length increases

In order to improve the performance of this system, we need to restrict the agents such that they only play with other agents who have opposite tags. As we discovered in our experiments with the Prisoner's Dilemma, the chance of an agent joining a tag group from outside is vanishingly small (and gets smaller as δ decreases). So in all likelihood any agent with the same tag as another agent is a copy of that agent (either directly or as a copy of a copy). So they will tend to have the same tag bit, and will both get low payoffs.

By this mechanism, the anti-coordination game actually discourages growth of homogeneous strategy groups, which totally negates the function of tags.

6   Conclusion

In this paper we show how and when tag-mediated agent interaction can promote and sustain cooperative behavior. In particular, we analyze how size of the tag space, mutation rate, and population size effect the evolution of cooperation in populations repeatedly playing the Prisoner's Dilemma game. Additionally, we have identified the function tags perform on influencing such systems: they promote mimicry, and not necessarily cooperation. We demonstrated this by studying the performance of a tagged society playing the Anti-Coordination Game. Our analysis and observations suggest that existing tag models primarily promote cooperative behavior in games where mimicry is the best strategy. While this means that tags can improve group performance in coordination games and games like the PD, they are inadequate for sustaining cooperation in general multiagent situations where effective cooperation requires complementary, and not identical, behaviors by the cooperators.

References

1. Banerjee, B., Sen, S., Peng, J.: Fast concurrent reinforcement learners. In: Proceedings of the Seventeenth International Joint Conference on Artificial Intelligence. (2001) 825–830
2. Bowling, M., Veloso, M.: Rational and convergent learning in stochastic games. In: Proceedings of the Seventeenth International Joint Conference on Artificial Intelligence. (2001) 1021–1026

3. Claus, C., Boutilier, C.: The dynamics of reinforcement learning in cooperative multiagent systems. In: Proceedings of the Fifteenth National Conference on Artificial Intelligence, Menlo Park, CA, AAAI Press/MIT Press (1998) 746–752

4. Hu, J., Wellman, M.P.: Multiagent reinforcement learning: Theoretical framework and an algorithm. In Shavlik, J., ed.: Proceedings of the Fifteenth International Conference on Machine Learning, San Francisco, CA, Morgan Kaufmann (1998) 242–250

5. Littman, M.L.: Markov games as a framework for multi-agent reinforcement learning. In: Proceedings of the Eleventh International Conference on Machine Learning, San Mateo, CA, Morgan Kaufmann (1994) 157–163

6. Littman, M.L.: Friend-or-foe q-learning in general-sum games. In: Proceedings of the Eighteenth International Conference on Machine Learning, San Francisco: CA, Morgan Kaufmann (2001) 322–328

7. Littman, M.L., Stone, P.: Implicit negotiation in repeated games. In: Intelligent Agents VIII: AGENT THEORIES, ARCHITECTURE, AND LANGUAGES. (2001) 393–404

8. Myerson, R.B.: Game Theory: Analysis of Conflict. Harvard University Press (1991)

9. Nash, J.F.: Non-cooperative games. Annals of Mathematics **54** (1951) 286 – 295

10. Brams, S.J.: Theory of Moves. Cambridge University Press, Cambridge: UK (1994)

11. Axelrod, R.: The Evolution of Cooperation. Basic Books (1984)

12. Dugatkin, L.A.: The evolution of cooperation: four paths to the evolution and maintenance of cooperative behavior. BioScience **47** (1997) 355–361

13. Sigmund, K., Nowak, M.A.: The alternating prisoner's dilemma. Journal of Theoretical Biology **38** (1994) 262–275

14. Stimpson, J.L., Goodrich, M.A., Walters, L.C.: Satisficing and learning cooperation in the prisoner's dilemma. In: Proceedings of the Seventeenth International Joint Conference on Artificial Intelligence. (2001) 535–540

15. Trivers, R.: The evolution of reciprocal altruism. Quarterly Review of Biology **46** (1972) 35–57

16. Hales, D., Edmonds, B.: Can tags build working systems? from mabs to esoa. In: Engineering Self-Organising Systems. Lecture Notes in AI-2977, Springer Verlag (2003) 186–194

17. Hales, D., Edmonds, B.: Evolving social rationality for mas using "tags". In: Proceedings of the Second International Joint Conference on Autonomous Agents and Multiagent Systems, Melbourne,Australia, ACM Press (2003) 497–503

18. Holland, J.H., Holyoak, K., Nisbett, R., Thagard, P.: Induction: Processes of Inferences, Learning, and Discovery. MIT Press, Cambridge, MA (1986)

19. Riolo, R.: The effects and evolution of tag-mediated selection of partners in populations playing the Iterated Prisoner's Dilemma. In: Proceedings of the Seventh International Conference on Genetic Algorithms, Morgan Kaufmann Publishers, Inc. (1997) 378–385

20. Riolo, R., Cohen, M.D., Axelrod, R.: Cooperation without reciprocity. Nature **414** (2001) 441–443

21. Allison, P.D.: The cultural evolution of beneficent norms. Social Forces **71** (1992) 279–301

22. Holland, J.: The effect of labels (tags) on social interactions. Technical Report Working Paper 93-10-064, Santa Fe Institute (1993)

23. Hales, D., Edmonds, B.: Change your tags fast! - a necessary condition for cooperation? In: Proceedings of the Joint Workshop on Multi-Agent and Multi-Agent-Based Simulation. (2004)

24. Hales, D.: Self-organising, open and cooperative p2p societies - from tags to networks. In: Proceedings of the 2nd Workshop on Engineering Self-Organsing Applications. (2004)

An Adaptive Approach for the Exploration-Exploitation Dilemma and Its Application to Economic Systems

Lilia Rejeb[1], Zahia Guessoum[1,2], and Rym M'Hallah[3]

[1] CReSTIC, MODECO Team, Rue des Crayères, Reims Cedex2, France
[2] Université de Paris-VI, LIP6, OASIS Team, 4 place Jussieu, 75252 cedex 5, France
[3] Kuwait University, Dep. of Statistics and Operations Research,
P.O. Box 5969, Safat 13060

Abstract. Learning agents have to deal with the exploration-exploitation dilemma. The choice between exploration and exploitation is very difficult in dynamic systems; in particular in large scale ones such as economic systems. Recent research shows that there is neither an optimal nor a unique solution for this problem. In this paper, we propose an adaptive approach based on meta-rules to adapt the choice between exploration and exploitation. This new adaptive approach relies on the variations of the performance of the agents. To validate the approach, we apply it to economic systems and compare it to two adaptive methods originally proposed by Wilson: one local and one global. Moreover, we compare different exploration strategies and focus on their influence on the performance of the agents.

1 Introduction

The exploration-exploitation dilemma, which is an important problem frequently encountered in reinforcement learning [19], is defined as follows. When an agent is faced with a state of the environment, it either chooses to explore its environment and try new actions in search for better ones to be adopted in the future [14], or exploit already tested actions and adopt them. When opting to explore, the agent is considering its long term performance whereas when opting to exploit tested actions, the agent is considering its short term performance [17].

Formally, the agent has to solve two subproblems. The first subproblem consists of choosing an exploration method. The exploration can be either directed or undirected. The second subproblem consists of identifying a method that switches the agent's mode between exploration and exploitation according to the state of the agent and the state of its environment. The two subproblems are important since they influence the learning speed, the performances and the actions of an agent. This influence is more critical when the agent environment is dynamic, which is the case of economic systems.

In this paper, we study the aforementioned two subproblems in the context of an economic system characterized by a set of firms in competition in a shared market. We propose an adaptive approach to the exploration-exploitation problem in a dynamic economic context where firms are modeled using the XCS-learning classifier system for their decision process [11]. We show that a firm performance can be improved when

K. Tuyls et al. (Eds.): LAMAS 2005, LNAI 3898, pp. 165–176, 2006.

it opts for directed exploration and uses a meta-rules based approach to choose between exploration and exploitation.

This paper is organized as follows. Section 2 presents the firm model and an overview of the learning classifier system XCS. Section 3 investigates exploration techniques. Section 4 presents the proposed meta-rules approach and the adaptation of Wilson's techniques to our context. Section 5 presents and analyzes the experimental results. Finally, Section 6 summarizes the contributions of this paper and provides future extensions.

2   Adaptive Firms

We study the exploration-exploitation dilemma in the context of a dynamic economic system where a set of firms are in indirect interaction in a shared market. We model the firms as adaptive agents with the XCS-learning classifier system for their learning. In Section 2.1, we present the model of a firm while in Section 2.2, we detail the characteristics of the XCS classifier system, and explain how agents learn when using it.

2.1   The Firm Model

We model firms using a resource-based approach [12]. We regard a firm as a collection of physical and human resources. We stipulate that the survival of a firm depends on the way it allocates its resources. A firm is characterized by:

- a set X of resources,
- a set $Y_t = (Y_t[1], Y_t[2])$ of performance indicators, where $Y_t[1]$ is profitability and $Y_t[2]$ is market share at time t ($Y_t[1] and Y_t[2]$ are measured using the statistical Lisrel Model),
- a capital K,
- a budget B (which when allocated updates the status of the firm resources),
- a set S of strategies available for the firm.

The allocation of the budget B to the different resources X according to the firm priority defines the firm strategy.

A firm behavior is dynamic over time. Each time period, a firm

- observes its environment and updates its competition model;
- updates its internal parameters (eg., its capital K and budget B);
- opts for a strategy; and
- updates its performance.

A firm chooses the strategy that best suits its current context. The context of a firm is determined by the its internal parameters ($K, B, X,$ and Y_t), and its perception of the environment which is strongly competitive and non-stationary. At the end of a time period, firms can either join or leave the market. A firm leaves the market either when its performance decreases over a number of successive periods or when its capital decreases and reaches an exit threshold. Its exit or extinction is the result of a bad strategy used by the firm not disposing of all the information about its rivals.

Each firm, represented by an agent, bases its perception of its current context on its environment. This perception is an aggregation of the performances and the capital of the firms present in the market. Based on this perception, the firm chooses the most suited strategy. The dynamic nature of the environment makes it difficult for a firm to anticipate all the possible outcomes of its strategy and/or to take into account the inadequate outcomes of its prior strategies. We propose then to endow the firm with a capacity of learning to build gradually its decision rules as it acquires knowledge from its environment. Herein, the XCS classifier system defined by Wilson [18]: constructs the model of the firm environment, updates the model as a firm acquires experiences and foresees the possible consequences of the decision before it is undertaken.

2.2   XCS and Adaptive Firms

We use XCS [18] to model the decision process of adaptive firms. XCS constructs a complete and accurate model of a firm environment. It develops a readable set of "condition-action" rules or classifiers which explain the evolution of the environment [10].

A classifier is also characterized by three parameters: its prediction p, its prediction error e and its fitness F which evaluates the quality of the prediction p. The condition part of a classifier is a representation of the context of the firm. The set of possible actions or strategies is defined by the economist. In our case, the set has twenty strategies oriented towards customers, suppliers and production. Table 1 presents an example of a classifier. This classifier associates the strategy one to the described context.

At each decision period, XCS undertakes a perception, prediction, action cycle. It determines the set [M] of classifiers whose conditions match the context of the firm. If [M] is empty, covering takes place; else the average prediction PS_i of each action a_i proposed by the classifiers in [M] is calculated:

$$PS_i = \frac{\sum F_{cl_j} p_{cl_j}}{\sum F_{cl_j}},\qquad(1)$$

where F_{cl_j} and p_{cl_j} are respectively the fitness and the prediction of classifier j when undertaking action a_i. The PS_i serves as the decisional basis for the firm strategy se-

Table 1. Example of a classifier

Classifier	Classifier in XCS
K ∈ [300,400[	0001
B ∈ [100,200[	0010
X = {x1 ∈ [0,10[, x2 e∈ [20,30[, x3 ∈ [10,20[, x4 ∈ [0,10[, x5 ∈ [0,10[, x6 ∈ [0,10[, x7 ∈ [0,10[, x8 ∈ [0,10[}	0000,0010,0001,0000, 0000,0000,0000,0000,
Y = {y1 ∈ [10,20[, y2 ∈ [10,20[}	0001,0001,
Average _K x3 ∈ [600,700[	0011,
Average_B ∈ [200,250[	0111,
Firms-Number ∈ [0,100[	0000,
Average_Y={y_aver1 ∈ [20,30[,y_aver2 ∈ [10,20[}	0010, 0001
Action = Strategy1	1,
(p)=0.5, (e)=0.01,(F)=100	0.5, 0.01, 100

lection which is either done by exploration (random choice) or exploitation (choice of the action having the largest PS_i). Exploration encourages a firm to take risks whereas exploitation incites a firm to avoid risks.

The firm adopts the chosen strategy and gets a reward r_t at time t. This reward is an aggregation of the variations of the firm performances:

$$r_t = aggreg \left(\frac{Y_t[1] - Y_{t-1}[1]}{Y_{t-1}[1]}, \frac{Y_t[2] - Y_{t-1}[2]}{Y_{t-1}[2]} \right) \tag{2}$$

where $aggreg$ is the average aggregation operator. r_t is used by the reinforcement learning component represented by the Q-Learning algotithm [16] to update the p, e and F of the classifiers proposing the chosen action. These classifiers are blocked in a set [A] which is updated by a Michigan genetic algorithm when possible.

The current version of XCS randomly chooses between exploration and exploitation. A number is randomly generated according to the continuous Uniform (0,1) distribution, and compared to the exploration probability fixed by the designer prior to the beginning of the simulation. In addition, the current version of XCS allows undirected exploration only. In the following section, we discuss the impact of the exploration strategy on a firm's performance and survival.

3   Exploration Techniques

Exploration techniques are classified as undirected and directed [15]. Undirected techniques are random. They are difficult to use in real-valued domains and in large state-action spaces. They increase the learning time exponentially. Directed exploration techniques seek to improve the knowledge of the environment by adopting more informative actions. They include techniques such as recency-based exploration and frequency-based exploration.

To compare the performance of firms under directed and undirected techniques, we need to integrate directed exploration techniques in XCS. In the following, we explain how we integrate, within XCS, the best known directed exploration techniques: recency based technique and frequency based technique.

The *recency-based technique* selects the oldest selected action independently of its number of occurrences. To do this, it determines the recency value which correspond to the smaller period from the last activation time of the action. It finds, for each action a_i, the matching classifiers $j, j = 1, \ldots, n$ and determine the recency value $Rec(a_i)$:

$$Rec(a_i) = \min_{j=1,n} \{t - ActivationTime(cl_j)\} \tag{3}$$

where $ActivationTime(cl_j)$ is the last activation date of classifier cl_j, and t is the current time. It selects then the action a_i having the highest recency value.

The *Frequency-based exploration* selects the least frequently used action a. It tallies for each action the frequency value $Freq(a_i)$ of the corresponding matching classifiers that were previously used and rewarded at least once.

$$Freq(a_i) = \sum_{j=1,n} (cl_j) : experience(cl_j) \geq 1 \tag{4}$$

where *experience* is the activation frequency of cl_j in a similar context of the firm. It then selects the action a_i having the lowest frequency value $Freq(a_i)$.

Wiering [17] states that when the firm is interested in immediate reward, it has to switch to exploitation and to gradually increase its rate of switching to exploitation. An exploitation-exploration tradeoff is therefore needed.

4   Exploration-Exploitation Tradeoff

Finding a balance between exploration and exploitation is not an easy task [5, 7]. Most existing methods, such as the "interval estimation" [7, 9] and the "Gittings index" [5, 1] techniques, deal with small non-complex problems [15]. Methods that are applicable to more complex contexts such as a multi-agent context are limited in number [13, 4]. Peres [13] underlined the necessity to link the changing rate of exploration and the changing indicators of performance to the changing prediction, but proposed no solution. Carmel [4] integrated an exploration technique to a learning-based model and applied to game theory with a small number of agents.

Wilson [19] proposed ten techniques that were tested on small simple test problems only. Their performance is sensitive to the constant gain factor fixed by the designer. The behavior of these techniques in complex systems remains however an open issue. In the following, we propose to test the behavior of two of these techniques in more complex settings.

4.1   Wilson Techniques

Wilson techniques focus on an "on-line "choice between exploration and exploitation in a dynamic environment. They are based on the rate of variation of the performance (prediction) or the prediction errors. These techniques could be *local* or *global*. A technique is local when the degree of exploration relies on the quantities raising from the immediate responses of the current state. A technique is global when the exploration degree is a statistic of the system overall behavior [19]. In this section, we adapt two adaptive Wilson techniques: a local and a global one to use them in the context of economic systems.

The adaptive **local technique** is applied at each activation of XCS. It determines the exploration probability p_1 based on the error variation of each action. When all the classifiers matching the current context are identified, the values of the moving average $\widehat{E}_i$ of the difference between the current and estimated error are computed for each action a_i. The exploration probability p_1 is then determined:

$$p_1 = min\left\{1, f\left(\widehat{E}_i\right) \times Gf\right\}, \tag{5}$$

where Gf is a given gain factor, and

$$f\left(\widehat{E}_i\right) = \frac{\sum_{i=1,na}(\widehat{E}_i)}{na} \tag{6}$$

where na is the number of the identified actions in the set of matching classifiers [M].

For a gain factor equal to 0.5 for example, if $\widehat{E}_j$ is large (equals 5 for example), the probability of exploration is set to 1: the action a_j generates a change in the prediction error; subsequently exploration must be pursued. On the other hand, if $\widehat{E}_j$ is small (equals 1 for example), the probability of exploration is set to 0: the firm should move to exploitation.

The adaptive **global technique** is applied after n steps of exploration. It determines the exploration probability p_1 based on the average prediction error during exploration periods. It estimates $\widehat{E}$ the average prediction error during exploration periods and determines the error rate of change $g\left(\widehat{E}\right)$ which is the difference between the moving averages of $\widehat{E}$ before and after n periods of exploration (where n is usually set to 100). The rate of change is then used to determine the probability p_1:

$$p_1 = min\left\{1, g\left(\widehat{E}\right) \times Gf\right\}. \tag{7}$$

Thus, if the average prediction error changes, n other steps of exploration are executed prior to switching to exploitation.

The performance of both of Wilson strategies -the local and the global- are sensitive to the gain factor Gf and to the exploration probability fixed in XCS. We avoid this shortcoming by using an approach based on meta-rules.

4.2   A Meta-rules Based Approach

We use meta-rules to control the activation of exploration and exploitation. These meta-rules adapt the choice between exploration and exploitation to the evolution of the firm performance. They account for the new variations of the environment, once the firm has learned. They are simple and make the behavior of the classifier system close to that of a decision maker. Contrary to some techniques of Wilson, they allow the return of a firm to exploration and do not use the gain factor.

After n periods of exploration and m periods of exploitation, the following meta-rules are applied:

- If $MY_{t+n} > MY_{t+n+m}$, the system must continue learning. Subsequently, m must be decreased: $m = m * (1 - Exploitation\_Rate)$.
- If $MY_{t+n} \leq MY_{t+n+m}$, the system has achieved enough learning. Subsequently, m must be increased: $m = m * (1 + Exploitation\_Rate)$.

MY_{t+n} and MY_{t+n+m} correspond to the moving average of the aggregation of the performances Y[1] and Y[2] during the exploration and exploitation periods, respectively. $Exploitation\_Rate$ represents the variation rate of m. Once the system has acquired enough learning, the value of m becomes very large. The value of n is maintained positive to allow the system to adapt to small changes of the environment.

5   Experimental Results

The objective of this experimentation is twofold. First, we investigate the impact of exploration techniques on the performance of a firm. Second, we study the impact of the meta-rules approach and compare it to other choice techniques of exploration and exploitation.

The XCS parameters are fixed as follows:

- the population size is 6000 (allowing the system to represent all the possible classifiers when the generalization is not used),
- the generalization probability is 0.5,
- the learning rate is 0.001,
- the crossover rate is 0.8,
- the mutation rate equals 0.02,
- the minimum error is 0.01,
- the genetic algorithm frequency is 10 (allowing an update of the classifiers population),
- the exploration probability equals 0.5.

Each simulation is replicated 20 times. The reported results correspond to the average values of these 20 replications.

5.1 Exploration Techniques

The first series of experiments compares exploration techniques. The comparison is based on the results of the simulation of three populations involving 300 firms each. These populations use respectively recency, frequency, and random based exploration techniques. The three populations use identical initial parameters and the same exploration-exploitation method.

Figures 1 and 2 show the difference between the directed and undirected exploration techniques. They show that directed exploration is interesting at the beginning of the simulation period. It directs the exploration towards the use of new actions; which is not always the case for random exploration. It enriches the classifier population at the beginning better than random exploration, and results in a larger accumulation of the environment knowledge. On average, directed exploration does not greatly improve the performance of a firm. The average percent improvement is 3.4 %, reaching a maximum

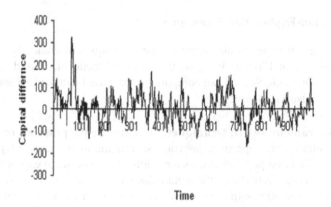

Fig. 1. Random vs. recency-based exploration techniques

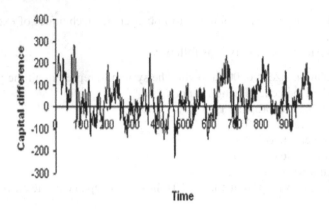

Fig. 2. Random vs. frequency-based exploration techniques

of 9.1% and a minimum of -7%. Table 2 displays the mean and standard deviation of the capital of firms from different simulation runs. The mean of the two techniques of directed exploration is greater than that of the random exploration but this difference is not statistically significant at the 99.95 % level. Therefore, directed-exploration alone is not sufficient to improve the performance of a firm. A balance between exploration and exploitation remains needed.

Table 2. Summary statistics for the capital of firms

Technique	Run	1	2	3	4	5
Random	Standard deviation	99.78	104.22	111.21	128.57	50.11
	Average	869.63	854.64	880.57	875.57	862.43
Frequency	Standard deviation	58.72	123.48	123.53	113.77	125.35
	Average	882.66	874.73	861.91	870.71	883.02
Recency	Standard deviation	123.87	118.44	131.30	122.32	55.35
	Average	872.38	869.61	880.31	886.91	877.57

5.2   Exploration-Exploitation Techniques

The second series of experiments compares the techniques of choice between exploration and exploitation. First, we compare the proposed meta-rules based approach to a random switch approach. Second, we compare the proposed meta-rules based approach to the adapted Wilson techniques.

Meta-rules vs. random switch techniques. To compare the proposed meta-rules approach to a random switch approach, we run a simulation involving two types of populations of firms. The first population uses a random choice between exploration and exploitation whereas the second uses the meta-rules with an $exploitation\_Rate = 20\%$. To focus on the exploration-exploitation switch technique, we endow these populations with identical parameters and with the same exploration technique. We set $n = 20$ and $m = 10$.

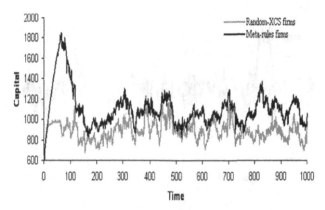

Fig. 3. Comparison of the capital of random XCS firms and meta-rules firms

Figure 3 shows that the use of meta-rules improves the performance of surviving firms. The comparison of the average life span for firms adopting meta-rules (112 periods) to the average life span for random-XCS firms (107 periods) shows that meta-rules improve the resistance of firms. The important degradation of firms performance when meta-rules are applied coincides with the beginning of the exploitation period. This degradation shows that firms should have pursued learning and that it was too early for them to consider exploitation.

Despite their positive impact on the performance of firms, the meta-rules are sensitive to the values of *n* and *m*. Large periods of exploration are advantageous at the beginning when a firm has not learned enough. However, large *n* values could become hazardous when the firm has acquired enough learning. At the end of the simulation, shorter periods of exploration are preferred.

Meta-rules vs. Wilson techniques. The following results are obtained by two simulations. The first includes a population of 300 firms adopting the meta-rules based approach and a population of 300 firms using Wilson adaptive local technique. The second includes the first population and a population of 300 firms using Wilson global adaptive technique. The gain factor for Wilson techniques is set to 0.5. The three populations share the same parameters and strategies except for the exploration-exploitation switch strategy. We compare Wilson local strategy to the meta-rules strategy on Figure 4 while we compare Wilson global strategy to the meta-rules strategy on Figure 5.

Figures 4 and 5 show that the use of meta-rules improves the performance of firms. This improvement is more pronounced with respect to Wilson global adaptive technique. In fact, this strategy does not allow firms to return to exploration once they have acquired enough knowledge and the environment has changed. The improvement is less pronounced when comparing the meta rules to Wilson local technique as the latter reconsiders the choice for each period. The local Wilson strategy is clearly better at the beginning of the simulation period as the meta-rules based approach engages only in exploration for long periods, at the beginning of the simulation. However, in the long run, meta-rules outperform Wilson local strategy. Basing decisions only on current information is not wise on the long run. The meta-rules based approach is promising and could be improved by adapting the *exploitation_Rate* to the age of the firm.

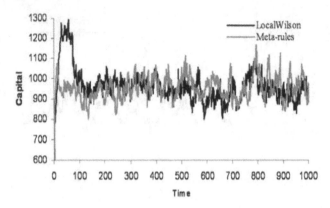

Fig. 4. Comparison of the meta-rules based approach to Wilson local technique

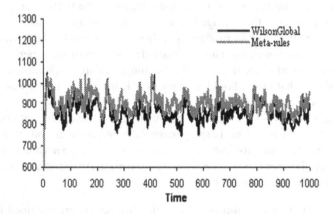

Fig. 5. Comparison of the meta-rules based approach to Wilson global techniques

Table 3. Summary statistics for the average capital of firms under different exploitation-exploration strategies

	Meta-rules	GlobalWilson	LocalWilson
Standard Deviation	44.65	47.97	85.07
Average	912.50	862.19	962.75

These conclusions are further confirmed when we compare the standard deviation and mean capital, displayed in Table 3, of the three populations. A smaller standard deviation of the capitals reflects a more stable behavior of an approach; thus, the meta-rules strategy is more stable than either Wilson Local or Global strategies. Even though its mean is the largest, Wilson local strategy is not necessarily the best strategy because of its very high variation: it could cause a large drop of the capital due to successive erroneous choices between exploration and exploitation and subsequently cause the disappearance of the firm. However, on the long run, the average capital doesn't greatly improve as all firms are simultaneously learning.

6   Conclusion

In this paper, we studied the exploration-exploitation dilemma and learning in the context of large scale economic systems. According to March [8], the choice between exploration and exploitation is the basic component of the organizational learning. It is important for the firm as much more exploitation (over-exploitation) sentences the firm to the obsolescence [6] whereas much more exploration (over-exploration) carries uncertainty and does not guarantee an immediate reward for the firm. The over-exploration and over-exploitation can cause the firm death. In this paper we propose an adaptive approach to avoid over-exploration and over-exploitation by finding a balance between exploration and exploitation. This approach is based on meta-rules that adapt this choice to the evolution of the performance and knowledge of the firm.

The experiments showed that the use of the meta-rules improves the performances of the firm and that the use of directed exploration is useful at the beginning for the construction of the classifiers population as it decreases the learning time of firms. The comparison of these meta-rules to two adaptive techniques, originally proposed by Wilson and adapted herein to a dynamic environment, showed that our approach is the best in the context of our application. However, the adaptation of the rate of change of the meta-rules to the age of the firm is needed.

References

1. Azoulay-Schwartz, R., Kraus, S., Wilkenfeld, J.: Exploration vs. exploitation: choosing a supplier in an environment of incomplete information. Elsevier Science (2003).
2. Baum, J.A.C., Rao, H.: Handbook of Organizational Change and Development: Evolutionary Dynamics of Organizational Populations and Communities. Oxford University Press (1999).
3. Butz, M. V., Wilson, S. W.: An algorithmic description of XCS. Journal of Soft Computing, **6** (2002) 144–153.
4. Carmel, D., Markovitch, S.: Exploration Strategies for Model-Based Learning in Multi-agent Systems. Autonomous Agents and Multi-agent systems. Nicholas Jennings and Katia Sycara and Michael Georgeff (eds.). **2(2)** (1999) 141–172.
5. Gittings, J. C.: Multi-armed bandit allocation indices. NY: John Wiley and sons (1989).
6. Roux-Dufort, C.: L'apprentissage organisationnel et le développement de l'organisation. Développement de l'organisation, Nouveaux regards. Durand, R., Economica (2002) 111-134.
7. Kaelbling, L. P., Moore, A. W.: Reinforcement learning: A survey. Journal of Artificial Intelligence Research, **4**, (1996) 237–285.
8. March, J. G. and Simon, H. A.: Les organisations, Editions Dunod,1991.
9. Meuleau, N., Bourgine, P.: Exploration of multi-state environments: Local measure and back-propagation of uncertainty. Machine Learning. **35(2)** (1999) 117–154.
10. Miramontes Hercog, L., Fogarty, T. C.: Social Simulation Using a Multi-agent Model Based on Classifier Systems: The emergence of Vacillating Behavior in the " El Farol" Bar Problem. In P.L. Lanzi, W. Soltzman and S. Wilson eds.: IWLCS 2001,Volume **2321** of Lecture Notes in Artificial Intelligence. (2002) 88-111.
11. Rejeb, L., Guessoum, Z.: Adaptive Firms. In Proc. AISTA'04 International Conference on Advances in Intelligent Systems - Theory and Applications. In cooperation with the IEEE Computer Society. Luxembourg November (2004).

12. Penrose, E. T.: The theory of the growth of the firm. Basil Blackwell, (1959).
13. Peres-Uribe, A., Hirsbrunner, B.: The risk of Exploration in multi-agent learning systems: a case study. Proc. Agents-00 Joint workshop on learning agents, Barcelona, June 3–7, (2000) 33–37.
14. Sutton, R. S., Barto, A.G.: Reinforcement learning, an introduction. The MIT Press, (1998).
15. Thrun S. B.: The role of exploration in learning control. In D A. Sofge (eds.). Handbook of Intelligent Control: Neural, Fuzzy and Adaptive Approaches. Florence, Kentucky: Van Nostrand Reinhold (1992).
16. Watkins, C., Dayan, P.: Q-Learning. Machine Learning, 8 (1999) 279-292.
17. Wiering, M.: Explorations in Efficient Reinforcement Learning. Ph.D. thesis. February (1999).
18. Wilson, S.W.: Classifiers Fitness Based on Accuracy. Evolutionary computation, 3(2) (1995) 149-175.
19. Wilson, S.W.: Explore/Exploit Strategies in Autonomy. In P. Maes, M. Mataric, J. Pollac, J.-A. Meyer and S. Wilson eds. From Animals to Animats 4, Proc. of the 4th International Conference of Adaptive Behavior, Cambridge (1996).

Efficient Reward Functions for Adaptive Multi-rover Systems

Kagan Tumer[1] and Adrian Agogino[2]

[1] NASA Ames Research Center,
Mail Stop 269-4, Moffet Field, CA 94035,
Phone:650-604-4940, Fax:650-604-4036
ktumer@mail.arc.nasa.gov
[2] UC Santa Cruz, NASA Ames Research Center,
Mail Stop 269-3, Moffet Field, CA 94035,
Phone:650-604-5985, Fax:650-604-4036
adrian@email.arc.nasa.gov

Abstract. This chapter focuses on deriving reward functions that allow multiple agents to co-evolve efficient control policies that maximize a system level reward in noisy and dynamic environments. The solution we present is based on agent rewards satisfying two crucial properties. First, the agent reward function and global reward function has to be aligned, that is, an agent maximizing its agent-specific reward should also maximize the global reward. Second, the agent has to receive sufficient "signal" from its reward, that is, an agent's action should have a large influence over its agent-specific reward. Agents using rewards with these two properties will evolve the correct policies quickly. This hypothesis is tested in episodic and non-episodic, continuous-space multi-rover environment where rovers evolve to maximize a global reward function over all rovers. The environments are dynamic (i.e. changes over time), noisy and have restriction on communication between agents. We show that a control policy evolved using agent-specific rewards satisfying the above properties outperforms policies evolved using global rewards by up to 400%. More notably, in the presence of a larger number of rovers or rovers with noisy and communication limited sensors, the proposed method outperforms global reward by a higher percentage than in noise-free conditions with a small number of rovers.

1 Introduction

Using learning agents to control a large distributed system is a difficult problem, especially when the environment is noisy and dynamic [4, 7, 14]. In particular, treating the collection of agents as a single entity and directly applying sucessful single-agent learning algorithms is problematic because of the exploding state space. Furthermore, many problems are naturally distributed, especially ones where agents have communication limitations. In this chapter we discuss how to extend successful single-agent learning algorithms (e.g., neuro-evolutionary algorithms) are to collectives. A collective is a large, distributed system of agents

K. Tuyls et al. (Eds.): LAMAS 2005, LNAI 3898, pp. 177–191, 2006.
© Springer-Verlag Berlin Heidelberg 2006

where each agent attempts to maxize its own reward and where there is a system-wide global reward to maximize [21, 17, 18]. Our application domain is a collective of data-gathering rovers whose task is to maximize the aggregate information collected by the full collective. In order to distinguish the members of the collective from the individuals in the population of an evolutionary algorithm, we will use "rovers" exclusively to refer to the members of a collective through this paper.[1]

Our approach is based on giving each rover in the collective its own reward function, which it tries to maximize using a learning algorithm. The key issue in such an approach is to ensure that the rover reward function possesses the following two properties: (i) it is aligned with the global reward, ensuring that the rovers that maximize their own reward do not hinder one another and hurt the reward of the collective; and (ii) it is sensitive to the actions of the rover, ensuring that it provides the right selective pressure on the rover (i.e., it limits the impact of other rovers in the reward function).

Our domain has a number of properties that make it particularly difficult for learning algorithms:

1. The environment is dynamic, meaning that the conditions under which the rovers evolve change with time. The rovers need to evolve general control policies, rather than specific policies tuned to their current environment.
2. The rovers have restrictions on their sensing abilities, meaning that the information they have access to is limited. The rovers need to formulate policies that satisfy the global reward function based on limited, local information.
3. The number of rovers in the system can be larger. The rovers need to decouple the impact of other rovers from their reward functions.

This paper provides methods to learn control policies in dynamic environments for large collectives of rovers with limited communication capabilities. In Sections 2 and 3 we discuss the properties needed in a collective, how to evolve rovers using reward functions possessing such properties along with a discussion of related work. In Section 4 we present the "Rover Problem" where planetary rovers in a collective use neural networks to determine their movements based on a continuous-valued array of sensor inputs. Section 5 presents the performance of the rover collective evolved using rover reward functions in dynamic and communication limited domains. The results show the the effectiveness of the rovers in gathering information is 400% higher with properly derived rover reward functions than in rovers using a global reward function. Finally Section 6 we discuss the implication of these results and their applicability to different domains.

2   Rover Reward Function Properties

Let us now derive effective rover reward functions based on the theory of collectives described in [21]. Let the **global reward function** be given by $G(z)$,

---

[1] Note, one can have individuals in a population of rovers or in a population of collectives, depending on where the evolutionary operators are applied.

where z is the state of the full system (e.g., the position of all the rovers in the system, along with their relevant internal parameters and the state of the environment). Let the **rover reward function** for rover i be given by $g_i(z)$. Let us further decompose z into two components: $z = z_i + z_{-i}$. In this decomposition z_i represents all the component of z that are affected by rover i and z_{-i} represents all components of z on which i has no effect.

First we want the private reward functions of each agent to have high *factoredness* with respect to G, intuitively meaning that an action taken by an agent that improves its private reward function also improves the global reward function (i.e. G and g_i are aligned). Formally, the degree of factoredness between g_i and G is given by:

$$\mathcal{F}_{g_i} = \frac{\int_z \int_{z'} u[(g_i(z) - g_i(z')) \, (G(z) - G(z'))] dz' dz}{\int_z \int_{z'} dz' dz} \tag{1}$$

where $z'_{-i} = z_{-i}$, that is z' differs from z only in the state of rover i, and $u[x]$ is the unit step function, equal to 1 when $x > 0$. Intuitively, a high degree of factoredness between g_i and G means that a rover evolved to maximize g_i will also maximize G.

Second, the rover reward function must be more sensitive to changes in that rover's actions than to changes in the actions of other rovers in the collective. Formally we can quantify the *rover-sensitivity* of reward function g_i, at z as:

$$\lambda_{i,g_i}(z) = E_{z'} \left[\frac{\|g_i(z) - g_i(z - z_i + z'_i)\|}{\|g_i(z) - g_i(z' - z'_i + z_i)\|} \right] \tag{2}$$

where $E_{z'}[\cdot]$ provides the expected value over possible values of z', and $(z - z_i + z'_i)$ notation specifies the state vector where the components of rover i have been removed from state z and replaced by the components of rover i from state z'. So at a given state z, the higher the rover-sensitivity, the more $g_i(z)$ depends on changes to the state of rover i, i.e., the better the associated signal-to-noise ratio for i is. Intuitively then, higher rover-sensitivity means there is "cleaner" (e.g., less noisy) selective pressure on rover i.

As an example, consider the case where the rover reward function of each rover is set to the global reward function, meaning that each rover is evaluated based on the actions of the full collective. Such a system will be factored by the definition of Equation 1. However, the rover reward functions will have low rover-sensitivity (the reward of each rover depends on the actions of all other rovers).

3 Difference Reward Functions

Let us now focus on improving the rover-sensitivity of the reward functions. To that end, consider **difference** reward functions [21], which are of the form:

$$D_i(z) \equiv G(z) - G(z_{-i} + c_i) \tag{3}$$

where c_i is a fixed vector. Intuitively, in the second term of Equation 3, all the components of z that are affected by rover i are replaced with the fixed vector c_i. Such difference reward functions are fully factored no matter what the choice of c_i, because the second term does not depend on i's states [21] (e.g., D and G will have the same derivative with respect to z_i). Furthermore, they usually have far better rover-sensitivity than does a global reward function, because the second term of D removes some of the effect of other rovers (i.e., noise) from i's reward function. In many situations it is possible to use a c_i that is equivalent to taking rover i out of the system. Intuitively this causes the second term of the difference reward function to evaluate the value of the system without i and therefore D evaluates the rover's contribution to the global reward.

Though for linear reward functions D_i simply cancels out the effect of other rovers in computing rover i's reward function, its applicability is not restricted to such functions. In fact, it can be applied to any linear or non-linear global utility function. However, its effectiveness is dependent on the domain and the interaction among the rover reward functions. At best, it fully cancels the effect of all other rovers. At worst, it reduces to the global reward function, unable to remove any terms (e.g., when z_{-i} is empty, meaning that rover i effects all states). In most real world applications, it falls somewhere in between, and has been successfully used in many domains including rover coordination, satellite control, data routing, job scheduling and congestion games [3, 19, 21]. Also note that the computation of D_i is a "virtual" operation in that rover i computes the impact of its not being in the system. There is no need to re-evolve the system for each rover to compute its D_i, and computationally it is often easier to compute than the global reward function [19]. Indeed in the problem presented in this paper, for rover i, D_i is easier to compute than G is (see details in Section 5).

4   Continuous Rover Problem

In this section, we show how evolutionary computation with the difference reward function can be used effectively in the Rover Problem[2]. In this problem, there is a collective of rovers on a two dimensional plane, which is trying to observe points of interests (POIs). Each POI has a value associated with it and each observation of a POI yields an observation value inversely related to the distance the rover is from the POI. In this paper the metric will be the squared Euclidean norm, bounded by a minimum observation distance, δ_{min}:[3]

$$\delta(x, y) = \max\{\|x - y\|^2, \delta_{min}^2\} .$$
(4)

---

[2] This problem was first presented in [3].

[3] The square Euclidean norm is appropriate for many natural phenomenon, such as light and signal attenuation. However any other type of distance metric could also be used as required by the problem domain. The minimum distance is included to prevent singularities when a rover is very close to a POI.

The global reward function is given by:

$$G = \sum_t \sum_j \frac{V_j}{\min_i \delta(L_j, L_{i,t})} \,, \tag{5}$$

where V_j is the value of POI j, L_j is the location of POI j and $L_{i,t}$ is the location of rover i at time t. Intuitively, while any rover can observe any POI, as far as the global reward function is concerned, only the closest observation matters[4].

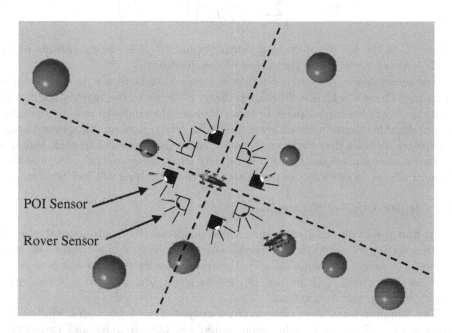

Fig. 1. Diagram of a Rover's Sensor Inputs. The world is broken up into four quadrants relative to rover's position. In each quadrant one sensor senses points of interest, while the other sensor senses other rovers.

4.1 Rover Capabilities

At every time step, the rovers sense the world through eight continuous sensors. From a rover's point of view, the world is divided up into four quadrants relative to the rover's orientation, with two sensors per quadrant (see Figure 1). For each quadrant, the first sensor returns a function of the POIs in the quadrant at time t. Specifically the first sensor for quadrant q returns the sum of the values of the POIs in its quadrant divided by their squared distance to the rover and scaled by the angle between the POI and the center of the quadrant:

---

[4] Similar reward functions could also be made where there are many different levels of information gain depending on the position of the rover. For example 3-D imaging may utilize different images of the same object, taken by two different rovers.

$$s_{1,q,j,t} = \sum_{j \in J_q} \frac{V_j}{\delta(L_j, L_{i,t})} \left(1 - \frac{|\theta_{j,q}|}{90}\right) \tag{6}$$

where J_q is the set of observable POIs in quadrant q and $|\theta_{j,q}|$ is the magnitude of the angle between POI j and the center of the quadrant. The second sensor returns the sum of inverse square distances from a rover to all the other rovers in the quadrant at time t scaled by the angle:

$$s_{2,q,i,t} = \sum_{i' \in N_q} \frac{1}{\delta(L_{i'}, L_{i,t})} \left(1 - \frac{|\theta_{i',q}|}{90}\right) \tag{7}$$

where N_q is the set of rovers in quadrant q and $|\theta_{i',q}|$ is the magnitude of the angle between rover i' and the center of the quadrant.

The sensor space is broken down into four regions to facilitate the input-output mapping. There is a trade-off between the granularity of the regions and the dimensionality of the input space. In some domains the tradeoffs may be such that it is preferable to have more or fewer than four sensor regions. Also, even though this paper assumes that there are actually two sensors present in each region at all times, in real problems there may be only two sensors on the rover, and they do a sensor sweep at 90 degree increments at the beginning of every time step.

4.2   Rover Control Strategies

With four quadrants and two sensors per quadrant, there are a total of eight continuous inputs. This eight dimensional sensor vector constitutes the state space for a rover. At each time step the rover uses its state to compute a two dimensional output. This output represents the x, y movement relative to the rover's location and orientation.

The mapping from rover state to rover output is done through a Multi Layer Perceptron (MLP), with eight input units, ten hidden units and two output units. The MLP uses a sigmoid activation function, therefore the outputs are limited to the range $(0, 1)$. The actual rover motions dx and dy, are determined by normalizing and scaling the MLP output by the maximum distance the rover can move in one time step. More precisely, we have:

$$dx = d_{max}(o_1 - 0.5)$$
$$dy = d_{max}(o_2 - 0.5)$$

where d_{max} is the maximum distance the rover can move in one time step, o_1 is the value of the first output unit, and o_2 is the value of the second output unit.

4.3   Rover Policy Selection

In this work, the MLP for a rover is selected using an evolutionary algorithm. This approach has a long history of success in continuous single agent control problems[20, 10, 7, 2, 11, 1]. In this case, we will assign a population of MLPs to each rover. At each N time steps (N set to 15 in these experiments), the rover uses ϵ-greedy selection ($\epsilon = 0.1$) to determine which MLP it will use (e.g., it it selects the best MLP from its population with 90% probability and a random MLP from its population with 10% probability). The selected MLP is then mutated by adding a value sampled from the Cauchy Distribution (with scale parameter equal to 0.3) to each weight, and is used for those N steps. At the end of those N steps, the MLP's performance is evaluated by the rover's reward function and re-inserted into its population of MLPs, at which time, the poorest performing member of the population is deleted. Both the global reward for system performance and rover reward for MLP selection is computed using an N-step window, meaning that the rovers only receive an reward after N steps.

While this is not a sophisticated evolutionary algorithm, it is ideal in this work since our purpose is to demonstrate the impact of principled reward functions selection on the performance of a collective. Even so, this algorithm has shown to be effective if the reward function used by the rovers is factored with G and has high rover-sensitivity. We expect more advanced algorithms from evolutionary computation, used in conjunction with these same reward functions, to improve the perform collective further.

4.4 Learning Control Strategies in a Collective

The key to success in this approach is to determine the correct rover reward functions. In this work we test three different reward function for rover selection. The first reward function is the global reward function (G), which when implemented results in approach two discussed in Section 2:

$$G = \sum_t \sum_j \frac{V_j}{\min_i \delta(L_j, L_{i,t})} \tag{8}$$

The second reward function is the "perfectly rover-sensitive" reward function(P):

$$P_i = \sum_t \sum_j \frac{V_j}{\delta(L_j, L_{i,t})} \tag{9}$$

The P reward function is equivalent to the global reward function in the single rover problem. In a collective of rover setting, it has infinite rover-sensitivity (in the way rover sensitivity is defined in Section 2). This is because the P reward function for a rover is not affected by the states of the other rovers, and thus the denominator of Equation 2 is zero. However the P reward function is not factored. Intuitively P and G offer opposite benefits, since G is by definition factored, but has poor rover-sensitivity. The final reward function is the difference reward function. It does not have as high rover-sensitivity as P, but is still factored like G. For the rover problem, the difference reward function, D, becomes:

$$D_i = \sum_t \left[\sum_j \frac{V_j}{\min_{i'} \delta(L_j, L_{i',t})} - \sum_j \frac{V_j}{\min_{i' \neq i} \delta(L_j, L_{i',t})} \right]$$

$$= \sum_t \sum_j I_{j,i,t}(z) \left(\frac{V_j}{\delta(L_j, L_{i,t})} - \frac{V_j}{\min_{i' \neq i} \delta(L_j, L_{i',t})} \right)$$

where $I_{j,i,t}(z)$ is an indicator function, returning one if and only if rover i is the closest rover to POI j at time t. The second term of the D is equal to the value of all the information collected if rover i were not in the system. Note that for all time steps where i is not the closest rover to any POI, the subtraction leaves zero. As mentioned in Section 3, the difference reward in this case is easier to compute as long as rover i knows the position and distance of the closest rover to each POI it can see (and the second closest when rover i is the closest). In that regard it requires knowledge about the position of fewer rovers than if it were to use the global reward function. In the simplified form, this is a very intuitive reward function yet it was generated mechanically from the general form if the difference reward function [21]. In this simplified domain we could expect a hand-crafted reward function to be similar. However the difference reward function can still be used in more complex domains with a less tractable form of the global reward, even when it is difficult to generate and evaluate hand-crafted solution. Even in domains where an intuitive feel is lacking, the difference reward function will be provably factored and rover-sensitive.

In the presence of communication limitations, it is not always possible for a rover to compute its exact D_i, nor is it possible for it to compute G. In such cases, D_i can be compute based on local information with minor modifications, such as limiting the radius of observing other rovers in the system. This has the net effect or reducing the factoredness of the reward function while increasing its rover-sensitivity.

5   Results

We performed extensive simulation to test the effectiveness of the different rover reward function under a wide variety of environmental conditions and rover capabilities. In these experiments, each rover had a population of MLPs of size 10. The world was 75 units long and 75 units wide. All of the rovers started the experiment at the center of the world. Unless otherwise stated as in the scaling experiments, there were 30 rovers in the simulations. The maximum distance the rovers could move in one direction during a time step, d_{max}, was set to 3. The rovers could not move beyond the bounds of the world. The minimum observation distance, δ_{min}, was equal to 5.

In these experiments the environment was dynamic, meaning that the POI locations and values changed with time. There were as many POIs as rovers, and the value of each POI was set to between three and five using a uniformly random distribution. In these experiments, each POI disappeared with probability 2.5%, and another one appeared with the same probability at 15 time step intervals. Because the experiments were run for 3000 time steps, the initial and final environments had little similarity.

All of the experiments (except the last one) were done in a non-episodic domain, where the environment continually changed with time. The dynamic environment experiments reported here explore how rover control policies can be generalized from one set of POIs to another, regardless of how significantly the

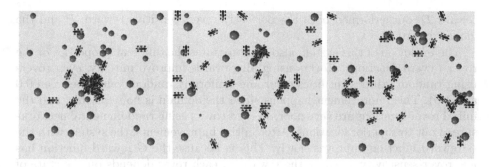

Fig. 2. Sample POI Placement. Left: Environment at time = 15. Middle: Environment at time = 150. Right: Environment at time = 1500.

environment changes. Figure 2 shows an instance of change in the environment throughout a simulation. The final POI set is not particularly close to the initial POI set and the rovers are forced to focus on the sensor input-output mappings rather than focus on regions in the (x, y) plane.

5.1 Learning Rates

The first set of experiments tested the performance of the three reward functions in a dynamic environment for 30 rovers. Figure 3 shows the performance of each reward function. In all cases, performance is measured by the same global reward function, regardless of the reward function used to evolve the system. All three reward functions performed adequately in this instance, though the difference

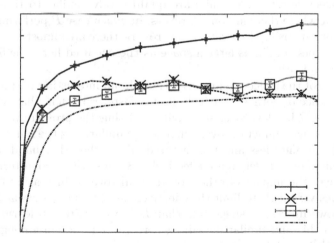

Fig. 3. Performance of a 30-rover collective for all three reward functions in noise-free environment. Difference reward function provides the best collective performance because it is both factored and rover-sensitive. (Random curve smoothed).

reward D_i outperformed both the perfectly rovers sensitive reward, P and the global reward G.

The evolution of this system also demonstrates the different properties of the rover reward functions. Rovers using all rewards improve initially, even rovers using random utilities (utilities returning uniformly random values between 0.0 and 1.0). This improvement happens since the domain is non-episodic, and the initial rover locations are very poor, so even rovers using random neural networks spread out to superior locations. After initial improvements, the system with the G reward function improves slowly. This is because the G reward function has low rover-sensitivity. Because the reward of each rover depends on the state of all other rovers, the noise in the system overwhelms the reward function. P on the other hand has a different problem: After an initial improvement, the performance of systems with this reward function decline. This is because though P has high rover-selectivity, it is not fully factored with the global reward function. This means that rovers selected to improve P do not necessarily improve G. D on the other hand is both factored and has high rover-sensitivity. As a consequence, it continues to improve well into the simulation as the reward signal the rovers receive is not swamped by the states of other rovers in the system. This simulation highlights the need for having reward function that are both factored with the global reward function and have high rover-sensitivity. Having one or the other is not sufficient.

5.2   Scaling Properties

The second set of experiments focused on the scaling properties of the three reward functions in a dynamic environment. Figure 4 shows the performance of each reward function at t=3000 for a collective of 10 to 70 rovers. For each different collective size, the results are qualitatively similar to those reported above, except where there are only 5 rovers, in which case P performs as well as G. This is not surprising since with so few rovers, there are almost no interactions among the rovers, and in as large a space as the one used here, the 5 rovers act almost independently.

As the size of the collective increases though, an interesting pattern emerges: The performance of both P and G drop at a faster rate than that of D. Again, this is because G has low rover-sensitivity and thus the problem becomes more pronounced as the number of rovers increases. Similarly, as the number of rovers increases, P becomes less and less factored. D on the other hand handles the increasing number of rovers quite effectively. Because the second term in Equation 3 removes the impact of other rovers from rover i, increasing the number of rovers does very little to limit the effectiveness of this rover reward functions. This is a powerful results suggesting that D is well suited to learning in large collectives in this and similar domains where the interaction among the rovers prevents both G and P from performing well. This result also supports the intuition expressed in Section 2 that Approach Two (i.e., evolving rovers based on the actions of the full collective) is ill-suited to evolving effective collectives in all but the smallest examples.

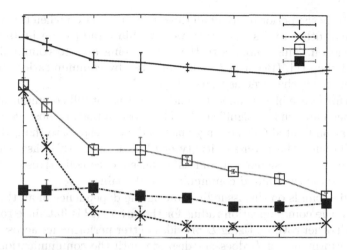

Fig. 4. Scaling properties of the three reward functions. The D reward function not only outperforms the alternatives, but the margin by which it outperforms them increases as the size of the collective goes up.

5.3   Learning with Communication Limitations

The third set of experiments tested the performance of the three reward functions in a dynamic environment where not only the rover sensors were noisy, but the rovers were subject to communication limitations. The communications limitations reduce the amount of information that is available to compute a rover's utility, by reducing the number of other rovers that a rover can observe.

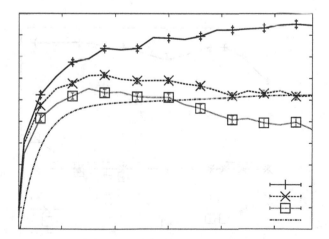

Fig. 5. Results for noisy domain under communication limitations. Rovers can only see of rovers covering an area of 1% of the domain. Difference reward is superior since it is both factored and rover-sensitive. (Random curve smoothed).

Figure 5 shows the performance of all three reward function when the rovers were only aware of other rovers when they were within a radius of 4 units from their current location. This amounts to the rovers being able to communicate with only 1% of the grid. (Because P is not affected by communication limitations, its performance is the same as that of Figure 3.)

The performance of D is almost identical to that of full communication D. G on the other hand suffers significantly. The most important observation is that communication limited G is no longer factored with respect to the global reward function. Though the rover-sensitivity of G goes up in this case, the drop in factoredness is more significant and as a consequence collectives evolved using G cannot handle the limited communication domain.

Figure 6 expands on this issue by showing the dependence of all three reward function on the communication radius for the rovers (P is flat since rovers using P ignore all other rovers). Using D provides better performance across the board and the performance of D does not degrade until the communication radius is dropped to 2 units. This is a severe restriction that practically cuts off the rover from other rovers in the system. G on the other hand needs a rather large communication radius (over 20) to outperform the collectives evolved using P. This result is significant in that it shows that D can be effectively used in many practical information-poor domains where neither G nor "full" D as given in Equation 3 can be accurately computed.

Another interesting phenomena appears in the results presented in Figure 6, where there is a dip in the performance of the collective when the communication radius is at 10 units for both D and G (the "bowl" is wider for G than D, but it is the same effect). This phenomenon is caused by the interaction between the degree of factoredness of the reward functions and their sensitivity. At the maximum communication radius (no limitations) D is highly factored and has

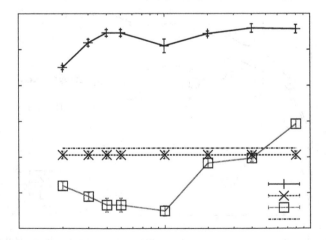

Fig. 6. Sensitivity of the three reward functions to the degree of communication limitations. Difference reward is not affected by communication limitations by as much as global reward.

high rover-sensitivity. Reducing the communication radius starts to reduce the factoredness, while increasing the rover-sensitivity. However, the rate at which these two properties change is not identical. At a communication radius of 10, the drop in factoredness has outpaced the gains in rover-sensitivity and the performance of the collective suffers. When the communication radius drops to 5, the increase in rover-sensitivity compensates for the drop in factoredness. This interaction among the rover-sensitivity and factoredness is domain dependent and has also been observed in previous applications of collectives [16, 18].

5.4 Leaning in Changing Episodic Environment

All the previous experiments were non-episodic, meaning that the environment is not reset over the course of a trial. In episodic domains, learning is performed over a series of episodes with the environment being reset at the beginning of each episode. This section shows results for the episodic version of the Rover Problem. In this problem the rovers move for fifteen time-steps to complete an episode and at the end of the episode the rovers are returned to their original position. In most episodic domains, the environment is also reset to its starting configuration at the beginning of the episode. However, to make this problem more difficult, we reset the POIs to new random positions at the beginning of each trial. By placing the POIs this way, the rovers have to learn a general policy for efficiently navigating using sensors, and cannot form a specific policy to a single environmental configuration.

Figure 7 shows that rovers using D performed best in this scenario. Rovers using D were effective in generalizing the knowledge gained from exploring previous POI configurations and applying that knowledge to new POI configurations. In contrast, rovers using the P rewards were especially ineffective in this scenario.

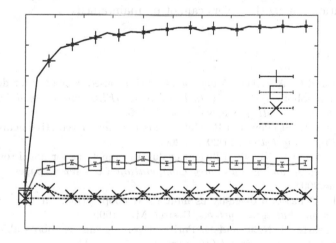

Fig. 7. Learning in an Episodic Domain with Changing Environment. Even in an episodic domain where the environment changes at the end of every episode, agents using the difference reward, D, are still able to achieve high performance.

We attribute this to the congested nature of the problem, where the rovers competed rather than cooperating with each other. Since a rover's P rewards only returns the value of what that rover observes, a rover using the P rewards tends to move towards the highest valued POI in its area. However all the other rovers in that vicinity are also moving towards the same high-valued POI, and thus many other POIs are not properly observed.

6   Discussion

This paper presented a method for providing rover specific reward functions to directly evolve individual rovers in a collective. The fundamental issue in this approach is in determining the rover specific reward functions that are both aligned with the global reward function and are as sensitive as possible to changes in the reward of each member.

In dynamic environments rovers using the difference reward function D, derived from the theory of collectives, were able to achieve high levels of performance because the reward function was both factored and highly rover-sensitive. These rovers performed better than rovers using the non-factored perfectly rover-sensitive reward and more than 400% better (over random rovers) than rovers using the hard to learn global rewards.

We then extended these results to rovers with limited communication capabilities and larger collectives. In each instance the collectives evolved using D performed better than alternatives and in most cases (e.g., larger collectives, communication limited rovers) the gains due to D increase as the conditions worsened. These results show the power of using factored and rover-sensitive reward functions, which allow evolutionary computation methods to be successfully applied to large distributed systems in real world applications where communication among the rovers cannot be maintained.

References

1. A. Agah and G. A. Bekey. A genetic algorithm-based controller for decentralized multi-agent robotic systems. In *In Proc. of the IEEE International Conference of Evolutionary Computing*, Nagoya, Japan, 1996.
2. A. Agogino, K. Stanley, and R. Miikkulainen. Online interactive neuro-evolution. *Neural Processing Letters*, 11:29–38, 2000.
3. A. Agogino and K. Tumer. Efficient evaluation functions for multi-rover systems. In *The Genetic and Evolutionary Computation Conference*, pages 1–12, Seatle, WA, June 2004.
4. T. Balch. Behavioral diversity as multiagent cooperation. In *Proc. of SPIE '99 Workshop on Multiagent Systems*, Boston, MA, 1999.
5. G. Baldassarre, S. Nolfi, and D. Parisi. Evolving mobile robots able to display collective behavior. *Artificial Life*, pages 9: 255–267, 2003.
6. M. Dorigo and L. M. Gambardella. Ant colony systems: A cooperative learning approach to the travelling salesman problem. *IEEE Transactions on Evolutionary Computation*, 1(1):53–66, 1997.

7. S. Farritor and S. Dubowsky. Planning methodology for planetary robotic exploration. In *ASME Journal of Dynamic Systems, Measurement and Control*, volume 124, pages 4: 698–701, 2002.
8. D. Floreano and F. Mondada. Automatic creation of an autonomous agent: Genetic evolution of a neural-network driven robot. In *Proc. of Conf. on Simulation of Adaptive Behavior*, 1994.
9. F. Gomez and R. Miikkulainen. Active guidance for a finless rocket through neuroevolution. In *Proc. of Genetic and Evolutionary Comp. Conf.*, Chicago, IL, 2003.
10. F. Hoffmann, T.-J. Koo, and O. Shakernia. Evolutionary design of a helicopter autopilot. In *Advances in Soft Computing - Engineering Design and Manufacturing, Part 3: Intelligent Control*, pages 201–214, 1999.
11. E. Lamma, F. Riguzzi, and L. Pereira. Belief revision by multi-agent genetic search. In *In Proc. of the 2nd International Workshop on Computational Logic for Multi-Agent Systems*, Paphos, Cyprus, December 2001.
12. A. Martinoli, A. J. Ijspeert, and F. Mondala. Understanding collective aggregation mechanisms: From probabilistic modelling to experiments with real robots. *Robotics and Autonomous Systems*, 29:51–63, 1999.
13. A. Martinoli and F. Mondala. Collective and cooperative group behaviors: Biologically inspired experiments in robotics. In O. Khatib and J. Salisbur, editors, *Proc. of the Fourth Intl. Symp. on Experimental Robotics*. Springer, New York, 1995.
14. M. J. Mataric. Coordination and learning in multi-robot systems. In *IEEE Intelligent Systems*, pages 6–8, March 1998.
15. K. Stanley and R. Miikkulainen. Efficient reinforcement learning through evolving neural network topologies. In *Proceedings of the Genetic and Evolutionary Computation Conference (GECCO-2002)*, San Francisco, CA, 2002.
16. K. Tumer and A. Agogino. Overcoming communication restrictions in collectives. In *Proceedings of the International Joint Conference on Neural Networks*, Budapest, Hungary, July 2004.
17. K. Tumer and D. Wolpert, editors. *Collectives and the Design of Complex Systems*. Springer, New York, 2004.
18. K. Tumer and D. Wolpert. A survey of collectives. In *Collectives and the Design of Complex Systems*, pages 1,42. Springer, 2004.
19. K. Tumer and D. H. Wolpert. Collective intelligence and Braess' paradox. In *Proceedings of the Seventeenth National Conference on Artificial Intelligence*, pages 104–109, Austin, TX, 2000.
20. D. Whitley, F. Gruau, and L. Pyeatt. Cellular encoding applied to neurocontrol. In *International Conference on Genetic Algorithms*, 1995.
21. D. H. Wolpert and K. Tumer. Optimal payoff functions for members of collectives. *Advances in Complex Systems*, 4(2/3):265–279, 2001.

Multi-agent Relational Reinforcement Learning

Explorations in Multi-state Coordination Tasks

Tom Croonenborghs[1], Karl Tuyls[2], Jan Ramon[1], and Maurice Bruynooghe[1]

[1] Department of Computer Science,
Katholieke Universiteit Leuven, Belgium
[2] Institute for Knowledge and Agent Technology,
Universiteit Maastricht, The Netherlands

Abstract. In this paper we report on using a relational state space in multi-agent reinforcement learning. There is growing evidence in the Reinforcement Learning research community that a relational representation of the state space has many benefits over a propositional one. Complex tasks as planning or information retrieval on the web can be represented more naturally in relational form. Yet, this relational structure has not been exploited for multi-agent reinforcement learning tasks and has only been studied in a single agent context so far. In this paper we explore the powerful possibilities of using Relational Reinforcement Learning (RRL) in complex multi-agent coordination tasks. More precisely, we consider an abstract multi-state coordination problem, which can be considered as a variation and extension of repeated stateless Dispersion Games. Our approach shows that RRL allows to represent a complex state space in a multi-agent environment more compactly and allows for fast convergence of learning agents. Moreover, with this technique, agents are able to make complex interactive models (in the sense of learning from an expert), to predict what other agents will do and generalize over this model. This enables to solve complex multi-agent planning tasks, in which agents need to be adaptive and learn, with more powerful tools.

1 Introduction

In recent years, Relational Reinforcement Learning (RRL) has emerged in the machine learning community as a new interesting subfield of Reinforcement Learning (RL) [7, 4, 20]. It offers to RL a state space representation that is much richer than that used in classical (or propositional) methods. More precisely, states are represented in a relational form, that more directly represents the underlying world and allows the representation of complex real world tasks as planning or information retrieval on the web in a more natural manner (see section 2 for an example).

Compared to single agent RL, learning in a MAS is a complex and cumbersome task. Typical for a MAS is that the environment is not stationary and the Markov property is not valid. These characteristics make the transition from a

K. Tuyls et al. (Eds.): LAMAS 2005, LNAI 3898, pp. 192–206, 2006.

one-agent system to a multi-agent system very hard. Furthermore, an agent in a MAS needs to take in account that other agents are also trying to attain the highest utility for their task. A possible solution would be to provide all possible situations an agent can encounter in a MAS and define the best possible behavior in each of these situations beforehand. However, such a solution suffers from combinatorial explosion and is not the most intelligent solution in terms of efficiency and performance.

Yet different approaches have been introduced to solve this multi-agent learning problem ranging from joint action learners [10] to individual local Q-learners. All of these approaches have as well their own merits as disadvantages in learning in a multi-agent context. In the first approach, i.e., the joint action space approach, the state and action space are respectively defined as the Cartesian product of the agent's individual state and action spaces. More precisely, if S is the set of states and $A_1, ..., A_n$ the action sets of the n different agents, the learning will be performed in the product space $S \times A_1 \times ... \times A_n$, where each agent has a reward function of the form: $S \times A_1 \times ... \times A_n \rightarrow \mathbb{R}$. This implies that the state information is shared amongst the agents and actions are taken and evaluated synchronously. It is obvious that this approach leads to very big state-action spaces, and assumes instant communication between the agents. Clearly this approach is in contrast with the basic principles of many contempo rary multi-agent applications such as distributed control, asynchronous actions, incomplete information, cost of communication. In the local or selfish Q-learners setting, the presence of the other agents is totally neglected, and agents are considered to be selfish reinforcement learners. The effects caused by the other agents also acting in that same environment are considered as noise. In between these approaches we can find examples which try to overcome the drawbacks of the joint action approach, examples are [13, 2, 15, 23, 17, 18]. There has also been quite some effort to extend these RL techniques to Partially Observable Markovian decision problems and non-Markovian settings [11].

However, to our knowledge, almost all of these different techniques have been used so far in combination with a state space which is in propositional form, where by no means relations between different features are expressed or exploited. To our belief, multi-agent RL in general could greatly benefit from the ideas of RRL, which has proved to be very successful in the single agent case. In this paper we illustrate the advantages of using RRL in MAS, by doing experiments in an abstract multi-state coordination task. This problem can be considered as a variation and extension of the abstract Dispersion Game (DG), introduced in [8]. More precisely, DGs are a stateless abstract representation of typical load-balancing problems. The goal of the game is to achieve coordination between the different participating agents and fast convergence to a maximally dispersed situation by avoiding to work on cross-purposes. This coordination problem has been acknowledged to be difficult and complex, but can be solved quite good by different RL approaches as for instance local Q-learning. Unfortunately, this problem remains stateless, which is of course a great simplification of real world complex coordination tasks. In this paper we study RRL in an abstract multi-state coordination problem in which tasks consists of multiple subtasks as opposed to in DGs. We believe that RRL can overcome many of the problems encountered by classical RL techniques when trying to solve this type of multi-agent learning problems. These issues include large state spaces, generalization of knowledge, building models of agents and computational cost of the problem. In a first step we study how agents can learn the relational structure of such a problem. We do not consider at this moment the allocation of tasks to agents. Interference of agents in different tasks will be subject of our future work. Questions we answer now include: Can agents learn the relational structure of the problem and other agents? Can they build models of each other improving learnability? Does this improve convergence properties and can agents generalize over the knowledge they learned about other agents?

The rest of this document is structured as follows. Section 2 introduces Relational Reinforcement Learning, Section 3 gives an overview of relevant existing work and introduces the multi-agent RRL task. The experiments are presented in Section 4 and finally Section 5 concludes.

2   Single Agent Relational Reinforcement Learning

2.1   Reinforcement Learning

Reinforcement Learning offers a general framework, including several methods, for constructing intelligent agents that optimize their behavior in stochastic environments with minimal supervision. The problem task of RL [19] using the discounted sum of rewards is most often formulated as follows: Given a set of possible states S, a set of possible actions A, unknown transition probabilities $t: S \times A \times S \rightarrow [0,1]$ and an unknown real-valued reward function $r : S \times A \rightarrow \mathbb{R}$, find a policy which maximizes the expected discounted sum of rewards $V(s_t) = \mathbb{E}\left(\sum_{i=0}^{\infty} \gamma^i r_t\right)$ for all s_t, where $0 \leq \gamma < 1$.

At every time step t, the learning agent is in one of the possible states s_t of S and selects an action $a_t = \pi(s_t) \in A$ according to his policy π. After executing action a_t in s_t, the agent will be in a new state s_{t+1} (this new state is chosen according to the transition probabilities) and receives a reward $r_t = r(s_t, a_t)$.

A drawback of most work on RL, using a propositional representation[1], is the difficulty to represent states that are defined by the objects that are present in this state and the relations between these objects. The real world contains objects. Objects with certain properties, that relate to each other. To apply RL in such complex environments, a structural or relational representation is needed.

To illustrate the need for these structural representations, we will describe the blocks world domain as a Reinforcement Learning problem. The blocks world consists of a number of blocks, which can be on the floor or onto each other. It is assumed that an infinite number of blocks can be put on the floor and that all blocks are neatly stacked onto each other, e.g. a block can only be on one other block at

---

[1] In propositional representations a feature vector is used with an attribute for every possible property of the agent's environment.

the same time. The possible actions consist of moving one clear block (e.g. a block with no other block on top of it) onto another clear block or onto the floor. It is impossible to represent such blocks world states with a propositional representation without an explosion of the number of states. Using First-Order Logic, a blocks world state can be represented as a conjunction of predicates, describing the relations between the blocks, e.g. $\{on(s, b, floor) \wedge on(s, a, b) \wedge clear(s, a) \ldots\}$.

2.2   Relational Reinforcement Learning

Relational Reinforcement Learning combines the RL setting with relational learning or Inductive Logic Programming (ILP). Because of this structural representation, it is possible to abstract from and generalize over specific goals, states and actions and exploit the results of previous learning phases when addressing new and possibly more complex situations.

Furthermore, because relational learning algorithms are used, there is the possibility to use background knowledge. Background knowledge consists of facts or general rules relevant to the examples or problem domain in the context of RL. E.g., in the blocks world, a predicate $above(S, A, B)$ could be defined as the transitive closure of the predicate $on(S, A, B)$. These predicates in the background knowledge can be used in the learning process, i.e., in the representation of a Q-function.

Although, RRL is a relatively new domain, several approaches have been proposed during the last few years, we refer to [20] for an overview.

One of the first methods within RRL, is relational Q-learning [7]. In this work, a Q-learning algorithm is proposed that allows a relational representation for states and actions. The Q-function is represented and learned using an incremental relational regression algorithm. So far, a number of different relational regression learners are developed[2].

Besides relational Q-learning, there has been some work on other methods which is not discussed here. So far, all work on RRL has focused on the single agent case. To our knowledge, there is no existing work on applying relational reinforcement learning in a multi-agent system. Earlier, van Otterlo et al. [24] already mentioned the possible benefits of using RRL in (multi-) agent systems. They state that cognitive and sapient agents especially need a learning component where the reinforcement learning paradigm is the most logical choice for this. Since these agents are (usually) logic-based, RRL is indicated as a very suitable learning method for intelligent agents.

Furthermore, there has been some work in the past on guiding learning agents [5] and combinations with behavioral cloning [14].

3   Relational Multi-agent Reinforcement Learning

During the 90's multi-agent systems have become a very popular approach in solving computational problems of distributed nature as for instance load bal-

---

[2] A thorough discussion and comparison can be found in [4].

ancing or distributed planning systems. They are a conceptually proved solution method for problems of this nature.

However, designing a cooperative multi-agent system with both a global high utility for the system and high individual utilities for the different agents is still a difficult problem [21, 9].The joint actions of all agents derive some reward from the outside world. To enable local learning, this reward has to be divided among the individual agents where each agent aims to increase its received reward. However, unless special care is taken as to how reward is assigned, there is a risk that agents in the collective work at cross-purposes. For example, agents can reach sub-optimal solutions in the blocks world example by competing for the same block or goal state, i.e., by inefficient task distribution among the agents as they each might only consider their own goals which can result in a Tragedy of the Commons situation, or policy oscillations [15].

In this setting different researches have already obtained some very nice results within the framework of stochastic Dispersion Games [8, 21, 9]. Dispersion games are an abstract representation of typical load balancing and niche selection problems. The games are played repeatedly, during which the agents learn to disperse. Still, these dispersion games are far more simple than for instance blocks world planning problems, as there is only one state to consider. We extend this type of work to large planning problems with multiple states, which we will try to solve by an agent-based system, consisting of learning agents in a relational state space.

Combining multi agent systems and relational reinforcement learning combines two complex domains. We believe that, in order to study the integration of these both settings, one should take care not to make the learning task too complex at once, as a mix up of the many different effects playing a role in both domains could make (especially experimental) results difficult to interpret. Therefore, we will first try to separate a number of effects we want to investigate as much as possible independently. In a second part of this section, we will then propose a number of settings of increasing difficulty in which we plan to conduct experiments.

3.1   Complexity Factors

One could describe the main complexity factors of multi agent systems as uninformedness, communication and interference. First, agents are often assumed to be unaware of parts of the world far away where the other agents are operating. This essentially makes the world only partially observable, and hence agents are less informed than in the Markovian situation. Second, agents are unaware of each other's knowledge and intentions. Though these cannot be observed, these can be (partially) revealed by communication. In fact, a lot of work has been published on the study of agent communication. Third, plans and actions of agents can interfere. To act optimally, an agent should take plans and actions of other agents into account (e.g. by knowing them, or by predicting them, or by making his own plan robust).

Relational learning adds extra complexity with increased state and hypothesis spaces, generalization and informedness. This does not necessarily mean that relational learning has a negative impact on the time complexity. First, RRL has been proposed in answer to the need to describe larger state spaces. Through their generalization ability, relational languages allow the compact representation of state spaces, policies, reward, transition and value functions. However, they do not take away the fundamental problem of difficult tasks that the optimal policy is complex and that the learning hardness increases with the state space size. This is illustrated by the fact that in the single agent relational case only some initial convergence results exist [12, 16], but no global guarantees that the policy will converge to an optimal policy in the case generalization over the state space is performed. Second, while the generalization ability is usually beneficial, it also often has the consequence that due to the generalization the world is only partially observable, i.e., it may be difficult to see the difference between states over which the agent generalizes. Third, while a reason for introducing relational languages was the ability to introduce background knowledge and hence make the agent better informed and put him in a better situation to act intelligently, the background knowledge will only be useful when the algorithm has the ability to exploit it. This often adds an extra level of complexity to the algorithm.

3.2 Settings

We will introduce first some terminology. A **setting** is a set of properties of the problem and the agent abilities under consideration. We say a setting has the `comm_reward` property iff the agents are trying to maximize the same common reward function (if one agent gets a reward, all other agents get the same reward). We say a setting has the `know_aim` property iff the agents know what function the other agents are trying to maximize. A setting has property `full_obs` iff the agents can observe the full world, including actions performed by other agents (but excluding internals of the other agents). A setting has property `know_abil` iff the agents know the ability of the other agents, i.e., how good they are at their task (e.g., whether an other agent will perform random actions, or whether an other agent always performs the optimal action). A setting has the property `comm_schedule` iff the agents have a way of communication for deciding who is performing actions at which time point. This e.g., would allow to let more experienced or specialized (but maybe also more costly) agents perform actions in certain types of situations. In a setting with the property `talk` the agents have the ability to communicate about their knowledge.

These properties are defined as general ones, but the same settings can of course be studied when some of these properties are only partially valid, e.g. there is only partial observability, based on some constraints like the kind of agents, their location or agents only know a part of the function other agents are trying to maximize etc. This will make the learning problem obviously more difficult, but the ideas about these properties and the settings in which they are used remain the same.

Table 1. A number of settings with their properties

Setting	other's ability	comm rew	know abil	know aim	observe full obs	observe learn beh	observe learn abil	comm or talk
0. Std. RRL (1 agent)	no			x	x			
1. Local learners	any	x						
2. Guidance	teacher	x		x	x			
3. Guided policy learning	perfect	x	x	x	x			
4. Active guidance	teacher	x		x	x			c
5. Actively guided policy learning	perfect	x	x	x	x			c
6. Describing the solution	perfect	x	x	x	x			c + t
7. Collaborative RRL	any	x		x	x			t
8. Find the teacher	any	x		x	x			
9. Learning behavior	any	x			x	x		
10. Learning abilities	any	x			x	x	x	
11. Learning who to imitate	any	x	x		x	x		
12. Knowing and learning abil	any	x	x		x	x	x	
13. Informed active guidance	any	x	x		x	x		c
14. Partially observable world	any	x		x	x			
15. Different interests	any			x				

If it is the case that the `full_obs` property holds, agents can use these observations to learn extra information. Therefore we define two properties based on the capabilities of the agents. We say the `learn_beh` property holds iff the agents are capable of learning the behavior of the agents they can observe. When agents use their observations about other agents to learn their abilities, the `learn_abil` holds.

We will now describe a number of settings. Table 1 lists these settings together with their properties. In the column "other's ability" we list the ability of the other agents in the world: 'teacher' means an agent having a good (but perhaps not optimal) policy; 'perfect' means an agent with an optimal policy. In the text we will refer to specific entries in the table with numbers between round brackets. The `comm` column has a 'c' if the `comm_schedule` property holds and a 't' if `talk` holds for that particular setting.

The first two settings, are the standard settings, (0) for the single agent case and (1) for the situation in which n single (R)RL-agents are put together in the same environment.

Probably one of the simplest settings is the case where `comm_reward`, `know_aim` and `full_obs` hold. Still, even this simple situation is not fully studied in the relational case. One empirical work is on "guidance" [5]. One can see guidance as a setting with two agents where one is a teacher, and the other is a learner (2). Both the teacher and the learner perform actions, and hence it is more likely that reward is obtained compared to the classical reinforcement learning case. This can be important in difficult planning domains where it would be unlikely to obtain a reward by only exploration. The main advantage is that the teacher directs the exploration towards difficult to reach parts of the state space.

If we also have know_abil and the teacher is known to make only optimal actions (3), the learner can directly use the actions performed by the teacher as examples of optimal actions. He could then use a direct learning algorithm that learns actions from states. Another interesting situation (4,5) is the case with comm_schedule where the learner may ask the teacher to perform an action (at a certain cost). This is described in [5], while several open questions remain. This can also be seen as a form of active learning.

In the presence of a perfect teacher, the talk property together with know_abil (6) makes the problem somewhat trivial as the learner can just ask the teacher for the optimal policy (at least if the learner is able to represent that policy). However, the situation gets much more interesting when we have only comm_reward, know_aim, full_obs, talk and maybe know_abil but no perfect teacher (7). We then have a situation where agents can discuss their learning experiences and even though there is full knowledge, the problem is far from trivial. Indeed, in the relational setting, agents can use very expressive languages to talk. Furthermore, extending the idea of Informed Reinforcement Learning [3], the agents can exchange their learned information. Possible interesting information to share could be subgoals, information about actions like pre- or postconditions but also learned options or macro-actions. No work has been published on which languages are suitable and which questions are most efficient. One could use a language which is a super language of the language to describe states and actions, and can also describe past episodes and statistics. E.g. one could imagine that one agent asks "did you ever see a state with four stacks containing each a red block above a light blue block?" And another agent might answer: "No, but I did see something very similar: I visited 13 states with four stacks containing each a red block above a dark blue one. Is that of interest to you?". Apart from the usual communication issues, one could investigate issues such as the following. What questions are useful in a communication? How to get the desired information at the lowest cost? What generalizations are needed for that? When is it cheaper to explore and find it out yourself?

Another unsolved task (8) occurs in the situation where an agent sees several other agents and knows that some of them are quite good agents. In such a situation it may be interesting to try and find the best agent to learn from. But as the reward is collective, it may not be trivial to detect who is performing the best actions. Or maybe, some agents are experts in certain areas of the state space, and it might be interesting to learn concepts describing the other agent's expertise (the areas where they perform well).

So far we have described settings that are determined by the environment, but agents can also learn information that is not provided by the environment. One such interesting setting is when learn_beh holds (9). Here the agents will use their observations to learn the behavior of the agents they observe. This can for instance be obtained by learning a model for every observable agent that predicts the probability that this agent will perform some action in a certain state. Examples to learn such a model can easily be generated if one can observe (some of) the actions made by other agents. Positive examples are the actual actions that are executed by that agent (at least according to their observation), actions executed by other agents can be used as negative examples or they can also be randomly generated. Interesting to note is that since negative examples can be easily generated, one can supply the learner with more examples per observation to accelerate the learning.

This setting becomes particularly interesting when also the know_abil property holds (11), because agents can then execute the actions they believe the expert would make in that situation. Note that this learning task boils down to behavioral cloning [1].

If know_abil does not hold, one can still have learn_abil where the agents can use their observations to try to learn these abilities (10). Learning these abilities can be based on the rewards the agents receive for their actions, but since this information is often not available, another possibility is for instance to learn the average time an agent is working on some task to estimate his abilities for that task. It is of course also possible to have both know_abil and learn_abil especially when the given information about the agents abilities is only partial (12).

When we also have the comm_schedule or even talk property (13), an extension of the active guidance settings occurs. This could be seen as informed active guidance since agents can use their learned knowledge about the other agents to restrict communication. The list of learnable knowledge from observations can of course be extended with models that learn what the results of an agents actions are, that learns what other agents are trying to achieve, i.e., the know_aim property, etc.

In what precedes, we have listed a number of (partly) unsolved tasks which may be assumed to be 'easy' for the learner. Of course, one can make the problems much more difficult by adding a number of supplementary complexity factors, such as partial observability (14) or situations where not all agents try to reach the same goal (15).

4   Experiments

In this section, we will present results from experiments in some of the settings of Table 1, more specifically on experiments where the full_obs property is used to learn extra information about the other agents and hence accelerate convergence. Previously, we reported on preliminary results where the RRL system is used in the blocks world with multiple agents to analyze the problem of interference and incomplete information, see [22] for more details. Here, we will concentrate on experiments showing the gain of learning the relational structure between the different agents in the system.

4.1   Experimental Setup

The test environment we use can be seen as a first step toward multi-state dispersion- and cooperation games, but since at the moment we would like to avoid the problem of interference between the agents, all agents are working on their own task without the possibility to interfere with each other. Not only is this still a challenging problem, an isolated study of the relations between the agents and methods that gain maximally from this, are necessary to tackle more complex problems involving communication and especially interference between agents as for instance in multi-state coordination tasks.

The agents need to fulfill some identical task, this task can be solved by sequentially solving a number of subtasks. Since all tasks are identical, all agents need to solve the same subtasks in the same order.

More specifically, the basic setting is a system with four agents, where each agent needs to solve a certain task by sequentially solving four subtasks. A subtask can only be solved by executing the optimal action and only one of a possible 40 actions is optimal.

When all subtasks are successfully solved, the agents are rewarded with a reward of 1.0, for all other actions they receive neither reward nor punishment. Episodes are ended when all agents have solved all of their subtasks or when a maximum of 800 actions is executed (by all agents together). When the quality of the learned policies are tested, episodes are ended after 40 actions to indicate how many agents learned at least a near-optimal policy.

It is also possible that some agents have prior knowledge about some subtask, i.e. they know what the optimal action is for that subtask. In the basic setting, each agent knows a priori how to solve one subtask optimally and hence he can be called an expert for that subtask. So, the goal of the agents is to learn how to optimally solve the full task.

The settings and language bias. We will compare results obtained with the basic setting where all agents are local learners (1) and the settings where observations are used to learn extra knowledge about the other agents and the environment (9-12). One can note that for this environment setting (1) converts to the single-agent case, but averaged over the different agents.

All the agents in the different settings use the same tree building regression algorithm (RRL-TG [6]). To guide this tree building a declarative bias can be specified. This declarative bias can contain a language bias to specify the predicates that can be used as tests in the tree to partition the state and action space. For all agents this language bias contains predicates that identify the subtask and inequalities to partition the action space.

If agents have the learn_beh property they can build a model, using the same algorithm and declarative bias, predicting the probability that an agent will perform some action for some subtask. The examples generated to learn these models consists of the actual actions taken as possible examples and for every positive examples, 10 random actions (different from the actual taken action) are generated as negative examples. In fact, different models will be learned for every subtask. Their language bias for building the Q-function is extended with predicates that test the probability that a specific agent will perform a specific action for some specific subtask, according to the learned model. Note, that it would be possible to test for the most probable action to be executed by an agent, but with the current implementation of the RRL-TG algorithm this requires to iterate over all possible actions every time this query would be posed. Due to their complexity such predicates are not used in the experiments here.

Agents having the `learn_abil` property will learn models that estimate the percentage of the time spent by some agent on some subtask during an episode. To use this information, tests that partition this probability space can be used in the Q-function.

4.2   Experimental Results

First, we will present the results obtained using the above described settings and test environment. In the following subsection, we will discuss the scaling possibilities of these settings and we conclude this section with some notes on generalization. The figures show the reward received by all agents averaged over ten test episodes and five test runs.

Basic settings. As illustrated by Figure 1 the learning rate increases significantly when the agents have the `learn_beh` property. It is also clear that having `know_abil` or `learn_abil` outperforms the setting with just `learn_beh`. These experiments also show that for this test environment `learn_abil` performs equally well as having `know_abil`, which means that the abilities of the other agents are easily learned for this environment setup. It is needless to say that in general there can be a big difference between these two properties. Consequently, it is no surprise that having both `know_abil` and `learn_abil` does not further increase the learning rate.

When `learn_beh` holds, the learned Q-functions make use of the subtask identification predicates and the expected actions by the experts for that subtask. Since the learning agent is only interested in distinguishing the optimal actions from the non-optimal actions, it is easier to learn this directly from positive and negative examples. Having this knowledge, it is easy for the learning agent to detect that the Q-values will be higher when executing this action (since he will progress to the next subtask). Hence, when also `know_abil` or `learn_abil` holds,

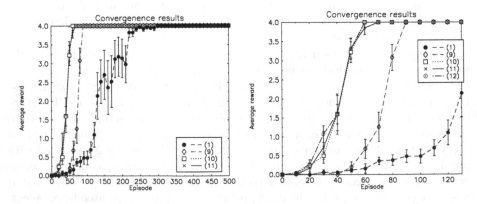

Fig. 1. Standard experiments

it becomes easier for the learning agent to know which agent to address for every subtask.

Scaling. In this section, we will show the results when the environment parameters are increased: the number of possible actions, the agents in the system and the number of subtasks. Since the settings (10), (11) and (12) performed more or less the same, we only show one in the following graphs. We have omitted the variances in order not to overload the images too much.

Figure 2(a) shows the results when we increase the number of actions to 80 possible actions (per subtask). This is a more difficult learning problem for setting (1), although the variance in these 5 runs was rather high, there is no significant change on the learning rate of settings (9) and (11). This can easily be explained by the structure of the learned Q-function as described above.

To test the settings with 8 agents (Figure 2(b)), the length of test episodes was increased to 80 in order to keep the number of available steps per agent constant. Since each agent still has prior expert knowledge about one subtask,

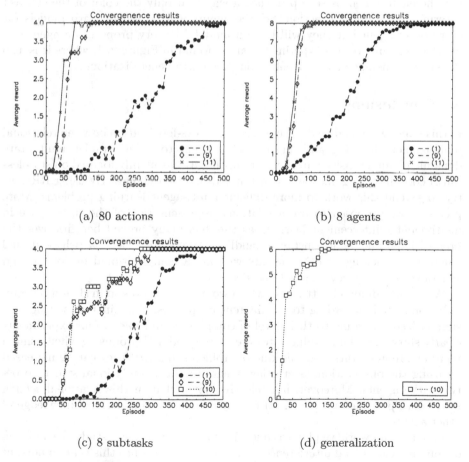

(a) 80 actions   (b) 8 agents

(c) 8 subtasks   (d) generalization

Fig. 2. Scaling and generalization experiments

the situation arises where two agents are expert in one subtask. This means that the learning task for every agent does not really become more difficult since the percentage of experts per subtask remains the same.

When we increase to number of subtasks to 8 (Figure 2(c)), the learning problem becomes more difficult, even if every agent is expert for two different subtasks, so that the results are not influenced by the lack of experts for some subtask.

Generalization. In the previous experiments, the agents learned a different model for every agent. In practice, there will often be a distinction between different kind of agents and the agents can be described by characteristics. The last experiment will show that it is also possible to learn models that generalize over several agents. The setup used for this experiment consists of 6 agents that need to solve 6 subtasks. The main difference with the previous experiments is that the agents and subtasks are described by their characteristics. The agents and subtasks all have a color (green, blue or yellow) and a size (small or large) and every agent is expert for the subtask that has the same characteristics, but the environment is set up in such a way that only the color of the subtask determines the optimal action. So, the agents will no longer learn models for every other agent but they will learn a model for every property an agent can have. The results of this experiment can be found in Figure 2(d) where it is also shown that the agents can benefit from this extra generalization.

5   Conclusions

In this paper we introduced the novel idea of cross-fertilization between relational reinforcement learning and multi-agent systems to solve complex multi-state dynamic planning tasks. Current state-of-the-art has mainly focused on stateless (anti) coordination games as for instance Dispersion Games. By using RRL we try to extend this work to more difficult multi-agent learning problems. More precisely, we proposed to use a relational representation of the state space in multi-agent reinforcement learning as this has many proved benefits over the propositional one, as for instance handling large state spaces, a rich relational language, modelling of other agents without a computational explosion, and generalization over new derived knowledge.

We defined different settings in which we believe this research should be carefully conducted, according to six different properties. The different settings are summarized according to their level of complexity in Table 1. Our experiments clearly show that the learning rates are quite good and promising when using a relational representation in this kind of problems and that they can be increased by using the observations over other agents to learn a relational structure between the agents. Moreover, it is clearly shown that in this relational setting it becomes possible and beneficial to generalize over new derived knowledge of other agents.

In our future work we plan to continue along this track and study the addition of communication and interference between the agents since this is an important part of every multi-agent system. A thorough theoretical study of the described properties and settings will also be part of our future research.

Acknowledgements

Tom Croonenborghs is supported by the Flemish Institute for the Promotion of Science and Technological Research in Industry (IWT). Karl Tuyls is sponsored by the Interactive Collaborative Information Systems (ICIS) project, supported by the Dutch Ministry of Economic Affairs, grant nr: BSIK03024. Jan Ramon is a post-doctoral fellow of the Fund for Scientific Research (FWO) of Flanders.

References

1. M. Bain and C. Sammut. *Machine Intelligence Agents*, chapter A Framework for Behavioral Cloning, pages 103–129. Oxford University Press, 1995.
2. C. Claus and C. Boutilier. The dynamics of reinforcement learning in cooperative multi-agent systems. In *Proceedings of the 15th International Conference on Artificial Intelligence, p. 746-752*, 1998.
3. T. Croonenborghs, J. Ramon, and M. Bruynooghe. Towards informed reinforcement learning. In P. Tadepalli, R. Givan, and K. Driessens, editors, *Proceedings of the ICML2004 Workshop on Relational Reinforcement Learning*, pages 21–26, Banff, Canada, July 2004.
4. K. Driessens. *Relational Reinforcement Learning*. PhD thesis, Department of Computer Science, Katholieke Universiteit Leuven, 2004. http://www.cs.kuleuven.be/publicaties/doctoraten/cw/CW2004_05.abs.html.
5. K. Driessens and S. Dzeroski. Integrating guidance into relational reinforcement learning. *Machine Learning*, 57(3):271–304, Dec. 2004.
6. K. Driessens, J. Ramon, and H. Blockeel. Speeding up relational reinforcement learning through the use of an incremental first order decision tree learner. In L. De Raedt and P. Flach, editors, *Proceedings of the 12th European Conference on Machine Learning*, volume 2167 of *Lecture Notes in Artificial Intelligence*, pages 97–108. Springer-Verlag, 2001.
7. S. Džeroski, L. De Raedt, and K. Driessens. Relational reinforcement learning. *Machine Learning*, 43:7–52, 2001.
8. T. Grenager, R. Powers, and Y. Shoham. Dispersion games: General definitions and some specific learning results. In *Eighteenth National Conference on Artificial Intelligence, Edmonton, Alberta, Canada, Pages: 398 - 403*, 2002.
9. P. Hoen and K. Tuyls. Engineering multi-agent reinforcement learning using evolutionary dynamics. In *Proceedings of the 15th European Conference on Machine Learning*, 2004.
10. J. Hu and M. P. Wellman. Experimental results on Q-learning for general-sum stochastic games. In *ICML '00: Proceedings of the Seventeenth International Conference on Machine Learning*, pages 407–414. Morgan Kaufmann Publishers Inc., 2000.
11. L. Kaelbling, M. Littman, and A. Moore. Reinforcement learning: A survey. *Journal of Artificial Intelligence Research*, 1996.

12. K. Kersting and L. De Raedt. Logical Markov Decision Programs and the Convergence of Logical TD(λ). In *Proceedings of the 14th International Conference on inductive logic programming.* Springer-Verlag, 2004. To appear.
13. M. Littman. Markov games as a framework for multi-agent reinforcement learning. In *Proceedings of the Eleventh International Conference on Machine Learning, p 157 - 163*, 1994.
14. E. F. Morales and C. Sammut. Learning to fly by combining reinforcement learning with behavioural cloning. In *ICML '04: Proceedings of the Twenty-First International Conference on Machine Learning*, page 76, New York, NY, USA, 2004. ACM Press.
15. A. Nowé, J. Parent, and K. Verbeeck. Social agents playing a periodical policy. In *Proceedings of the 12th European Conference on Machine Learning, p 382 - 393, Freiburg*, 2001.
16. J. Ramon. On the convergence of reinforcement learning using a decision tree learner. In *Proceedings of ICML-2005 Workshop on Rich Representation for Reinforcement Learning, Bonn, Germany*, 2005. URL = http://www.cs.kuleuven.ac.be/cgi-bin-dtai/publ_info.pl?id=41743.
17. S. Sen, S. Airiau, and R. Mukherjee. Towards a Pareto-optimal solution in general-sum games. In *in the Proceedings of the Second Intenational Joint Conference on Autonomous Agents and Multiagent Systems, (pages 153-160), Melbourne, Australia, July 2003*, 2003.
18. P. Stone. Layered learning in multi-agent systems. *Cambridge, MA: MIT Press*, 2000.
19. R. Sutton and A. Barto. *Reinforcement Learning: An Introduction.* The MIT Press, Cambridge, MA, 1998.
20. P. Tadepalli, R. Givan, and K. Driessens. Relational reinfocement learning: An overview. In *Proceedings of the ICML'04 Workshop on Relational Reinfocement Learning*, 2004.
21. K. Tumer and D. Wolpert. COllective INtelligence and Braess' Paradox. In *Proceedings of the Sixteenth National Conference on Artificial Intelligence, pages 104-109.*, 2000.
22. K. Tuyls, T. Croonenborghs, J. Ramon, R. Goetschalckx, and M. Bruynooghe. Multi-agent relational reinforcement learning. In K. Tuyls, K. Verbeeck, P. J. 't Hoen, and S. Sen, editors, *Proceedings of the First International Workshop on Learning and Adaptation in Multi Agent Systems*, pages 123–132, Utrecht, The Netherlands, July 25-26 2005.
23. K. Tuyls, K. Verbeeck, and T. Lenaerts. A selection-mutation model for Q-learning in Multi-Agent Systems. In *The second International Joint Conference on Autonomous Agents and Multi-Agent Systems. ACM Press, Melbourne, Australia*, 2003.
24. M. van Otterlo. A characterization of sapient agents. In *International Conference Integration of Knowledge Intensive Multi-Agent Systems (KIMAS-03)*, Boston, Massachusetts, 2003.

Multi-type ACO for Light Path Protection

Peter Vrancx, Ann Nowé, and Kris Steenhaut

Vrije Universiteit Brussel
{pvrancx, ann.nowe, kris.steenhaut}@vub.ac.be

Abstract. Backup trees (BTs) are a promising approach to network protection in optical networks. BTs allow us to protect a group of working paths against single network failures, while reserving only a minimum amount of network capacity for backup purposes. The process of constructing a set of working paths together with a backup tree is computationally very expensive, however. In this paper we propose a multi-agent approach based on ant colony optimization (ACO) for solving this problem. ACO algorithms use a set of relatively simple agents that model the behavior of real ants. In our algorithm multiple types of ants are used. Ants of the same type collaborate, but are in competition with the ants of other types. The idea is to let each type find a path in the network that is disjoint with that of other types. We also demonstrate a preliminary version of this algorithm in a series of simple experiments.

1 Introduction

High speed optical transport networks (OTNs) have been gaining importance during the last years. By using Wavelength Division Multiplexing these networks are able to transmit multiple signals simultaneously over the different wavelengths on a single optical link. In these wavelength-routed networks optical cross-connects can be used to establish light paths, or end-to-end high speed optical links. These light paths allow signals to be sent through the network without having to convert them between optical and electrical signals at each network node. In this paper we consider the problem of protecting a set of these lightpaths against single network failures through the use of a backup tree (BT). We propose a heuristic approach based on ant colony optimization to route these light paths and establish a backup tree to protect them.

We first explain the concept of backup trees and clearly state the problem at hand. In the next section we give a short overview of the ant colony optimization metaheuristic. We then explain how we extended the original metaheuristic to include multiple competing types of ants and explain our Ant Colony Optimization (ACO) algorithm for finding BTs.

2 Backup Trees

In many networks it is crucial that the network can recover quickly from single (node or link) failures. This is especially the case in OTNs were a single failure

K. Tuyls et al. (Eds.): LAMAS 2005, LNAI 3898, pp. 207–215, 2006.

can affect an enormous amount of traffic. One approach used in Multi-Protocol Label Switched (MPLS) IP networks is to have a backup path (BP) for each working path (WP). This means that each source node in the network keeps 2 (node) disjoint paths for every destination node it has to address in the network: a working path and a backup path. As long as the primary working path does not fail, this path is used to forward all packets to the destination node. If the working path fails, the node switches to the backup path. Such a pre-configured scheme has the advantage that it is very fast and minimizes network outages.

In optical networks this approach causes problems because of the use of wavelength domain multiplexing. Each optical link offers a number of wavelengths or channels that can be used to transmit data over. When we establish a (light) path in an OTN we reserve a channel on each link from the source node to the destination node. The wavelength used by the light path is then no longer available for other traffic until the light path is removed. As we want our backup paths to be ready at the instant that a failure occurs, this circuit based approach means we need a dedicated wavelength on each link used by a backup path. This leads to a large amount of network capacity being reserved for backup purposes. Earlier studies [10] have reported savings in network capacity of about 15% by using backup trees over a dedicated path scheme.

Backup trees [9] are a strategy to minimize the capacity drain while still protecting the working paths. The idea is to join backup paths that lead to the same destination node into a single backup tree. In Figure 1 we see an example of how 2 backup paths are combined into a single tree. Using a tree instead of a set of distinct paths means that the wavelengths on common links are shared, thus reducing the amount of capacity reserved.

It should be noted that this scheme only protects against *single* path failures. Multiple failures can still cause interruptions as they can disable multiple paths protected by the same backup tree or both the working path and backup tree. To make sure that the network can deal with single failures all working paths and the backup tree protecting them should be mutually node disjoint.

The optimization problem of routing the working paths and protecting them by a backup tree was stated by Groebbens et al [9, 10] as follows:

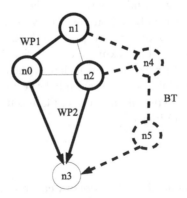

Fig. 1. Example of 2 working paths (bold) protected by a backup tree (dashed)

- Working Paths should fulfill the connection demand,
- a Backup Path should be (node) disjoint with its Working Path,
- Working Paths to the same destination node should be mutually disjoint as much as possible,
- Backup Paths of disjoint Working Paths to the same destination should overlap as much as possible,
- Backup Paths of disjoint Working Paths to the same destination that overlap should form a tree structure (a BT) to that destination (so once they overlap they should continue to overlap until the destination node is reached),
- The objective is to minimize the cost in terms of wavelengths that are consumed by the WPs and the BTs (note there are several BTs to each destination node).

In this paper we propose a heuristic approach for routing the WPs and an associated backup tree. Given a destination and a number of source nodes, our algorithm will try to route the working paths and the associated backup paths in a way that satisfies the above constraints. It should be noted that this is not a dynamic, but a static routing problem. Typically the working paths and backup trees are routed before the network is set up. The traffic demands for which we have to find paths and backup trees are assumed to be known in advance. Because the problem is highly coupled, however, it remains very hard to solve and a heuristic approach is called for. In [9, 10] an heuristic approach based on Integer Linear Programming is suggested. Our ultimate goal is to develop an ACO algorithm for this problem and compare its performance with these "traditional" algorithms. ACO algorithms have already been proposed for dynamic routing problems [3, 14] and recently ACO approaches for static (edge) disjoint path problems were introduced [12, 1].

3   Ant Colony Optimization

Ant Colony Optimization [6, 5] is a relatively new metaheuristic based on the observation that real ants are capable of finding the shortest path between 2 locations. To do this ants rely on a system of indirect communication through pheromones. An ant leaves a trail of pheromones while it walks. Other ants that encounter this trail have a high probability of following it, and reinforcing it with their own pheromones. When faced with multiple possible paths this system allows an ant colony to converge on a single path. In addition, since shorter paths allow faster travel, they accumulate pheromones faster and are more likely to be selected by the colony.

Based on this mechanism Colorni et al [7, 4] proposed the first algorithm of the ant colony metaheuristic. The metaheuristic consists of a number of algorithms that mimic the pheromone communication of real ants in order to solve a wide range of optimization problems. In ACO algorithms a number of antlike agents construct solutions by adding (problem specific) solution components to a partial solution. In our particular case these solution components are network links that are added to an ant's path. The decision of which component to add is made probabilistically, based on an artificial pheromone associated with each component. The original Ant System [7] assigned following probability to each possible next component c:

$$P(c) = \frac{[\tau(c)]^\alpha [\eta(c)]^\beta}{\sum_a [\tau(a)]^\alpha [\eta(a)]^\beta} \tag{1}$$

The probability of adding a solution component depends on the pheromone τ that is associated with it as well as a problem specific heuristic value η. The powers α and β are algorithm parameters that determine an ant's sensitivity towards both factors. The probability is normalized by taking the sum over all possible next components a.

When an ant agent completes its solution, it updates the pheromones concentrations for each of the solution components it used. The update for each component depends on the global quality of the solution the agent produced. Pheromone updates consist of two parts: an evaporation and a pheromone deposit.

$$\tau(c) \leftarrow \rho\tau(c) + \Delta\tau(c) \tag{2}$$

Pheromone evaporation is simulated by multiplying the current amount of pheromones with a factor $0 \leq \rho \leq 1$. Evaporation is needed to bound the increase in pheromone concentrations and prevent early stagnation of the algorithm [2, 8]. Pheromone evaporation can be global (all pheromones are evaporated at regular intervals) or can be performed only when a component receives a pheromone deposit.

The pheromone deposit adds additional pheromones $\Delta\tau(c)$ to the components that were used in an ant's solution. The amount of pheromones deposited depends on the quality of the solutions that the component was used in. Generally a solution cost function $cost(S)$ is used to calculate the cost of a solution S. The pheromone deposit obtained from an ant with solution S, is calculated as $1/cost(S)$ if the component was used in S, and 0 otherwise. Several different strategies have been proposed [8] for the pheromone deposit ranging from an elitist system that only lets the best ant deposit pheromones to systems in which each ant is allowed to deposit pheromones.

4   Multi-type ACO

Multi-type ACO extends the original Ant Colony algorithms with multiple types of competing ants, each using their own type of pheromones. The purpose is to better adapt the algorithms to problem situations where there is an inherent amount of competition present. An example of this arises in network routing, where ants need to collaborate to find good paths, but at the same time ants from different source nodes are in competition for the use of good links.

In the multi-type system this is modeled by using different types of ants that each work on their own solution (e.g. a source-destination path in routing problems). The ants still collaborate with other ants of the same type, but compete with ants of different types. This collaboration and competition system is modeled through the pheromones the ants deposit. Ants are still attracted to pheromone of their own type, but repulsed by pheromones left by other types. A multi-type system for the Multiple Edge Disjoint Paths problem was previously reported in [12, 16]. Similar systems were proposed earlier by Varela and Sinclair [15] for routing and wavelength assignment in optical networks, and by Kawamura et al.[11] with the aim of increasing variation in the ACO search process.

4.1   Our Algorithm

In this section we outline the multi-type algorithm for light path protection. The algorithm routes a set of working paths together with their backup tree. Currently we assume sufficient wavelengths are available. In practice we will also need to consider the problem of wavelength assignment.

Problem decomposition. The algorithm we propose finds a set of WPs and a backup tree to a single destination. This is a subproblem of the problem stated in section 2. Typically we will have several destinations each possibly requiring more than 1 BT, depending on the number of sources sending to the destination. This means that in order to apply our algorithm we must group together a number of sources sending to the same destination. During this grouping we must take in account which nodes can effectively share a BT and the number of feasible disjoint paths. The degrees of both source and destination nodes together with the topology of the network play an important role in determining the number of feasible paths. One possible method for grouping source nodes is proposed in [9].

Given a group of source nodes and a destination node in the network, the algorithm will look for a set of working paths and a backup tree so that following constraints are met:

- Working paths should be mutually disjoint.
- Each working path should be protected by a node disjoint backup path.
- Backup paths should form a tree rooted at the destination node, sharing as many links as possible.
- The total cost of all paths should be minimal.

Solution construction. The algorithm assigns 1 ant type to find each working path and 1 type to build the backup tree. The WP ants types each start from a their own source node, the backup ants are distributed equally among the source nodes. The idea is that the BT ants starting from different source nodes will be attracted by each other, but repulsed by the ants looking for working paths. This will lead BT ants to share links with BT ants starting form other source nodes, while trying to avoid sharing with WP ants. The working path ants are repelled by both other WP types and the BT type. Their goal is to find a path that is completely node disjoint with that of all other types.

In order to build a path each ant makes a number of probabilistic choices. These choices are based on the pheromones left on networks links by the ants.

An ant considers 2 quantities of pheromones: pheromones of its own type and foreign pheromones which are the total amount of pheromones deposited by all other ant types. In each node the ant uses Formula 3 to assign a probability to each outgoing link leading to an unvisited neighbour node. The ant then chooses the next node according to the assigned probabilities. The formula we use is an extension of the original Ant System formula that was stated earlier:

$$P(i,j) = \frac{[\tau(i,j)]^\alpha [\eta(i,j)]^\beta [1/\phi(j)]^\gamma}{\sum_l [\tau(i,l)]^\alpha [\eta(i,l)]^\beta [1/\phi(l)]^\gamma} \tag{3}$$

The powers α, β and γ are parameters that dictate the ants sensitivity towards the different factors. $\tau(i,j)$ is the pheromone associated with the link (i,l) that belongs to the ant's own type. $\phi(l)$ represents the total foreign pheromone associated with the possible next node l. We explain below how this is calculated. The η heuristic factor is equal to $\frac{1}{cost(i,j)}$ so that the ant initially has a preference towards using lower cost links. The probabilities are normalized with the sum of the probabilities of all possible links (i,l).

It has been shown in earlier papers that repulsion by foreign pheromones can be used to obtain edge disjoint paths [12]. In [12] the total foreign pheromones were defined as the sum of all pheromones on the link deposited by other ant types. In the application studied here we want to obtain node disjoint paths, however. In order to achieve this we do not simply consider the foreign pheromones on the link. In the backup tree algorithm we consider all foreign pheromones associated with the destination node of the link an ant is considering. The foreign pheromone associated with a node is taken to be the maximum amount of foreign pheromones on any link arriving or starting from the node. This amount indicates how intensively the node is used by other ant types. Nodes that are heavily used by other ant types will have at least one incoming or outgoing link that has a high amount of foreign pheromones.

5   Experimental Results

In this section we show some experimental results obtained for the proposed algorithm. We use here a simplified version that operates on a graph. The algorithm runs for a number of iterations. Each iteration the source nodes simultaneously launch a fixed number of ants. When all ants have finished their paths, the pheromones in the graph are updated. The purpose of this section is only to indicate the possibilities of the proposed approach. Parameter values were based on settings found to be appropriate for the edge disjoint path problem. These settings seem to give reasonable results but a more thorough investigation of the influence of parameter settings is still needed.

The algorithm was run on a graph based on the Qwest North American Telecom network [13]. This network has 14 nodes corresponding to major North American cities. The nodes are connected by 25 links which we assume to be bidirectional. Each link in the network has an associated cost that is proportional to the link length.

Table 1. Finding disjoint paths. Column 1 shows the number of sources considered. Column 2 shows the percentage of tries in which the algorithm successfully found disjoint paths. Column 3 shows the average number of shared nodes in non disjoint paths. Results were taken over 100 algorithm runs. Settings: $\alpha = 1, \beta = 1, \gamma = 3, \rho = 0.99$, 10 ants , 500 iterations.

sources	disjoint	shared
3	94	1
4	86	1.2
5	96	1

Table 2. Building trees. Column 1 shows the number of sources used. Column 2 shows the percentage of tries in which a valid tree was produced. Column 3 shows the average percentage of edges shared in the trees. Results were taken over 100 runs. Settings: $\alpha = 2, \beta = 1, \gamma = 0, \rho = 0.9$, 5 ants , 500 iterations.

sources	valid trees	%shared
3	100	72.3102
4	100	59.2742
5	100	56.8921

5.1   Finding Node Disjoint Paths

This experiment was performed to show that the pheromone system we proposed is indeed capable of discovering node disjoint paths. We chose 3 fixed nodes as destination nodes. For each node we randomly chose 3, 4 and 5 nodes respectively as sources. The results are shown in Table 1. We see that the algorithm succeeds in finding node disjoint paths in most runs. In cases were the algorithm does not find a valid set of disjoint paths only a very low number of nodes are shared.

5.2   Building Backup Trees

In this experiment we investigated whether ants that are launched from different source nodes, heading for the same destination node can actually build a tree. All ants used in this experiment are of the same type; no foreign pheromone or repulsion is considered in this setting. In Table 2 we show the percentage of runs in which ants found a valid tree for different numbers of source nodes. A valid tree is found if the ants stay on the same route to the destination node once their paths meet. In this experiment the same destination nodes as above were used with randomly selected source nodes. The results show that the algorithm always succeeds in building a valid tree.

5.3   The Complete Algorithm

In the last experiment we consider the complete algorithm. The working path ants try to find disjoint paths, while the backup tree ants try and build a valid tree that is node disjoint with the working paths. Fixed sources and destinations

Table 3. Working path protection. Column 1 shows the number of sources used. Column 2 shows the percentage of runs in which a valid disjoint solution was produced. Column 3 shows the average number of shared edges in the backup tree and column 4 shows the average percentage reduction in cost of the tree by sharing these edges. Results were taken over 50 algorithm runs. Settings $\alpha = 1, \beta = 1, \gamma = 4, \rho = 0.96$, 10 ants per type, 500 iterations.

sources	valid	shared edges	shared cost
2	100	1	40.0
3	32	3.75	43.2
4	94	4	59.1

were used because the network topology constraints often prevent a valid solution if the nodes are chosen randomly. In Table 3 we see that the algorithm finds valid solutions, but results for the case of 3 nodes are much worse than other cases. This is possibly due to topology constraints that make a disjoint solution harder to find. In a realistic setting we would need to solve this problem, possibly by regrouping the source nodes.

6   Conclusion

In this paper we described a Multi-type ACO algorithm for light path protection in optical networks. Different ant types in this system compete by using pheromones that repel ants of other types. This mechanism allows them to find disjoint paths in a network.

Our proposition is to use this system to route working paths and their associated backup trees in optical networks. To do this we assign an ant type to each WP and a type to the backup tree. In a number of simplified experiments we showed that the algorithm is capable of finding WPs and a BT in a graph. Further research is needed to determine if it is feasible to use the algorithm in a realistic optical network setting.

References

1. M.J. Blesa and C. Blum. Ant colony optimization for the maximum edge-disjoint paths problem. In *EvoWorkshops 2004*, volume 3005 of *LNCS*, pages 160–169, 2004.
2. Eric Bonabeau, Marco Dorigo, and Guy Theraulaz. *Swarm Intelligence, From Natural to Artificial Systems*. Santa Fe Institute studies in the sciences of complexity. Oxford University Press, 1999.
3. Gianni Di Caro, Marco Dorigo, and Luca Maria Gambardella. Antnet: A mobile agents approach to adaptive routing. Technical report, IRIDIA, Université Libre de Bruxelles Brussels, Belgium, 1997.
4. A. Colorni, M. Dorigo, F. Maffioli, V. Maniezzo, G. Righini, and M. Trubian. Heuristics from nature for hard combinatorial optimization problems. *International Transactions in Operational Research*, 1996.

5. Marco Dorigo, Gianni Di Caro, and Luca Maria Gambardella. Ant algorithms for discrete optimization. *Artificial Life 5*, pages 137–172, 1999.
6. Marco Dorigo and Gianno Di Caro. The ant colony optimization meta-heuristic. *D.Corne, M.Dorigo and F.Glover (Eds.), New Ideas In Optimization, Maidenhaid, UK: McGraw-Hill*, 1999.
7. Marco Dorigo, Vittorio Maniezzo, and Alberto Colorni. The ant system: Optimization by a colony of cooperating agents. *IEE Transactions on Systems, Man, and Cybernetics*, 1996.
8. Marco Dorigo and Thomas Stützle. *Ant Colony Optimization*. The MIT Press, 2004.
9. Adelbert Groebbens, Lan Tran, Didier Colle, Kris Steenhaut, Sophie De Maesschalck, Ann Nowe, Ilse Lievens, Mario Pickavet, and Piet Demeester. Efficient protection in mplambdas networks using backup trees: Part1- concepts and heuristics. *Photonic Network Communications*, vol 6(3):p207–222, 2003.
10. Adelbert Groebbens, Lan Tran, Didier Colle, Kris Steenhaut, Sophie De Maesschalck, Ann Nowe, Ilse Lievens, Mario Pickavet, and Piet Demeester. Efficient protection in mplambdas networks using backup trees: Part2- simulations. *Photonic Network Communications*, vol 6(3):p191–206, 2003.
11. H. Kawamura, M. Yamamoto, K. Suzuki, and A. Ohuchi. Multiple ant colonies algorithm based on colony level interactions. *IEICE Transactions on Fundamentals*, E83-A, no. 2:371–379, 2000.
12. Ann Nowé, Katja Verbeeck, and Peter Vrancx. Multi-type ant colony: the edge-disjoint paths problem. In M. Dorigo, M. Birattari, C. Blum, L. M. Gambardella, F. Mondada, and T. Stützle, editors, *Ant Colony Optimization and Swarm Intelligence, 4th International Workshop, ANTS 2004*, volume 3172 of *LNCS*, pages 202–213, Berlin, Germany, 2004. Springer-Verlag.
13. Qwest Nationwide network: http://www.qwest.com/about/inside/network/nationip.html.
14. D. Subramanian, P. Druschel, and P. Chen. Ants and reinforcement learning: A case study in routing in dynamic networks. *Proceedings of IJCAI-97, International Joint Conference on Artificial Intelligence*, pages 832–838, 1997.
15. G. Navarro Varela and M.C. Sinclair. Ant colony optimisation for virtual-wavelength-path routing and wavelength allocation. *Proceedings of the Congress on Evolutionary Computation (CEC'99)*, 1999.
16. P. Vrancx. Multi-type ant system: Introducing competition to ant algorithms. Master's thesis, Vrije Universiteit Brussel, 2004.

Author Index

Lecture Notes in Artificial Intelligence (LNAI)

Vol. 3684: R. Khosla, R.J. Howlett, L.C. Jain (Eds.), Knowledge-Based Intelligent Information and Engineering Systems, Part IV. LXXIX, 933 pages. 2005.

Vol. 3683: R. Khosla, R.J. Howlett, L.C. Jain (Eds.), Knowledge-Based Intelligent Information and Engineering Systems, Part III. LXXX, 1397 pages. 2005.

Vol. 3682: R. Khosla, R.J. Howlett, L.C. Jain (Eds.), Knowledge-Based Intelligent Information and Engineering Systems, Part II. LXXIX, 1371 pages. 2005.

Vol. 3681: R. Khosla, R.J. Howlett, L.C. Jain (Eds.), Knowledge-Based Intelligent Information and Engineering Systems, Part I. LXXX, 1319 pages. 2005.

Vol. 3673: S. Bandini, S. Manzoni (Eds.), AI*IA 2005: Advances in Artificial Intelligence. XIV, 614 pages. 2005.

Vol. 3662: C. Baral, G. Greco, N. Leone, G. Terracina (Eds.), Logic Programming and Nonmonotonic Reasoning. XIII, 454 pages. 2005.

Vol. 3661: T. Panayiotopoulos, J. Gratch, R.S. Aylett, D. Ballin, P. Olivier, T. Rist (Eds.), Intelligent Virtual Agents. XIII, 506 pages. 2005.

Vol. 3658: V. Matoušek, P. Mautner, T. Pavelka (Eds.), Text, Speech and Dialogue. XV, 460 pages. 2005.

Vol. 3651: R. Dale, K.-F. Wong, J. Su, O.Y. Kwong (Eds.), Natural Language Processing – IJCNLP 2005. XXI, 1031 pages. 2005.

Vol. 3642: D. Ślęzak, J. Yao, J.F. Peters, W. Ziarko, X. Hu (Eds.), Rough Sets, Fuzzy Sets, Data Mining, and Granular Computing, Part II. XXIII, 738 pages. 2005.

Vol. 3641: D. Ślęzak, G. Wang, M. Szczuka, I. Düntsch, Y. Yao (Eds.), Rough Sets, Fuzzy Sets, Data Mining, and Granular Computing, Part I. XXIV, 742 pages. 2005.

Vol. 3635: J.R. Winkler, M. Niranjan, N.D. Lawrence (Eds.), Deterministic and Statistical Methods in Machine Learning. VIII, 341 pages. 2005.

Vol. 3632: R. Nieuwenhuis (Ed.), Automated Deduction – CADE-20. XIII, 459 pages. 2005.

Vol. 3630: M.S. Capcarrère, A.A. Freitas, P.J. Bentley, C.G. Johnson, J. Timmis (Eds.), Advances in Artificial Life. XIX, 949 pages. 2005.

Vol. 3626: B. Ganter, G. Stumme, R. Wille (Eds.), Formal Concept Analysis. X, 349 pages. 2005.

Vol. 3625: S. Kramer, B. Pfahringer (Eds.), Inductive Logic Programming. XIII, 427 pages. 2005.

Vol. 3620: H. Muñoz-Ávila, F. Ricci (Eds.), Case-Based Reasoning Research and Development. XV, 654 pages. 2005.

Vol. 3614: L. Wang, Y. Jin (Eds.), Fuzzy Systems and Knowledge Discovery, Part II. XLI, 1314 pages. 2005.

Vol. 3613: L. Wang, Y. Jin (Eds.), Fuzzy Systems and Knowledge Discovery, Part I. XLI, 1334 pages. 2005.

Vol. 3607: J.-D. Zucker, L. Saitta (Eds.), Abstraction, Reformulation and Approximation. XII, 376 pages. 2005.

Vol. 3601: G. Moro, S. Bergamaschi, K. Aberer (Eds.), Agents and Peer-to-Peer Computing. XII, 245 pages. 2005.

Vol. 3600: F. Wiedijk (Ed.), The Seventeen Provers of the World. XVI, 159 pages. 2006.

Vol. 3596: F. Dau, M.-L. Mugnier, G. Stumme (Eds.), Conceptual Structures: Common Semantics for Sharing Knowledge. XI, 467 pages. 2005.

Vol. 3593: V. Mařík, R. W. Brennan, M. Pěchouček (Eds.), Holonic and Multi-Agent Systems for Manufacturing. XI, 269 pages. 2005.

Vol. 3587: P. Perner, A. Imiya (Eds.), Machine Learning and Data Mining in Pattern Recognition. XVII, 695 pages. 2005.

Vol. 3584: X. Li, S. Wang, Z.Y. Dong (Eds.), Advanced Data Mining and Applications. XIX, 835 pages. 2005.

Vol. 3581: S. Miksch, J. Hunter, E.T. Keravnou (Eds.), Artificial Intelligence in Medicine. XVII, 547 pages. 2005.

Vol. 3577: R. Falcone, S. Barber, J. Sabater-Mir, M.P. Singh (Eds.), Trusting Agents for Trusting Electronic Societies. VIII, 235 pages. 2005.

Vol. 3575: S. Wermter, G. Palm, M. Elshaw (Eds.), Biomimetic Neural Learning for Intelligent Robots. IX, 383 pages. 2005.

Vol. 3571: L. Godo (Ed.), Symbolic and Quantitative Approaches to Reasoning with Uncertainty. XVI, 1028 pages. 2005.

Vol. 3559: P. Auer, R. Meir (Eds.), Learning Theory. XI, 692 pages. 2005.

Vol. 3558: V. Torra, Y. Narukawa, S. Miyamoto (Eds.), Modeling Decisions for Artificial Intelligence. XII, 470 pages. 2005.

Vol. 3554: A.K. Dey, B. Kokinov, D.B. Leake, R. Turner (Eds.), Modeling and Using Context. XIV, 572 pages. 2005.

Vol. 3550: T. Eymann, F. Klügl, W. Lamersdorf, M. Klusch, M.N. Huhns (Eds.), Multiagent System Technologies. XI, 246 pages. 2005.

Vol. 3539: K. Morik, J.-F. Boulicaut, A. Siebes (Eds.), Local Pattern Detection. XI, 233 pages. 2005.

Vol. 3538: L. Ardissono, P. Brna, A. Mitrović (Eds.), User Modeling 2005. XVI, 533 pages. 2005.

Vol. 3533: M. Ali, F. Esposito (Eds.), Innovations in Applied Artificial Intelligence. XX, 858 pages. 2005.

Vol. 3528: P.S. Szczepaniak, J. Kacprzyk, A. Niewiadomski (Eds.), Advances in Web Intelligence. XVII, 513 pages. 2005.

Vol. 3518: T.-B. Ho, D. Cheung, H. Liu (Eds.), Advances in Knowledge Discovery and Data Mining. XXI, 864 pages. 2005.

Vol. 3508: P. Bresciani, P. Giorgini, B. Henderson-Sellers, G. Low, M. Winikoff (Eds.), Agent-Oriented Information Systems II. X, 227 pages. 2005.

Vol. 3505: V. Gorodetsky, J. Liu, V.A. Skormin (Eds.), Autonomous Intelligent Systems: Agents and Data Mining. XIII, 303 pages. 2005.

Vol. 3501: B. Kégl, G. Lapalme (Eds.), Advances in Artificial Intelligence. XV, 458 pages. 2005.

Vol. 3492: P. Blache, E.P. Stabler, J.V. Busquets, R. Moot (Eds.), Logical Aspects of Computational Linguistics. X, 363 pages. 2005.

Vol. 3490: L. Bolc, Z. Michalewicz, T. Nishida (Eds.), Intelligent Media Technology for Communicative Intelligence. X, 259 pages. 2005.